What

The   s

Outside (Fe
"... most u
It's readable, ...
charts), and comprehensive, covering pretrip preparations, first-aid kits,
preventive measures, diagnosis and treatment of specific maladies, and
more — but it's still slim enough to take along."

Library Journal (January 1991)
"comprehensive. . . advises readers on how to prepare for serious health
hazards that may be encountered when traveling in developing countries.
Focusing on the needs of people planning extended trips or travel outside
modern urban areas, it covers first-aid kits, dental remedies for
emergencies, and prescription medications. The book also includes
extensive food and water guides, quick reference charts to help diagnose
common illnesses, maps showing areas where infectious diseases are
prevalent, and a list of Travel Clinics in the United States and Canada. A
valuable addition to collections where patrons travel."

Travel & Leisure (Jan 1992)
"If you're. . . more at home in a Brazilian rain forest than a Paris boîte,
pick up a copy of The Medical Guide for Third World Travelers . . .
there are sections on immunizations, jet lag and first aid kits, but the
emphasis is on responsible self-care for far-flung adventurers who might
be days away from modern medical facilities. You'll learn how to
diagnose and treat a range of ailments (from minor skin wounds and
insect bites to intestinal disorders) and how to determine whether you can
handle something yourself or need professional help."

Turn page for more reviews

Free Nutshell™ Guide for Healthy Traveling

See page 341 for details on how to get your free,
wallet-size Nutshell™ Guide for Healthy Traveling

Journal of Wilderness Medicine (Vol. 2, No. 3 1991)
"The format used certainly is more practical for the average tourist traveling abroad than that of other self-help books. . . I would recommend *The Medical Guide for Third World Travelers* specifically for persons traveling to areas where medical help will not be available, and/or immediate medical evaluation might be required."

Islands (June 1991)
"not only a basic manual to healthy traveling, but a disorder-by-disorder guide to virtually every kind of exotic ailment an independent traveler is likely to encounter . . . in the remote corners of the world . . . including specific, up-to-date medications — and what to do when medical care is not available. Stash it in your backpack, and save a copy for your doctor if a strange fever breaks out after you return."

TMA Update (Travel Medical Alert) July/Aug. 1991
"This book contains many helpful hints and is recommended for any person who is anticipating adventure travel or prolonged residence in developing areas of the world. The book is easily portable. . . ."

Sierra (March/April 1991)
"Trekking in the developing world requires being especially attentive to your health. As a resource to help you stay fit . . . the book gives detailed advice on diagnosing and treating everything from intestinal disorders to sexually transmitted diseases."

Footprints (Winter 1990)
". . . by far the most comprehensive and detailed self-care manual available for travelers to Third World countries. Authors Robin and Dessery . . . did it exceptionally well . . . **Any traveler** would benefit from this information especially in the area of preventive health measures. And if problems do come into play, detailed, educated information is available."

International Travel News (Feb. 1991)
"a thorough, self-doctoring guide for travelers to the Third World . . . the best part of this book is the field-guide-type diagnosis and treatment sections, which compose a major part of the book. . . . you don't need to be a doctor to understand the symptoms and undertake treatment if there isn't a good doctor around. Even medicines are listed in their generic equivalents — important since trade names sometimes change from country to country but generic names never do. (★★★ Excellent)"

San Diego Peace Corps Association (July-Aug. 1991)
"Don't leave home without one."

The Medical Guide for Third World Travelers

A Comprehensive Self-Care Handbook

Bradford L. Dessery

and

Marc R. Robin
Coordinator, International Traveler's Clinic
San Diego, California

San Diego, California

Ordering Information

Additional copies of this book may be purchased at your local bookstore or directly from the publisher at the address below. Remit $14.95 plus $4.00 for shipping and handling. California residents add applicable sales tax. See **page 341** for a handy order form.

For information concerning bulk purchases or course adoptions, write:

> K-W Publications
> 11532 Alkaid Dr., San Diego, CA 92126-1370
> 619-566-6489, FAX: 619-271-1425

Disclaimer

See **page 18** for important information on using this book.

Book design by Mike Kelly, K-W Publications, San Diego, California

Library of Congress Catalog Card Number: 92-073362
ISBN 0-929894-06-5

Printing History: 1st Edition printed August 1990;
2nd Edition printed August 1992

Printed in the United States of America
10 9 8 7 6 5 4 3 2 1

Contents — Overview

Charts

Contents — Detailed

Appendices

Acknowledgements

We would like to thank the following people for their editing, comments, and suggestions in various parts of this book:

Dr. Michelle Ginsberg, Epidemiologist; Michael Heumann, Epidemiologist; Dr. Jim Lewis, Dermatologist; Dr. Pierre Rivet, Ear, Nose & Throat; Dr. C.C. Smith, Pulmonary Medicine; Dr. Sue Drier, Pharmacist; Dr. Gerry Graff, Pharmacist; Dr. John Westwood, Dentist; Dr. Joe Stein, Diving Medicine; Gerald Dessery; Rise Burdman; Kathy Dessery; and Yvette Doyle.

A very special thanks to Lesley Robin for her support, ideas, editing, and typing. Also to Dr. Gary Fujimoto, Internal Medicine, for his editing suggestions and answers to all of our long-distance telephone questions and pleas for assistance.

And finally to our racquetball club jacuzzi where the idea for this book was conceived, developed, and after a record gestation period finally grew to term.

Disclaimer

This book is written by applying standard medical principles for the general public. It's meant to help you plan in advance for possible medical eventualities in the area of the world you are visiting. While planning your trip, consult your physician before utilizing the recommendations discussed in this book, especially if you have any medical problems.

Our book is also meant to help you find competent medical care in a foreign country should you need it. It will also alert you to potentially dangerous medical practices in some countries — such as using unsterilized syringes or dangerous medications that have been banned elsewhere. Medical treatment varies in different parts of the world and is constantly changing. We urge any reader who is ill to seek medical help if it is available before utilizing any of the medical recommendations or suggestions contained in this book. The authors emphasize that this book is not a substitute for the medical advice of a physician.

The authors disclaim responsibility from adverse consequences or effects resulting from use of the contents of this book.

Introduction

How To Use This Book ▬▬▬

Anyone living or traveling in Third World countries — whether for work, business, research, vacation, volunteer work, or adventure — will encounter increased and unaccustomed health risks. These new risks are a challenge, requiring increased responsibility for your health and well-being. Travelers to Europe — East or West — and other destinations will also find much of this book useful.

Part I
Pre-Trip Medical Planning

Preventing illness is the key to successful travel in Third World countries. Understanding the health risks, you can avoid and minimize them. Part I will help you identify potential health problems and prepare appropriately. From immunizations to first aid kits, health insurance to birth control measures, physical exams to food and water precautions, we'll help you get ready for your trip. Read Part I before your departure, and know the preventive measures to follow during travel in any Third World country.

Part II
Diagnosis and Treatment of Medical Disorders

In spite of precautions, illness and injury may occur. Part II will help you with the interpretation of symptoms and identification of commonly encountered illnesses. Use the table of contents and the index to locate specific information quickly. To identify possible causes and find relevant information when you know only the symptoms, consult the Quick Reference guides in each chapter. A guide to identification of a mysterious rash, for example, will be found at the end of Chapter 5, "Skin Problems". In addition, there are guidelines to help determine when you must obtain medical evaluation.

We provide treatment schedules in Part II for use when medical care isn't available. Also use this information to ensure that when care is available, the medications prescribed for you are appropriate and safe.

Part III
Medications and How To Use Them

Part III helps you safely evaluate and use a variety of pharmaceutical tools. You'll find information on contraindications, as well as how to maximize the effectiveness — and minimize potential side effects — of medications. Read this information before taking any medication we or others recommend for use while traveling. You'll also find the generic equivalents or chemical compositions of brand name medications we mention in the text. Throughout the text we capitalize brand, but not generic, names.

All dosages and medications are for adult usage only. Children have specialized medical needs which are beyond the scope of this book.

Appendices

Appendices detail information on vaccinations and the precautions to take when obtaining any injection while traveling. Zone maps show geographical areas of high risk for certain diseases. Check them to see if precautions against malaria, yellow fever, schistosomiasis, dengue fever, meningococcal meningitis, and other diseases are necessary.

The information in this book will help you stay healthy and cope with illness, whether traveling for 3 weeks or 3 years. It should enable you to assume responsibility for a substantial part of your medical care when the need arises, particularly in isolated areas.

Travel, even to remote rural areas of the world, need not entail major health risks. Both the hazards and anxiety of new, possibly exotic locations, can vanish with proper preparation.

Part I _____

Pre-Trip Medical Planning _____

Preparing for any trip depends on several factors. These include the length of the trip, your general state of health, and your destination — urban or rural, temperate or tropical.

Wherever you travel in developing countries, you must take measures to safeguard your health. Food and water precautions are essential. Vaccinations, insect precautions, sun protection, malaria prophylaxis, and other preventive measures depend primarily on your destination. The first aid kit you assemble, the self-examination skills you learn, and the medical and dental checkups you obtain, depend mainly on the duration of your stay.

It's essential to allow sufficient time to complete all the necessary immunizations and medical preparations. Many travelers to Third World countries will need 6–8 weeks. Injectable typhoid vaccination alone requires 4 weeks. Make the best preparations possible, and you'll be well on your way to a healthy stay abroad.

Use the checklist on the next page for travel planning, and for quickly locating specific information.

✓ Medical Checklist: Planning Your Trip

All Travelers (including travel to urban areas for two to three weeks or less)

❑ first aid kit (pp. 42–43)
❑ food and water precautions (pp. 77–87)
❑ health insurance (pp.45–46)
❑ insect precautions and repellents (pp. 38–40)
❑ jet lag (pp. 26–30)
❑ locating health care while traveling (pp. 44–45)
❑ motion sickness (pp. 30–31)
❑ prevention of malaria (pp. 34–38)
❑ prevention of traveler's diarrhea (pp. 40–41)
❑ sun exposure and sunscreens (pp. 31–34)
❑ traveling with prescription drugs (p. 31)
❑ vaccinations (pp. 23–27)
❑ water purification (pp. 80–83)

Special Individual Needs

❑ allergies to stinging insects (pp. 59–60)
❑ altitude sickness precautions (pp. 91–94)
❑ birth control measures (pp. 62–68)
❑ disabled travelers (pp. 60–62)
❑ medical alert tags (p. 58)
❑ pregnancy and travel (pp. 55–58)
❑ prevention of sexually transmitted diseases (pp. 89–90)
❑ special health problems, including diabetes and chronic medical conditions (pp. 50–55)
❑ traveling with prescription glasses and contacts (pp. 68–69)

Extended Travel

❑ blood typing (p. 71)
❑ dental checkup (pp. 71–72)
❑ self-examination skills (pp. 72–74)
❑ TB skin test (p. 71)

Vaccinations and Other Preventive Measures

1

Vaccinations

Your travel itinerary determines the vaccinations you need. You may need them to legally enter a country. More often, the risk of disease in an area you're visiting or living in is sufficiently high to warrant vaccination.

Almost everyone gets the routine childhood immunizations necessary to attend public schools, such as polio, measles, rubella, tetanus, and diphtheria. If you didn't get them, by all means obtain them before departure. To determine which other vaccinations you need, consult the Public Health Service, your doctor, a local travel clinic, or the information we provide here and in Appendix A. In general, travel agents are not reliable sources of information about your health needs. This is not their area of expertise, nor their responsibility.

Start immunizations early. You can't take some together — and others require a series of injections at intervals of a week or more. If you need a vaccination while traveling, check with a local university, public health clinic, private medical practice, or obtain referrals from local embassies. Be certain all vaccinations, as well as any other injections you obtain while traveling, are given with sterile, disposable equipment. You may even want to take your own sterile, disposable syringes (see our First Aid Kit recommendations, p. 42–43).

Documentation

Document vaccinations in a yellow *International Certificate of Vaccination,* which is available from travel clinics or the public health service. Don't use a pediatric (childhood) shot card from your doctor. Each injection should be properly entered and signed, not stamped, by the medical provider or their representative. You must show this book on request at international points of entry. Keep it with your passport. It's a good idea to make a photocopy of these documents to keep separately.

If, for medical reasons, a legally required vaccination can't be given, obtain documentation from your medical provider. A signed and dated statement on letterhead stationery is sufficient. It should explain the medical reasons why you are unable to receive the vaccine.

Cautions and Contraindications

Under some circumstances, you should either avoid a vaccination or take it only under medical supervision. For any of the following conditions, get medical advice before obtaining or omitting a recommended vaccine.

1. Pregnancy (or potential pregnancy when not practicing birth control). See pp. 55–58 for more information.

2. A history of allergic reaction to a particular vaccine.

3. Allergy to eggs (may be a contraindication for yellow fever, measles, or influenza vaccine).

4. Allergy to neomycin, or certain vaccine preservatives.

5. Presence of immune deficiencies, undergoing immunosuppressive or radiation therapy, or history of an HIV (AIDS virus) positive blood test.

6. Illness accompanied by fever above 102°F (38.9°C).

Breastfeeding

Vaccinations are acceptable for breastfeeding mothers.

Overview of Vaccination Schedules

The following overview will help you determine and schedule the vaccinations you require for travel. Appendix A contains detailed information on each vaccine. Consult it to determine if you need any of the vaccines in Groups 2 and 3 for your itinerary or situation.

Group 1: for all Third World Travel

Tetanus-diphtheria (Td)
Obtain a booster shot prior to travel if you haven't had one in the previous 10 years. If potential tetanus exposure occurs from a deep or dirty wound, a booster is needed if you haven't had one in the previous 5 years.

Immune globulin (IG, gamma globulin)
This should be your last shot prior to departure. Booster shots every 5 months are necessary for ongoing protection against hepatitis A. Revaccination with IG in Third World countries is not necessarily recommended — see Appendix A.

Polio
Get a single booster of oral (OPV) or enhanced inactivated vaccine (eIPV) if you had the primary series more than 5 years prior to travel.

Measles (rubeola)
A single booster is recommended for anyone born after 1956.

Rubella (German measles)
Exposure to the disease or a single immunization provides lifetime protection.

Group 2: for Travel in Some Geographic Areas (See Appendix A)

Yellow fever
A single injection provides immunity for 10 years. A booster is recommended at 10-year intervals for continued exposure. This vaccine is required for entry into many countries.

Japanese B encephalitis
After primary vaccination a booster is needed at 12–18 months, then at 4-year intervals for ongoing protection.

Meningococcal meningitis
One dose, with a booster every 3 years for ongoing protection.

Tickborne encephalitis
Vaccine available in Europe; not available in U.S.

Group 3: Special Situations (Some Individuals Only — See Appendix A)

Rabies, pre-exposure (HDCV, Human Diploid Cell Vaccine)
Three doses are required. See Appendix A for details.

Influenza
Vaccination annually.

Pneumococcal pneumonia
One dose provides lifetime immunity; no booster necessary.

Plague
After the primary series, two boosters are needed at 6-month intervals – thereafter at 1–2 year intervals for ongoing protection. (Travelers genuinely at risk for exposure to plague should see their doctor for possible use of tetracycline preventively, 500 mg. 4 times a day, during periods of exposure.)

Hepatitis B vaccine (Engerix)
Three doses, the second 4 weeks after the first and the third 5 months after the second.

Typhoid
Orally — One dose every other day for 4 doses. An identical booster dose is recommended every 5 years.
Injections — Preferably 2 doses, the second 4 or more weeks after the initial dose. Vaccination is possible with 3 doses, 1 each at weekly intervals for 3 consecutive weeks, if time is short. A booster every 3 years for continued exposure.

Cholera
Not recommended for general travel. If medically required, 2 doses 1–4 weeks apart. Boosters every 6 months for continued exposure.

Group 4: Unnecessary Vaccinations

Smallpox
This disease has been officially eradicated.

Typhus
No longer of concern to travelers.

Other Preventive Measures

Jet Lag

Traveling east or west across 3 or more time zones puts daily biological rhythms out of synch with their environmental cues. These rhythms are chemically regulated daily cycles of hunger, sleep, and wakefulness. They also involve changes in hormone levels, kidney function, brain and heart activity, and body temperature. The chief environmental cue for these cycles is sunlight. Until your body reorients to sunrise, sunset, and the living routines of a new location, you are likely to suffer the discomforts known as jet lag.

Vaccination Record

Keep a record here of your vaccination history. Be sure to also keep your yellow international certificate of vaccination up to date.

Vaccine	Date given (month/day/year)	Date next dose due

Flying east produces the most severe, prolonged effects of jet lag. Daytime sleepiness and insomnia are the most frequent effects. Other symptoms include poor concentration, fatigue, indigestion, depression, irritability, slowed reflexes, headaches, and memory loss. It's worth noting that north-south travel does not produce jet lag.

After exposure to sunlight on 2 successive days, the body clock effectively resets following exposure to sunlight on the third day. Although the exact mechanism is unknown, the hormone melatonin apparently governs the biological rhythm. Light passing along the optic nerve affects its production in the brain. Consequently, most symptoms of jet lag disappear within 3 days. Travelers who spend daylight hours indoors may take up to a week to fully recover from jet lag symptoms.

There are many strategies to cope with jet lag. They may not all work for everyone, but they should help adjustment to new time zones in the shortest time possible.

Preflight

1. Fly east, fly early; fly west, fly late. Make reservations accordingly. This allows arrival at your destination with the least loss of rest due to the flight itself. It works best for flights of 6 time zones or less.

2. Change sleep patterns to fit more closely the destination time zone. Do this by adjusting your bedtime. For example, on westbound flights go to bed 1 hour later each night for 3 successive nights prior to departure. On eastbound flights, go to bed 1 hour earlier for three nights before departure. This also works best for flights of up to 6 time zones.

3. One dietary approach that is popular is to alternate feasting on a high protein, high calorie diet, with fasting on weak soups, salads, and dry toast prior to travel. Initiate this regime 4 days before departure. On the first day, feast on 3 high protein meals. On the following day fast on liquids, fruits, and salads. Alternate until the day of departure, which will be a fasting day. Upon arrival at your destination eat light meals according to the local time schedule. Although there is no scientific documentation for this diet, many travelers swear by it. The complete system is in the book *Overcoming Jet Lag*, by Dr. Charles F. Ehret. (For a summary of the jet lag diet printed on a wallet-sized card, send a stamped self-addressed envelope to: Anti Jet Lag Diet, OPA, Argonne National Lab., 9700 S. Cass Avenue, Argonne, IL 60439.)

4. If possible, plan to break up very long flights with one day layovers at locations en route to your destination.

5. At the airport, walk around before boarding the plane. Avoid sitting and waiting. Stay active.

6. Avoid overeating and drinking alcohol prior to the flight.

7. Set your watch to the destination time when boarding the plane. This may help psychological adjustment to local time upon landing.

Inflight

1. During the flight do stretching exercises in your seat. Walk up and down the aisles as permitted. Avoid cramped positions to help minimize fatigue.

2. Drink water and juices on the plane. Avoid caffeine and alcohol which, along with the dry, pressurized air, promote dehydration. Dehydration makes it harder to sleep at night and may make it more difficult for body rhythms to adjust. On flights from Third World countries, drink only water that is bottled or purified.

3. Unfortunately, the quality of sleep on long flights is usually poor, rarely providing adequate rest. Use of sleeping pills is controversial, although many travelers use them to increase the ease and duration of sleep. The 2 most frequently prescribed are Halcion (triazolam), 0.125–0.25 mg., or Restoril (temazepam) 15–30 mg. These should be used in the lowest dose possible, and only when there will be at least 6 hours of uninterrupted flight time. Don't use alcohol with sleeping pills, especially Halcion, as the combination may cause retrograde amnesia. This type of amnesia allows you to function normally, but unable later to recall what transpired. The phenomenon is temporary and resolves without residual effects. Don't use Halcion or Restoril during pregnancy.

Postflight

1. Adopt local time and routines immediately upon arrival.

2. For the first 72 hours, allow plenty of time to sleep and rest to compensate for reduced sleep quality and to make the adjustment period easier. You may use Halcion or Restoril for a few nights after arrival to help adjust sleep patterns. Avoid prolonged use of sleeping pills — they can be habit forming.

3. Take walks outdoors for several hours daily for the first 3 days. Sunlight exposure helps reset your biological clock for the new time zone. Following eastbound travel across 6 time zones or less, exposure to bright morning sunlight advances daily rhythms, preparing the body to accept an earlier bedtime. Westbound, exposure to afternoon sunlight

appears to delay body rhythms so that the need to sleep comes later. For travel east or west across more than 6 time zones, exposure to midday sun appears to be most effective in resetting the body's biological clock.

Motion Sickness

Motion sickness is a common problem. On highways, even seasoned travelers may succumb to a combination of rutted roads, dead shock absorbers, and broken seat springs. Travel by several different modes of transportation can overwhelm balance centers in the inner ear and result in nausea, vomiting, fatigue, and loss of equilibrium.

Prevention

Preventing motion sickness is much easier than treating the symptoms once they occur. While medications to prevent motion sickness work fairly well, other preventive measures can be taken. If you're prone to illness, reduce your exposure to modes of transportation that cause you problems. On a bus, plane, boat, or train, it is often helpful to sit near the midsection. If possible, lie back in a reclining position and close your eyes. Don't try to read. When looking out the window, look as far ahead to the horizon as possible — not to the sides. Eat only small amounts of light foods, and avoid fried foods, alcohol, and overeating both before and during travel.

Sea Bands

"Sea Bands" are light weight, elastic knitted stretch bands with a small, noncorrosive plastic button. Worn on the wrists, they apply pressure to an acupuncture site used to treat motion sickness. They both treat and prevent symptoms. They're a drugless alternative, ideal during pregnancy or conditions such as glaucoma because of the absence of side effects. They're worth a try if you are susceptible to motion sickness.

Medications to prevent motion sickness

Scopolamine — The medication of choice for preventing motion sickness, Transderm-Scop, is a small circular patch. Place the patch behind your ear and it works for up to 72 hours. Apply it 8 hours before travel.

After putting on the patch, wash your hands thoroughly. Otherwise if you rub your eyes, the pupils may become uncomfortably dilated. Transderm-Scop can't be used by anyone with glaucoma. Travelers over 65 should use Dramamine instead, as Transderm-Scop commonly produces a dry mouth and urinary retention as side effects.

Antihistamines — Many drugs in this class of medications are also commonly used to prevent motion sickness. They include Phenergan (promethazine), Dramamine (dimenhydrinate), Marezine (cyclizine), Antivert or Bonine (meclizine), and Benadryl (diphenhydramine). The main problem with these, especially Benadryl, is that they may cause drowsiness. Start these medications 1–2 hours prior to travel.

Treatment

"The only cure for seasickness is to sit on the east side of a barn in the country." The truth is that once vomiting from motion sickness starts, none of the preventive medications have much effect. If possible, stop traveling until symptoms disappear, then take preventive medications before resuming travel. If this is not possible, treat symptoms with a drug to stop vomiting such as Compazine (see Part III, p. 270). If you can't keep pills down, use the suppository form. It may also help you to get fresh air, find a quiet spot to sit or lie down and rest, or nibble on dry crackers.

Traveling with Prescription Drugs

Carry each medication in a container with a proper prescription label. Don't mix different medications in the same container. These are legal as well as medical precautions. In some countries, carrying any kind of unmarked medication without a prescription is an invitation to harassment. However unjustified, local officials are sometimes in a position to delay travel, deny entry, exact a bribe, or even toss you in jail for smuggling. Proper identification of prescription drugs is a sound precaution.

Travelers who take medicine regularly should carry with them a sufficient quantity for the entire trip. Some medications may not be readily available. Carry at least a one-month supply, properly marked, on your person. If luggage is stolen or lost, you won't be caught short while awaiting replacement, which may take *weeks*.

For the same reason, carry a written prescription for each medication *separate* from the medications themselves. This prescription should contain the generic name of the drug. Trade names vary from one country to another, but the generic name should enable you to find the equivalent medication if you require a replacement.

Liquid medications require spill-proof containers. If you are flying, leave space in the container for expansion of the liquid.

Sunburn

Excessive sun exposure is a potential hazard to any traveler, especially in the tropics. In addition to fried skin, other dangers include sunstroke, heat cramps, heat exhaustion, and dehydration. Drink plenty of fluids, avoiding alcohol, to prevent dehydration. Limit your physical activity, especially during the hottest part of the day.

Most of the skin damage caused by the sun is cumulative. Excessive exposure to sunlight results in degenerative changes such as wrinkling and skin aging. It may eventually cause precancerous or cancerous skin lesions. It's the ultraviolet (UV) portion of the light spectrum which is responsible for these changes, and for tanning as well as sunburn.

Ultraviolet further divides into UV-A and UV-B. UV-A contributes to skin damage and is the main cause of photosensitivity reactions from drugs. Severe sunburn on exposed areas of the skin characterizes these reactions. UV-B is the major cause of sunburn (as well as tanning) and chronic skin injury, including aging and skin cancer.

Factors Affecting Sun Exposure

Time of day
The earth's ozone layer, or what's left of it, filters out ultraviolet light. When the sun is directly overhead more UV light reaches the earth's surface. Minimize direct sun exposure from 10 am to 3 pm if possible.

Altitude
For every increase of 1,000 feet (305 meters), there is a 4% increase in ultraviolet light. The intensity of the sun at 6,000 feet (1,830 meters) is 24% greater than at sea level.

Clouds
Cloudy days cut exposure to ultraviolet light by about 40%. Since it's usually cooler, people stay outdoors longer and often by much more than 40%. Light overcast or haze is especially deceptive. Cloudy days warrant extra vigilance about sun exposure.

Reflective surfaces
Ultraviolet light reflects off white sand or snow by up to 20% and 85%, respectively. Near these surfaces, sun exposure often intensifies.

Prevention
To avoid sunburn, tan slowly — no more than 30 minutes sun exposure the first day. Increase exposure by 5–10 minutes daily thereafter. Use a hat, light-colored protective clothing, and sunglasses to avoid overexposure outdoors. Make liberal use of sunscreens and sunblocks on exposed skin, and use protective lip balm with a sunblock. Be especially careful of

sunburn during high exposure activities such as swimming or snorkling. In the water, people stay cool and often lose track of time while their sunscreen washes away. Even a T-shirt may be inadequate protection. Thin clothing, when wet, is transparent to UV light.

Sunscreens and sunblocks

Use a broad spectrum sunscreen that blocks both ultraviolet A and B rays. Look for products with a combination of blocking ingredients, such as "Photoplex." UV-A blocks are especially important when taking medication such as tetracycline which may cause a photosensitivity reaction. A list of other sensitizing drugs is in Part III, pp. 272–273.

Some people may be sensitive to PABA or other sunscreen ingredients, especially when applied to the face. Try a PABA-free product such as "Neutrogena Sunblock" or "Shade."

Most sunblocks are opaque products which totally block out sunlight and look like warpaint. They usually contain either zinc oxide or titanium dioxide, and protect against both UV-A and UV-B.

SPF (Sun Protection Factor) designations — SPF numbers from 2–50 or higher measure the degree of protection from a given sunscreen preparation. In theory, it would take that many times as long to produce a sunburn with the sunscreen as it otherwise would without it. SPF #2 provides minimal protection, while SPF #15 or higher provides closer to maximum protection.

For serious skin protection, use both a sunscreen and a lip balm with an SPF rating of at least 15. If you're prone to acne, sunscreens over 15 may aggravate this condition. Use a sunblock for sensitive areas prone to burn, such as nose, ears, and lips. In practice, of course, the numbers are meaningless if the sunscreen or sunblock washes off from bathing or sweat.

Sunglasses

The sun's ultraviolet light can damage your eyes just as it does the skin. UV light can cause corneal and retinal damage, increase the risk for cancer of the eye and eyelid, and may contribute to the development of cataracts. To protect from UV light, sunglasses must be UV rated and labeled, or endorsed by the American National Standards Institute.

Sunglasses will also help protect the eyes from dust, dirt, and the glare which causes squinting. Lenses of green or gray plastic are best and should be dark enough so that the eyes cannot be seen through them. In areas of intense glare, such as snow, ice, water, and sand, polarized lenses will help filter out reflected light. They will not, however, reduce exposure to UV light. Artificial tears are a good addition to a first aid kit. They will help protect your eyes from dryness in the desert, or following prolonged exposure to the tropical sun.

Preventing Malaria (Malaria Prophylaxis)

The red blood cell parasite "Plasmodium" causes malaria. It's spread by the bite of the female Anopheles mosquito. Measures against malaria are not legally required for travel in any country. However malaria is on the rise worldwide and we *strongly* recommend antimalarial medications.

Individuals with little or no previous exposure to malaria may rapidly progress to severe or sometimes even fatal illness. While you can't prevent all cases of malaria, you can prevent the deaths associated with it by the the use of preventive measures and by immediate treatment when preventive measures fail. We can't overemphasize the importance of prophylactic medications and protection from mosquito bites for travel in malaria zones. All travelers should use them in any malarial zone, for travel *as brief as a single day*.

Check with your local public health department, travel clinic, or the Centers for Disease Control (CDC) malaria hotline (1-404-332-4555) to see if your travel plans include a visit to a malarial zone. Areas of risk include parts of Mexico, Haiti, Central and South America, Africa — particularly in the region of the sub-Sahara — the Middle East, Turkey, the Indian subcontinent, Southeast Asia, China, the Indonesian archipelago, and Oceania. (There are 200–500 million cases of malaria yearly throughout the developing world, where it's the leading cause of illness and death. Among U.S. travelers, 1534 cases of malaria due to P. falciparum were reported during the period 1980-1988. 80% were acquired in sub-Saharan Africa, 7% in Asia, and 7% in the Caribbean and S. America. Of 37 fatal infections, 27 were acquired in sub-Saharan Africa. Here there are 1–2 million deaths from malaria annually among the native population.) Canada, Europe, Japan, and Australia are considered free of malaria. See map in Appendix B, p. 310.

Malaria Prevention During Pregnancy

See Chapter 2, pp. 56–57.

Travel in Malarial Zones

Details for insect precautions are covered later in this chapter. Preventing mosquito bites prevents malaria! This is just as important as taking pro-phylactic medications. Even while taking antimalarial medications it's possible to contract malaria, as the medications may fail.

Symptoms may develop as early as 8 days following exposure, or up to months and occasionally even up to 3 years after leaving a malarial zone. It's also possible for symptoms to develop after completing all rec-ommended antimalarial medications.

> *Anyone who develops recurrent fevers, sweats, malaise, and head-ache during or following travel in a malarial zone should obtain medical evaluation as soon as possible, including blood tests for malaria.*

Malaria is most effectively treated in the early course of disease. De-laying treatment may have serious or even fatal consequences.

Recommended Preventive Drug Regimes for Travel in Malarial Zones

Recommendations for the prevention and treatment of malaria change regularly. Check with your local public health department, travel clinic, or the CDC for current recommendations. The existence of several spe-cies of Plasmodium, and the recent spread of drug-resistant strains of the species Plasmodium falciparum complicates the prevention of malaria. The other significant species, P. ovale, P. vivax, and P. malariae, are gen-erally not resistant to antimalarial medications, except for a resistant strain of P. vivax centered around Papua New Guinea.

Travel in nonresistant Plasmodium falciparum areas

This includes Haiti, the Dominican Republic, Central America west of the Panama Canal, Mexico, Egypt and the Middle East, and a few other countries in Africa and elsewhere.

Chloroquine phosphate — 500 mg. salt (equivalent to 300 mg. base). The most common brand name is Aralen.

Chloroquine — Should be taken orally, on the same day, once a *week*. Start 1–2 weeks prior to entering the malarial zone, continue weekly dur-ing your stay, and for 4 weeks after leaving the zone.

Other formulations of chloroquine are available, including chloroquine hydrochloride and hydroxychloroquine sulfate (Plaquenil). These are the same as chloroquine phosphate and you can substitute equivalent doses.

Most people do not experience any side effects from chloroquine. If you do have side effects, try taking the medication with food, or take 1/2 dose twice a week. If nausea, vomiting, diarrhea, abdominal cramps or an upset stomach occur, instead of chloroquine take hydroxychloroquine sulfate which is sometimes better tolerated.

Travel in areas of chloroquine-resistant Plasmodium falciparum

Malaria caused by species of P. falciparum that are resistant to chloroquine is increasing worldwide. The recommended antimalarial medication is:

Mefloquine 250 mg. — Take one tablet once a week, starting one week before entering a malarial zone, each week while in the zone, and for four weeks after leaving the malarial zone. Recent cases of malaria in West Africa occurred in spite of this regime. Observe mosquito precautions religiously in this area.

Alternative antimalarial medications for areas of chloroquine-resistant P. falciparum

If you're unable to take mefloquine (see contraindications in Part III, p. 286), then take either doxycycline or chloroquine as described below:

Doxycycline 100 mg. — Take one tablet orally once a day beginning 1-2 days before arrival in a malarial zone, daily while in a malarial zone, and for four weeks after leaving the zone.

Note: doxycycline is contraindicated during pregnancy and breastfeeding. It's also photosensitizing and can result in severe sunburn. Take precautions against sun exposure (see pp. 31–34).

Chloroquine — Take weekly as prescribed for nonresistant areas; **and** carry a single dose (3 tablets) of **Fansidar**. If you develop a flu-like illness accompanied by fever and chills, and *medical care is not available*, take all 3 pills together promptly. Continue taking chloroquine weekly, and seek medical attention as soon as possible for malarial blood tests and treatment. This is a temporary measure and prompt medical evaluation is essential. If medical care is available, do not take the Fansidar. Get medical evaluation and blood tests for malaria instead.

Note: do not take Fansidar if you are allergic to sulfa drugs. Anyone with severe allergies or asthma should consult their doctor before taking this medication.

Use of Fansidar — Don't take weekly doses of Fansidar. Continuous use (more than 2 doses) is associated with severe, even fatal, drug reactions. Following any use of Fansidar, get immediate medical attention if side effects develop. Watch especially for changes in the skin or mucous membranes. Changes may include *itching, redness, development of a rash,* *mouth or genital lesion(s)*, or a *sore throat*. These may be life-threatening.

There are now documented cases of Fansidar-resistant P. falciparum malaria in East Africa. Resistance to Fansidar is also high in certain rural areas of Thailand, especially along the Thai-Burma border.

If you are unable to take mefloquine and are traveling to the jungles of Indonesia, Papua New Guinea, or the Solomon Islands, it has been suggested that combining weekly chloroquine and daily doxycycline may provide increased protection.

Travel in areas with Plasmodium ovale and Plasmodium vivax

Unlike P. falciparum, P. ovale and P. vivax can persist in the liver. They may cause relapses for as long as 4 years after you discontinue preventive drugs.

Travelers in these areas who develop symptoms suggesting malaria after returning home should seek medical help immediately. Report your travel history and the possibility of malaria to your doctor. If malaria is the diagnosis, the drug primaquine can be prescribed. This medication acts against the liver stages of malaria, preventing relapse.

The routine use of primaquine is controversial. It's not recommended for most travelers. Use of primaquine preventively (without the diagnosis of P. ovale or P. vivax malaria) should be limited to Peace Corps Volunteers, missionaries, or others who will spend an extended period in a malarial zone exposed to either of these Plasmodium species. Prior to taking primaquine, a blood test is required to rule out a particular blood deficiency (G_6PD).

If possible, take primaquine at home under medical supervision rather than abroad. This will be feasible for many travelers because the drug is taken once a day for 14 days, usually during the last 2 weeks of the chloroquine or mefloquine treatment following departure from the malarial zone.

Other antimalarial medications

In the past Amodiaquine was used as an alternative drug against chloroquine-resistant P. falciparum, particularly in Africa. This drug is no longer recommended — under any circumstances — due to adverse and potentially deadly side effects.

Proguanil (Paludrine) — This medication is not available in the U.S. It's considered effective in East Africa but not in West Africa, Thailand, or Papua New Guinea. It's taken daily (200 mg.) in combination with the weekly chloroquine.

Travelers transiting Heathrow airport in London, England can obtain both Proguanil and chloroquine without prescription from the airport pharmacy. Ask the pharmacist for the medication. Allow 2–3 hours to get to the pharmacy and back through customs to your airplane.

Use of antimalarial medications during breastfeeding

With the exception of tetracycline or doxycycline, the use of antimalarial medications is considered safe for infants who are breastfeeding. No protection from malaria is provided to the infant.

Overdose of Antimalarial Medications

Never exceed the prescribed amount of medication. Overdosage can be fatal. Store medications, especially chloroquine, in childproof containers out of reach of children.

Treatment of Acute Malaria in Isolated Areas

Some adventurous travelers may acquire malaria while working, trekking, or exploring far from medical help. It may be wise to carry medication to treat an acute attack of malaria, especially in highly drug-resistant malarial zones in Burma, Papua New Guinea, Tanzania, and East and Central Africa. See Chapter 7, "Infectious Diseases," pp. 159–160 for recommended medications and treatment schedules in isolated areas.

Mosquito and Tick Precautions

Clothing

Besides causing itching and discomfort, insects carry a number of formidable diseases, including malaria, yellow fever, dengue fever, Japanese B encephalitis, and tickborne encephalitis. The first line of defense is protective clothing, backed up by use of repellents. Many insects are active at dawn and dusk. The mosquitoes that spread malaria, yellow fever, and Japanese B encephalitis are active at night and the mosquito which carries dengue fever is active during the day. Insect precautions can therefore be a 24-hour concern.

When you venture outside where mosquitoes are active, avoid using scented preparations such as perfume, hair spray, or deodorants. Wear clothing that covers the neck, arms, legs, and ankles. White or light-colored clothing is least likely to attract insects. Avoid dark colored clothing.

For maximum protection, treat clothing with "Duranon Tick Repellent."

It's a permethrin spray which kills mosquitoes, ticks, and chiggers upon contact. It's odorless and doesn't stain clothing. Spray on outer surfaces of clothing and allow to dry before wearing. This may take up to 2 to 4 hours in humid weather. The treated clothing retains its effectiveness through numerous washings up to 2 weeks.

If not available locally, it can be mail ordered from:

Buck Rub Archery
157 Bank St., Waukesha, Wisconsin 53188 • (414) 547-0535
The manufacturer is

Coulston International
Easton, Pennsylvania • (215) 253-0167.

Insect Repellents

Apply insect repellent to all areas of exposed skin except around the eyes and mouth. Use only insect repellents containing DEET (diethyl-m-toluamide). DEET repels a variety of mosquitoes, chiggers, ticks, fleas, and biting flies. On mosquitoes, it apparently works by blocking their heat receptors so they don't know where to land. Repellents are not effective against stinging insects such as bees and wasps.

DEET requires some caution. Some formulations are absorbed through the skin and can cause toxic and allergic reactions such as itching, skin rashes, blisters, and swelling. If a reaction occurs, wash the DEET off thoroughly and seek medical attention. If unavailable, see pp. 113–115 for treatment. Ingestion of DEET can be fatal. Topical repellents are often washed off by rain or sweat, or when swimming or diving. Repellent is also lost from absorption, evaporation, or wiping the skin. To maintain effectiveness, repellents must periodically be reapplied.

"Ultrathon" is a new formulation of 35% DEET with a polymer that prevents absorption into the skin and resists removal from sweat, rain, and water exposure. It provides protection for up to 12 hours.

Some people report that vitamin B_1 supplements act as an insect repellent. Avon's "Skin So Soft" has also come into popular use as a repellent. Although we haven't tried it, it's certain to be kinder to the skin and better smelling than most other products. One study showed it may only provide protection for 10–30 minutes, so repeated applications are necessary.

Indoor Precautions

Houses and sleeping quarters may also need protection, especially in rural areas. Window and door screens, if present, must fit tightly. They must be free of holes, with a mesh small enough to prevent the entrance of insects such as mosquitos. Use a pyrethrum insect spray in living or sleeping areas during the evening and nighttime hours. Mosquito coils, burned in your room at night, will also help keep insects away.

In some areas mosquito nets for the bed are crucial, whether or not you have screens on the rest of the house. Rectangular shapes are preferrable to cone shapes. Otherwise, skin contact with the netting might allow insect bites. Netting should have a tightly woven border so it can be tucked under a mattress. It should also be white so that insects can be seen against it or through it. A zipper is a nice extra, allowing easy entrance and exit.

Free standing, portable rectangular mosquito netting is now available from IAMAT (for address, see p. 44). "La Mosquette" weighs 5 pounds, adjusts to single or double bed size, and is easy to assemble and pack away.

Netting with a minimum of 26 holes per square inch will keep out the smallest mosquito. Tears should be patched with needle and thread, or with tape (duct tape works well). Use the tape back to back, inside and out. Mosquito netting will not, however, keep out sand flies. These insects sometimes transmit *leishmaniasis*. While sand fly netting is available, it's very hot and stuffy to use.

In summary, to obtain maximum protection from mosquitoes:

1. use an insect repellent containing DEET on exposed skin;

2. wear protective clothing treated with a permethrin spray;

3. use mosquito netting and coils when necessary.

Other Precautions

If necessary, shake out your shoes and clothing before dressing in the morning. This will help protect you from other unwanted guests — scorpions, spiders, and the like.

Prevention (Prophylaxis) of Traveler's Diarrhea

There's no vaccination available to prevent traveler's diarrhea, and we don't expect one in the near future. Strict adherence to food and beverage precautions is the best prevention. These are summarized in the Nutshell Guide™ (see pp. 97–98).

For travel of 3 weeks or less, Pepto Bismol can be taken as a preventive regimen. The dosage is 2 chewable tablets, 4 times a day. Liquid Pepto-Bismol, 2 tablespoons 4 times a day, is usually too bulky for practical use. Start one day before departure and continue until 2 days after your return. This regimen prevents traveler's diarrhea in a majority of cases.

Pepto-Bismol contains salicylic acid (an aspirin-like compound). Don't use it if you are pregnant, have an ulcer, or take Coumadin or aspirin routinely as treatment for a medical condition. Avoid Pepto-Bismol if your doctor has advised you not to take aspirin. Diabetics on either insulin or oral medications should discuss use of Pepto-Bismol with their doctor. There is an increased risk of low blood sugar (hypoglycemia). Pepto-Bismol may turn the tongue and/or stools black and cause mild constipation. These are harmless side effects which disappear after stopping the medication. If ringing in the ears or a burning sensation in the stomach occur, immediately discontinue use.

Antibiotics once used to prevent traveler's diarrhea are no longer recommended. Adverse consequences include antibiotic-induced intestinal problems, vaginal yeast infections, and the emergence of drug resistant bacteria. If you're pregnant refer to Chapter 2, p. 57 for details on which medications to take or *not* to take.

Several dangerous products once popular for treating diarrhea in western travelers **must be avoided**. These include Enterovioform, chloramphenicol, Clioquinol, Iodoquinol, Mexaform, and Intestopan. These medications can cause severe neurological or other problems. Treatment of traveler's diarrhea is discussed in Chapter 6, "Stomach and Intestinal Disorders," pp. 134–137.

First Aid Kit

A first aid kit can be anything from aspirin and Band-aids to a miniature MASH warehouse. If travel will only be to major cities where doctors and pharmacies are available, take the basics. A rural Peace Corps Volunteer or New Guinea anthropologist will need something more extensive.

When preparing a first aid kit remember that in developing countries all types of medicines are available without prescription. They're often cheaper. There's no need to carry everything, or to carry large quantities.

Have your medical provider assist in planning the kit, particularly if you have any drug allergies, chronic medical conditions, or are pregnant, breastfeeding, or have other special medical needs. Write down specific instructions in the book.

Following is a list of recommended medicines and first aid kit supplies. You can customize the kit depending on several factors. These include the destination, length of stay, anticipated activities, and the local availability of medical supplies and care.

People living and working in rural areas face special problems when medical help isn't readily accessible. Some of the medications will be

 **Basic First Aid Kit**

antacids
antibiotics for traveler's diarrhea
antimalarial medications (if traveling in malarial zones)
aspirin or acetaminophen (Tylenol)
Band-Aids
chapstick with sunblock
condoms (if any new sexual contact is even a remote possibility)
cotton swabs
dental floss
hydrogen peroxide

insect repellent (with DEET)
Pepto-Bismol and/or other anti-diarrheal medications (Lomotil, Immodium)
safety pins
scissors
suntan lotion with sunscreen
thermometer
topical antibacterial ointment
tweezers
water purification system (iodine, iodine contact filter, or apparatus for boiling)

Optional:
anaphylaxis (allergy) kit if allergic to bee or other insect stings
antihistamines for allergies
artificial tears
"Extractor" for removing animal venom"*
motion sickness medications

medication to prevent altitude sickness (Diamox)
mole skin (for blisters)
mosquito net, permethrin clothing spray, knockdown spray (if needed for mosquitoes, insects)

---

*This substitutes for a snakebite kit—but **not** *for medical treatment in case of snakebite!* We highly recommend it for travel in rural areas. It can be used in the treatment of almost all venomous bites and stings. The "Extractor" is a hard plastic vacuum pump in the shape of a syringe, which creates very powerful suction. It is designed to remove venom through the injection site, whether a bite or a sting. Because of the strong suction, *no cutting is needed*—not even for snakebite. The "Extractor" is supplied with a variety of suction cups, for bites to different parts of the body. Because suction is created by pushing in on the plunger rather than by pulling, it can be applied with one hand. The manufacturer states that it can be used to treat envenomization from snakes, scorpions, bees, wasps, hornets, and spiders.

✔ Basic First Aid Kit (Continued)

Optional for women:

medications for menstrual cramps
medications for urinary tract infections

medications for vaginal yeast infections
tampons or sanitary napkins

Reminders: flashlight, Swiss Army Knife, sunglasses, extra prescription glasses, contact lens solution, copy of lens prescription, hearing aid batteries, contraceptives, soap, medications for chronic conditions (see "Special Individual Needs"), and your doctor's phone number. Keep prescription medications in their original labeled containers.

For travel in rural areas for less than 1 month, add:

Ace wrap, 3" width
adhesive tape, 1" width
antibiotics for bacterial skin infections
antifungal topical cream for fungal
  skin infections
anti-inflammatory medications
aspirin or acetaminophen (Tylenol)
  with codeine for pain
Benadryl or other antihistamine (for
  itching, allergies, or sleep)
betadine swabsticks
butterfly bandages or steri-strips,
tincture of benzoin

CAVIT (a temporary dental filling)
cotton
fine forceps for tick removal (in tick-
  infested areas)
hydrocortisone topical cream
muscle relaxants
oil of cloves (a dental anesthetic)
oral rehydration solutions
Sam splint*
sterile disposable syringes and
  needles**
sterile gauze, 2" x 2" and 4" x 4"
sterile gauze roll, 2" or 3" width

For travel in rural areas for up to 6 months, add:

antibiotics for bacterial respiratory infections (see Chapter 13).
Silvadene Cream

If living or working in rural areas for more than 6 months, add:

antibiotics for eye and ear infections
medicines for intestinal parasite
Kwell

---

*The Sam Splint is a compact, versatile splint that can be molded into almost any shape and used on any part of the body. It is made by:

Seaberg Company, Inc.
P. O. Box 734, South Beach, OR 97366 USA • (503) 867-4726.

**The purpose of carrying syringes and needles is to protect yourself from having blood drawn or shots given with possibly contaminated equipment. This would increase the risk for both AIDS and hepatitis. If you carry these items you must have a written prescription accompanying them to avoid legal problems.

useful when medical help is not available, or if you choose to be your own doctor under certain conditions.

Basic CPR and first aid classes are highly desirable for all travelers. These are available through the Red Cross, the American Heart Association, and other organizations. The Red Cross has an excellent first aid book with information on the use of triangular bandages, Ace wraps, dressings, and covers other first aid skills. Such preparation is of particular importance for anyone planning to visit remote or rural areas for any length of time.

Parts II and III of this book provide information that you'll need in order to use the medicines in your first aid kit appropriately and safely. Part II also provides guidelines to help determine when medical care is mandatory. These guidelines, together with your first aid kit, will prepare you to cope with most medical contingencies even when help is not immediately available.

Finding Health Care in Foreign Countries

Falling ill in a foreign land can be a terrifying experience. Part II, "Diagnosis and Treatment of Medical Disorders," offers guidelines to help determine when medical care is needed. When it is, who do you turn to for help? Are they qualified? Do they speak English? How much do they charge? Depending on circumstances, there will be a lot of choices, or very few. But there will almost always be a way of locating medical assistance.

Finding Help Before You Go

By far the best way to locate help is to identify potential resources in advance. This can be done inexpensively through one of the following organizations:

1. IAMAT (Internat'l Association for Medical Assistance to Travelers): 417 Center St. , Lewiston, NY 14092 • (716) 754-4883

IAMAT is the best known traveler's assistance organization. It's a nonprofit group that provides a worldwide directory of physicians, hospitals, and health care centers. If you become ill, locate the nearest IAMAT center in the directory. It will provide you with a list of approved English-speaking doctors, including those on 24-hour call.

A physician does an appropriate medical workup, makes referrals if necessary, and even reports to your personal physician at home upon request. He or she will furnish a medical report if you need it for the remainder of your trip.

IAMAT pledges that their physician referrals will meet a high standard of medical practice, adhere to a fixed fee schedule, and speak English. Furthermore, there is no charge for joining IAMAT, although they do request donations.

2. American Express Travel Related Services
   World Financial Center, New York, NY 10285-3600 • (212) 640-2000

American Express has a telephone hotline referral service for their cardholders while traveling. It's a worldwide 24-hour emergency medical referral service. They'll also refer translators if needed and notify family members and your office upon request.

If you already have an American Express card this may meet your needs. If not, you'll have to join. Other issuers of "premium" credit cards are establishing similar referral services.

Pre-arranged Health Insurance and Emergency Services

A variety of insurance plans provide medical coverage and emergency services for international travelers. Costs and coverage vary considerably. Some programs include emergency evacuation and 24-hour telephone hotline services to track down English-speaking doctors or provide quick medical advice. Other programs provide directories of English-speaking doctors, but may require treatment from an MD on their approved list. Some health insurance is available only as an option to comprehensive travel insurance, which usually includes trip cancellation, interruption, baggage loss, and other features. Such plans may or may not fit your needs.

When considering insurance, check the fine print. Many policies exclude coverage for accidents from skiing or other winter sports, skin or scuba diving, mountaineering, and other activities. Some policies exclude coverage in certain countries, such as El Salvador, Nicaragua, Iran, or Iraq. They may exclude problems related to pregnancy or illness diagnosed or treated within a period, usually 2–6 months, preceding your trip. Some limit medical payments to one or two thousand dollars, which would not be sufficient to cover hospitalization for serious illness or surgery.

Individual health insurance coverage for extended travel should be available for $3.00 a day or less. The following is a partial list of agencies with health insurance plans for travelers:

1. Access America, Inc.
   600 Third Avenue Box 807
   New York, NY 10163
   1-800-851-2899 M-F or
   1-800-654-6686 after hours

2. HealthCare Abroad
   243 Church St. N.W.
   Suite 100D
   Vienna, VA 22180
   1-800-237-6615

3. WorldCare Travel Assistance
   1995 W. Commercial Blvd.
   Fort Lauderdale, FL 33307
   1-800-521-4882

4. International SOS Assistance
   Box 11568
   Philadelphia, PA 19116
   1-800-523-6586

5. Internat'l Travelers Assistance
   Box 10623
   Towson, Maryland 21204
   1-800-732-5309

6. Carefree Travel Insurance
   ARM Coverage, Inc.
   120 Mineola Blvd.
   Box 310
   Mineola, New York 11501
   1-800-645-2424

7. Travel Guard International
   P.O. Box 1200
   Stevens Point, WI 54481
   1-800-826-1300

8. The Travelers Insurance Co.
   One Tower Square
   Hartford, CT 06183
   1-800-243-3174

9. Tele-Trip Co.,
   Mutual of Omaha
   3201 Farnham St.
   Omaha, NE 68131
   1-800-228-9792

10. Nationwide/Worldwide Emergency Ambulance Return
    1900 N. MacArthur Blvd
    Oklahoma City, OK 71327
    1-800-654-6700.

11. Travel Safe Network
    Bank America
    201 Mission St., 29th Floor
    San Francisco, CA 91405
    1-800-227-3460

12. Global Assistance Network
    999 Summer St.
    Stamford, CT 06905
    1-800-368-2110

Finding Help Abroad

All of the telephone referral services, no matter how extensive, assume you have access to a telephone. They also assume that calls can be put through to the U.S. without difficulty. Obviously, this is not always the case — especially in Third World countries outside the major cities. What other options exist?

In Large Urban Areas

There are usually many alternatives in large urban areas:

1. Your local embassy or consulate will have a list of medical services available in the vicinity. Information can be obtained during office hours, and frequently from a duty officer at other times. U.S. consulates provide names, addresses, fee schedules, and qualifications of local English-speaking physicians. In the U.S., information on U.S. consular services, including addresses, can be obtained by calling

   1-202-632-3444.

2. Large hospitals, medical schools, or university hospitals will usually have English-speaking staff.

3. Major tourist hotels will usually have a list of English-speaking doctors available, or they may be able to tell you who to contact.

4. International agencies, such as the Red Cross, CARE, Catholic Relief Services, American Friends Service Committee, and other development or relief agencies, or their employees, may be able to make a medical referral — especially in an emergency.

5. Other Americans or foreigners living abroad, or English-speaking nationals are often willing and able to provide medical referrals. Find them by checking foreign-based U.S. companies, American church missions, offices of international airlines, even telephone operators — or anywhere else you can think of.

6. In an emergency, head for the emergency room of the nearest large hospital.

In Isolated or Rural Areas

In small towns or rural areas you will be more on your own. Check locally with missionaries, Peace Corps volunteers, Red Cross personnel, or any other foreigners living in the area. Local hotels may be able to locate a doctor, although fees, language, and the quality of care could present difficulties.

If all else fails, check the local pharmacies. In developing nations, especially in isolated areas, the pharmacist frequently finds him- or herself in the position of community doctor. Though language and qualifications are problematic, the local pharmacist is in an ideal position to learn about and respond to the medical needs of the community. The information in Parts II and III of this book will be useful in conjunction with this approach.

In an Emergency

If an international phone line is accessible, call *The Overseas Citizens Emergency Center* in Washington, D.C., which is part of the U.S. State Department. In case of serious illness or other medical emergency, they will help find local medical care through the nearest U.S. embassy or consulate. They can also contact family and friends at home, obtain medical records and send them abroad, help with the transfer of emergency funds, or arrange a medical evacuation. Their phone number is:

1-202-647-5225.

In Case Of Death

Report the death of a relative or traveling companion in a foreign country to your nearest consular or embassy office. They will provide further instructions.

After Obtaining Medical Care

It's important to keep a record of any diagnosis made or treatment obtained while traveling. This information may be vital for follow-up or if problems occur upon returning home. Write down both the brand name and the chemical name of any unfamiliar medication taken. Save the original package or package insert if one is provided. When symptoms of illness occur after returning home, give this information to your doctor. He or she should also be informed of your itinerary, especially after visits to malarial zones or areas of high risk for other illnesses.

Use the form on the following page to record your information.

Travel Medical Record

Date of Visit _____
MD Name, Address, Phone # _____
Symptoms _____
_____
Diagnosis_____
Medications Prescribed_____
Lab Tests Obtained_____
Lab Results _____

Date of Visit _____
MD Name, Address, Phone # _____
Symptoms _____
_____
Diagnosis_____
Medications Prescribed_____
Lab Tests Obtained_____
Lab Results _____

Date of Visit _____
MD Name, Address, Phone # _____
Symptoms _____
_____
Diagnosis_____
Medications Prescribed_____
Lab Tests Obtained_____
Lab Results _____

Special
Individual Needs

2

Special Health Problems

If you have a medical condition, chronic illness, or regularly take medications, discuss travel plans with your doctor in advance. Inquire about aspects of travel that may affect you medically. For instance, some people with anemia or chronic heart or lung disease may not tolerate high altitudes. If you anticipate using new medications during travel, including any suggested in this book, find out if there are any contraindications. If so, have your doctor recommend an alternative. For chronic medical conditions ask your doctor to provide you a written medical summary to carry on your trip. It should be written on letterhead stationery, and include current therapy as well as copies of recent EKG results, lab reports, diagnostic tests, or other relevant data. This information could be of great value if you develop or exacerbate medical problems while traveling.

Other conditions which may require medical consultation prior to travel include a recent heart attack, angina, pregnancy, diabetes, asthma, drug and food allergies, or a previous allergic reaction to insect bites or stings. With proper preparation almost anyone's desire to travel can be accomodated, even when chronic medical conditions exist.

Air Travel with Special Medical Conditions

Most airlines can meet the needs of travelers with specific health problems and special requirements when notified at least 48–72 hours in advance. They can order oxygen, wheelchairs, and special diets (diabetic, low salt, gluten-free, vegetarian, Kosher, low cholesterol).

Chronic medical conditions, pregnancy, and some acute illnesses may require medical consent prior to flying. Other conditions may require avoidance or postponement of air travel, or medical assistance during flight. Some recent surgical, medical, or dental procedures, severe anemia, and a recent stroke or heart attack fall into the latter category. Anyone taking medication should carry a supply of their medication with them on the airplane, not in their luggage.

Flying with Supplemental Oxygen

Supplemental oxygen requires a prescription. Airline regulations prohibit use of your own oxygen on board the plane. Some airlines require advance notice of 48–72 hours; others may require airline approval before a ticket can be purchased. Airlines provide oxygen only during the flight — *not* during stopovers. Oxygen during stopovers must be contracted separately.

Consider using a wheelchair to board and disembark. This will decrease the work involved and consequently decrease oxygen requirements. Drink plenty of fluids during the flight because the lower air humidity is dehydrating. Make sure the airline seats you in the no smoking area.

Anemia, if Severe

You may require supplemental oxygen if your hemoglobin level is below 9. Obtain medical evaluation and consent before flying.

Lung Disease

With emphysema or Chronic Obstructive Pulmonary Disease (COPD) consult your doctor when flying. Supplemental oxygen might be necessary.

Heart Disease

If you had a heart attack within the 3 months preceding the flight, or if you have angina stabilized by medications, take along a recent copy of your EKG. Check with your doctor to see if supplemental oxygen is necessary. For all other heart conditions, consult your doctor before flying. Notify the steward or stewardess immediately if chest pain develops during the flight.

Pacemakers

Pacemakers are not affected by airport security devices, and flying is not a contraindicated activity. Carry the model and lot number, and a copy of your baseline EKG. Make sure the battery's lifespan is sufficient to last the full length of the trip. Note that electronic telephone checks are *not* relayed by international satellite.

Travelers with heart conditions can obtain a wallet card that provides a recent EKG, a list of current medications, a medical history summary, and pacemaker information. The card is available from:

Heart Chart
PO Box 221, New Rochelle, New York • (914) 632-3388

Varicose Veins or a History of Phlebitis

Sitting on long plane flights may aggravate these conditions. Stand up and walk around at 30–45 minute intervals, and do isometric exercises when sitting down. If necessary, use support hose during the flight.

Sinus and Ear Conditions

Flying with clogged ear, nose, or sinus passages can cause symptoms which vary from annoying to painful. Most problems occur during descent, but ascent can also produce symptoms.

Avoid flying if you have a cold, ear or sinus infection, or severe sinus and nasal congestion. If flying is unavoidable, or if you have chronic or acute serous otitis or allergic rhinitis, you may need a decongestant. Take Entex LA, or Sudafed (pseudoephedrine HCl) 60 mg.— if Entex LA is unavailable — about 45 minutes before departure. Use a 1% Neosynephrine or Afrin nasal spray 15 minutes before takeoff and landing. Wait 5–10 minutes, then clear your ears. Close your mouth, pinch your nose shut and pop your ears by blowing outward against the closed passages. Blowing your nose, swallowing, yawning, and chewing gum may also help clear air passages. If ear or sinus pain persist after flying, or for recurrent problems, obtain medical evaluation.

Blind with a Guide Dog

Check with airlines prior to travel to be sure you can bring your dog on board. Embassies of the countries you'll be visiting can inform you of any regulations regarding guide dogs. Some countries don't permit guide dogs, while others require a quarantine period. Carry a certificate of rabies vaccination for your dog.

Diabetes and Travel

Travel presents some challenges to diabetics who use medications to control their blood sugar level. This is due to changes in time zones, irregular meal schedules, unfamiliar food, varying levels of physical activity, and other factors. With a little effort and preparation it should be possible to keep blood sugar levels under control and travel safely almost anywhere. Get off to a good start by ordering a diabetic diet from the airline 24 hours in advance. It's also important to avoid nausea, vomiting, and diarrhea. Take preventive medications as needed. Know how to treat low blood sugar and ketoacidosis prior to travel.

Insulin Dependent Diabetics

Observe the following precautions:

1. Take enough insulin to last the entire trip. Insulin is good for 3 months unrefrigerated, but should be kept as cool as possible.
2. Carry enough U100 syringes for the entire trip. In many areas of the world only U40 and U80 syringes are available. Carry a prescription from your doctor for the insulin, syringes, and other supplies.
3. Take a sufficient quantity of lancets and reagent strips for blood glucose monitoring, and strips or tablets for urine ketone testing. Travel may require more frequent blood tests to keep glucose levels under control.
4. Have packets of sugar, crackers, dried fruit, or candy bars at hand for a quick snack if needed.
5. Carry a medical card with your insulin type and dosage, doctor's name and telephone number. Also wear a diabetic ID bracelet or necklace.

Insulin adjustment across time zones

For travel east or west across 6 or more time zones, make dosage adjustments for a longer or shorter day. Traveling north or south, or across 5 time zones or less, does not require insulin adjustment. Monitor blood sugar levels every 6 hours and before meals. See the chart on the next page.

Insulin Adjustment Schedules

Check with your doctor before using this schedule to make sure it's appropriate and that there are no contraindications.

Westbound, 6 or more time zones (day is lengthened).

Dosage schedule	Day of departure	18 hours after morning dose check blood glucose; if greater than:	Morning of destination
single dose	usual dose	240, take one third of usual dose followed by a snack or meal	usual dose
2 doses	usual a.m. & p.m. dose (10–12 hours after a.m. dose)	240, take one third of usual a.m. dose followed by a snack or meal	usual 2 doses

Eastbound, 6 or more time zones (day is shortened).

Dosage schedule	Day of departure	Morning of destination	10 hours after a.m. dose, test blood glucose; if greater than:	2nd day
single dose	usual dose	two thirds usual dose	240, take remaining one third of a.m. dose	usual dose
2 doses	usual a.m. and p.m. dose	two thirds a.m. dose	240, take usual p.m. dose plus remaining one third of a.m. dose	usual 2 doses

Oral Diabetic Medications

Take an adequate supply of medications for the entire trip. Carry them on your person — don't risk losing them with your luggage. Also carry an extra prescription for each medication, with the generic name of the drug as well as the trade name.

Medication timing is not crucial as it is with insulin. Take the pills according to local time, regardless of how many time zones you have crossed. It's prudent to carry extra snacks, as well as a medical ID card with your doctor's name and phone number, and a diabetic ID necklace or bracelet.

Foot Care

Feet require even greater attention and care when traveling than at home. In all likelihood you will be using them more. Good walking shoes, well broken in, are a must. New shoes require close monitoring of your feet for blistering or possible infection. If signs of infection or skin breakdown are noted, obtain medical evaluation at the earliest opportunity.

Travel Services for Diabetics

The Diabetic Service Club provides information on emergency assistance while traveling, and information on diets, foot care, and exercise. A nominal membership fee is charged. Their address:

Diabetic Travel Services, Inc.
349 E. 52nd St., New York, NY 10022

The American Diabetic Association publishes a booklet "Traveling With DM, Not From DM." It's available free by writing to:

American Diabetic Association
500 5th Ave., New York, NY 10029

Other sources of information on diabetes and travel are:

The Diabetic Traveler   International Diabetes Federation
PO Box 8223 RW   10 Queen Street
Stamford, CT 06905   London W1M OBD, England

Pregnancy and Travel

Healthy women with normal pregnancies can travel freely to most areas of the world. Travel is safe throughout pregnancy, although the period from the fourth–sixth month (second trimester) is usually safest. Follow the routine preventive health measures pertaining to food and water, insects, and skin exposure to contaminated soil and water. Discuss travel plans with your obstetrician before leaving, and go over all the medications you plan to take on your trip.

Avoid travel if:

1. multiple births are expected;

2. you have a history of pregnancy-induced hypertension;

3. your pregnancy is considered high risk. If you have a high risk pregnancy and choose to travel during the final 3 months of pregnancy, carry urine dipsticks to check for sugar and protein. Blood pressure should also be checked weekly. An unexpected elevation in any of these requires medical attention as soon as possible.

Pregnancy increases the likelihood of developing a vaginal yeast infection. Wear appropriate loose clothing (see vaginal infections, pp. 234–236) and consider carrying medication for treatment.

Immunizations

It's prudent to avoid all vaccinations, especially influenza, during the first 3 months of pregnancy. Avoid the live virus vaccines — measles, mumps, rubella, yellow fever, oral polio, and oral typhoid — throughout pregnancy. There's no convincing evidence of risk to the fetus from other vaccines, toxoids, or immune globulin.

If a vaccination previously produced a high fever, inform your doctor prior to revaccination. It may be prudent to avoid that particular vaccine. After receiving any of the live attenuated vaccines, avoid pregnancy for a period of 3 months.

Only if visiting areas of high risk for yellow fever or polio should these vaccines be taken, preferrably after the first 3 months of pregnancy. Oral polio vaccine is the preferred polio vaccine. Better yet, avoid travel in areas of high risk for yellow fever and polio during pregnancy if not previously vaccinated against these diseases.

Air Travel

If you're 35 weeks or more pregnant, you're not allowed to board international flights. To prevent problems, carry a letter from a doctor on letterhead stationery stating the due date. Women with a high risk pregnancy or a history of blood clots (thromboembolic disease) should avoid flying.

Wear the seatbelt low around the hips to avoid the possibility of injury during take off, landing, or air turbulence. To help circulation, get up and walk around at 30–45 minute intervals. Bulkhead seats (the ones in front of compartment partitions) may allow more leg room, and are easier to get in and out of during flight. Aisle seats are the next best choice.

Drink lots of fluids inflight to avoid dehydration. If your hematocrit is 25 or less, supplemental oxygen may be advisable during the flight. Avoid unpressurized planes. One thing not to worry about is the metal detectors used for airport security. They aren't harmful.

Malaria Prevention

See Chapter 1 for an overview of malaria. There are special concerns for women which we discuss here. Malaria infection may be more severe in women who are pregnant. There is an increased risk of complications including premature delivery, spontaneous abortion, and stillbirth.

While the use of chloroquine is safe throughout pregnancy, preventive drugs for chloroquine-resistant areas are usually contraindicated, except under special circumstances and only under a doctor's care. (An exception is proguanil which can be used for travel to resistant areas of East Africa. This medication is not available in the U.S.) Women who are pregnant or likely to become pregnant should avoid travel to areas of choroquine-resistant P. falciparum malaria. Don't take Fansidar, doxycycline, primaquine, or quinine. Mefloquine should also be avoided during pregnancy. Use of protective clothing and mosquito nets is encouraged, as well as the sparing use of low percentage Deet insect repellents or Avon's Skin-So-Soft. See "Mosquito and Tick Precautions," pp. 38–40.

Treating Traveler's Diarrhea

Follow food and water precautions religiously. Purify water by boiling or by use of a micropore filter with an iodine element, such as the "PUR." You may use iodine for water purification during pregnancy for a maximum of three weeks.

You shouldn't use many of the medications for prevention and treatment of traveler's diarrhea during pregnancy. Avoid Pepto-Bismol, Bactrim (Septra), doxycycline, norfloxacillin, and Cipro (ciprofloxacin). Drugs which you can use safely include ampicillin, erythromycin, and Imodium (loperamide).

Medical Coverage

Check your travel health insurance for the gestational date cutoff, and for coverage for delivery or prolonged confinement due to premature delivery while traveling.

Activity Precautions

It's best to avoid high altitudes during pregnancy. As a general rule, confine your travels to places under 7,000 ft. (2,135 meters) elevation. Running, jogging, and other activities are fine, but avoid getting overheated. Swimming is excellent exercise, but water skiing is associated with a risk of tearing the vaginal wall. Avoid scuba diving throughout pregnancy.

Indications for Medical Attention

Obtain medical evaluation immediately for any of the following:

1. high blood pressure;
2. elevated urine protein;
3. severe abdominal pain;
4. ruptured membranes ("water breaking");
5. headaches or visual disturbances;
6. contractions;
7. vaginal bleeding;
8. severe swelling of the face or extremities, or sudden weight increase.

Medical Alert Tags

We strongly recommend wearing a medical identification bracelet or necklace for certain conditions. These include:

1. common drug allergies (such as penicillin);
2. allergies to stinging insects;
3. conditions such as diabetes or epilepsy;
4. use of certain medications, such as the anticoagulant coumadin.

Remember that a card in a wallet may not always be found, or may be indecipherable in a foreign country. For the conditions mentioned use a medical alert tag during travel — even if you do not use one at home.

Many pharmacies carry medical identification tags. If you can't locate what you need, write to:

Medic Alert Foundation International • 800-344-3226
PO Box 1009, Department AZ, Turlock, CA 9538

It's a nonprofit organization which provides medical information in the form of a bracelet or necklace. There's also a 24-hour hotline that accepts collect calls in a medical emergency from anywhere in the world. The hotline has immediate computer access to its members' medical records. They issue a wallet card annually to ensure medical information is current, although it can be updated at any time. There is a lifetime membership fee.

For those who don't want to wear a medical alert tag, a free medical ID card can be obtained from the AMA. The address is:

American Medical Association
535 N. Dearborn St., Chicago, IL 60610.

Allergies to Stinging Insects

If you have had a generalized reaction to the sting of any flying insects (wasps, bees, etc.),

wear a medical alert tag and carry emergency medications as part of a sting or anaphylaxis kit when traveling. It could save your life.

Commercial kits are available, or one can be assembled with your doctor's help. It should contain:

1. injectable epinephrine;
2. oral Benadryl or other antihistamine;
3. a strip of material for a loosely constrictive band;
4. any other medications your doctor advises.

Always have a prescription for any kit which contains needles and syringes. If you have angina, use epinephrine only with the prior consent of your physician.

Traveling companions should also be made aware of your situation. They must know how to use the kit on your behalf in any environment where you might encounter stinging insects. Always carry your kit with you while traveling. It does no good in your luggage or hotel room.

The EpiPen

For the injectable epinephrine in your kit, the EpiPen is highly recommended. This product contains a premeasured dose of epinephrine with an autoinjector that is simple and easy to use in an emergency. By pushing a small tube against the skin, epinephrine is automatically injected.

Other Recommendations

Because the "Extractor" can be used to remove venom from stings, we recommend it along with an allergy kit. See "First Aid Kit," pp. 42 - 43.

Precautions for Hypersensitive Individuals

Observe the following precautions to minimize the chance of an insect sting:

1. Avoid shiny jewelry and floral or scented perfumes, deodorants, soaps, or hair sprays outdoors.
2. Avoid wearing dark clothing outdoors. Brown, black, dark red and floral prints are said to be the most attracting, while white is the least.
3. Never go barefoot or wear sandals outdoors especially in clover or grass. Bees are attracted to flowering ground cover and yellow jackets are burrowing ground dwellers.
4. Avoid orchards and ripe fruit. Do not kick dead logs.
5. Use a small can of hairspray to quickly immobilize an insect. This works both outdoors or in a closed space such as a car. As an alternative, use a knock-down spray (Raid, Ortho).
6. Always carry an allergy kit when hiking, camping, or traveling where stings can occur. It's best to keep the kit on your person, rather than in luggage or a backpack. Replacement may be difficult if these are lost or stolen.
7. Avoid taking drugs from the class known as "beta-blockers." These block the effect of epinephrine if needed during an emergency.

Allergy Desensitization

Desensitization is recommended by some medical specialists for anyone with a generalized reaction to insect stings or a large local reaction greater than 6 inches (15 cm) across. Although it works well, desensitization to insect venom (unlike pollens) is effective only with ongoing treatment. Travelers working or residing in major cities in foreign countries might be able to arrange or continue a desensitization program. Desensitization must be done with sterile, disposable needles and syringes.

Disabled Travelers

Relatively few organized services exist for disabled travelers in Third World nations. Most of the services which do exist are provided in the U.S., Canada, Iceland, Europe, Israel, Australia, New Zealand, Japan, Hong Kong, and to a limited extent the Caribbean.

Some published books detail the resources available to disabled travelers in these areas. They include:

Frommer's — A Guide for the Disabled Traveler
by Frances Barish

Access to the World: A Travel Guide for the Handicapped
by Louise Weiss (Henry Holt & W.)

Travel for the Disabled, A Handbook of Travel Resources and 500 Worldwide Access Guides;
by Helen Heckler, R.N.
Twin Peaks Press, P.O. Box 8097, Portland, OR 97207

Access to transportation, food, lodging, museums, and other services are provided in international access guides. Two sources for these are:

RIUSA (Rehabilitation Int'l USA
1123 Broadway
New York, NY 10010
(212) 972-2707

Travel Information Center
Moss Rehabilitation Hospital
12th St. and Tabor Rd.
Philadelphia, PA 19141
(215) 329-5715

The Travel Information Center has an interesting approach. They will provide limited information by phone. For a $5 fee, they provide detailed access information on up to 3 destinations by mail. They tailor the information to your special interests and level of disability.

There are a number of associations and travel agencies providing special international tours and services for disabled travelers. Among these are:

THETA Association, Inc.
1058 Shell Blvd. Bldg. #1,
P.O. Box 4850
Foster City, CA 94404
(415) 573-9701

Society for the Advancement of
Travel for the Handicapped
26 Court St.
Brooklyn, NY 11242
(718) 858-5483

The Guided Tour
555 Ashbourne Rd.
Elkin Park, PA 19117
782-1370

Directions Unlimited
344 Main St.
Mount Kisco, NY 10549
1-800-533-5343

Handy-Cap Horizons
3250 E. Loretta Dr.
Indianapolis, IN 46227
(317) 784-5777

Flying Wheels Travel Group
143 West Bridge Street
Box 382
Owatonna, MN 55060
1-800-533-0363

Evergreen Travel Service
19505L 44th Ave.
West Lynwood, WA 98036
(206) 776-1184

Rambling Tours
Box 1304
Hallendale, FL 33009
(305) 456-2161

Coston-Clark and Associates
123-33 83rd Ave., Suite 1801
Kew Gardens, NY 11415
(212) 263-3835

Whole Person Tours
137 West 32nd St.
Bayonne, NJ 07002-1084
(201) 858-3400, ext. 10

Tours and services for the deaf or hearing-impaired can be arranged through the following agencies:

Signed Seekers
Box 53354
Washington, DC 20009
(202) 265-5451

Interpret Tours /Encino Travel Service
16660 Ventura Blvd.
Encino, CA 91436
(818) 788-4118

Birth Control for Travelers

Birth control is an important consideration for people who may be sexually active during their travels. Don't ignore the reality of your sexuality, especially given the stress that living or traveling in a foreign country can sometimes produce. Make good preparations in this area. The reward will be a safer and happier experience.

Women, whether or not currently using a birth control method, may need to make preparations well before departure. Some methods of birth control are not suitable for extended travel. Others should not be implemented either during or immediately preceding a trip.

It's just as important for male travelers to be concerned with contraception as it is for women. This is particularly true in Third World countries where women may be less likely to employ birth control measures. You can obtain information about or access to contraceptives in these countries through a regional office of the International Planned Parenthood Federation. A "World List of Family Planning Addresses" is available from the Planned Parenthood Federation of America. Their address is:

Planned Parenthood Federation of America (PPFA)
810 Seventh Ave., New York, NY 10019 • (212) 541-7800.

Birth Control Measures for Men

Men who take responsibility for contraception have only 2 viable alternatives, and withdrawal is not one of them. Unless you have had a vasectomy, there is little choice but to use a condom during sexual intercourse. Whether you normally disdain them or have never given them a thought, seriously consider their use. Whatever reluctance you have should be measured against your feelings about unintended pregnancy, and the array of circumstances, foreseen and unforeseen, this consequence entails. Assuming responsibility for preventing conception should make you feel better about sex, and about yourself.

Condoms have other advantages as well. Use of a *latex* (not lambskin) condom provides good protection against sexually transmitted infections such as gonorrhea, chlamydia, herpes, warts, and AIDS. Condoms are also inexpensive and widely available throughout the world. They come plain or lubricated, and in a variety of colors and styles. Know how to use them before departure.

Condoms should be stored in a cool, dry place — never in a wallet. Don't use a condom that was stored in a wallet. Condoms are disposable — reuse is unsafe as well as unesthetic.

When putting on condoms with a reservoir tip, gently press the tip to expel air. Air interferes with sensitivity and safety. Condoms without a receptacle tip need 1/2 inch free on the end. Place the condom on the erect penis, and roll it all the way down to the base. Following intercourse withdraw gently, holding the base of the condom to avoid either leaving the condom behind or spilling the contents.

It's appropriate and desirable to use a water-based lubricant in conjunction with the condom. Don't use Vaseline or other oil-based lubricants. Lubricants with the spermicide nonoxynol-9 add a further degree of protection not only against pregnancy, but also against disease including the AIDS virus.

Concurrent use of a vaginal spermicide foam raises the effectiveness of condoms to a level approaching that of birth control pills. For the touch of thoroughness, add spermicide to your packing list. In addition to being effective, it makes customs inspections a lot more interesting.

Birth Control Measures for Women

Women have a variety of alternatives for birth control. The discussion which follows focuses on safety, availability, convenience, and appropriateness for travel. This should help you to choose the method which is best.

Most forms of birth control require a trial period of at least 3 months prior to departure. This will provide some protection against the occurrence of unexpected problems while traveling.

Barrier Methods of Birth Control

Barrier methods of birth control include the diaphragm, cervical cap, contraceptive sponge, and condom. All these methods are well-suited for use by travelers. They avoid the potentially dangerous complications of an IUD. They're noninvasive, easy to use, and take up little space in a backpack or suitcase.

Barrier methods offer further advantages. Studies indicate that women using a barrier method have a significantly reduced rate of pelvic inflammatory disease (PID, "Sexually Transmitted Diseases, Gynecology," pp. 229–230). There's an approximate 40% decrease of PID compared to women using no contraceptive measures, or using nonbarrier forms of contraception. Studies also show that barrier methods reduce the incidence of other sexually transmitted diseases.

Barrier methods require concurrent use of a spermicidal preparation. This must be added prior to insertion, except for the contraceptive sponge which already contains spermicide. Barrier methods must be used to be effective, which sometimes requires assertive behavior. It's OK to let someone wait while the barrier is prepared, placed, and the correct positioning verified. Use of any barrier method can be creatively integrated into the sexual experience.

Contraindications

All barrier methods except condoms are contraindicated if you have ever had toxic shock syndrome. Barrier methods are also contraindicated if you develop an allergic reaction. This is usually caused either by the material the barrier is made from, or the spermicide employed. Switching to a different spermicide, product manufacturer, or barrier method usually eliminates the problem.

Diaphragms

Excellent for travel, diaphragms rarely present problems for most users. Used properly with a spermicide jelly or cream, diaphragms are almost as effective as birth control pills. Diaphragms can, however, cause recurrent urinary tract infections in some people. In this case you should use an alternative form of birth control.

Diaphragms must fit correctly to be effective. This requirement may present problems for travelers because *diaphragms must be refitted following any weight change (gain or loss) of 10 pounds (4.5 kg) or more.* Since extended travel may cause variations in weight from dietary changes and other factors, diaphragm size changes may be required periodically. If planning to use a diaphragm, it's a good idea to be fitted prior to departure. If you've had a diaphragm a long time, have a practitioner recheck the fit.

Know how to use, care for, and inspect the diaphragm before traveling. A diaphragm must be cleaned well, properly stored, and checked regularly for leaks. Do the latter by holding it up to the light or filling it with water. Take along a spare diaphragm and carry enough spermicide jelly or cream. These are available in major cities but may be hard to find in smaller towns or rural areas.

Cervical Cap

Excellent for travel, the cervical cap is similar to a diaphragm except that it fits directly over the cervix. It has the advantage of not needing to be refitted following normal changes in body weight. It may also be left in place for up to 48-72 hours.

For extended travel take along a spare and a sufficient supply of spermicidal jelly. Don't fill the cap more than 1/3 full of jelly, as it may interfere with suction. Many women find the cap effective even without the spermicide. This is an advantage during extended travel if spermicide is not readily available.

Condom and Foam

The use of a condom and spermicidal foam together is an excellent form of contraception, well suited for travel. This combination is virtually as effective as the pill. In addition, both products are readily available almost anywhere in the world. They do not require a prescription. Besides contraception, use of a latex (not lambskin) condom provides good protection against most sexually transmitted diseases. Condoms should be stored in a cool, dry place. Don't use a condom that has been kept in a wallet. Condoms are disposable and should never be reused.

Spermicidal foam can be used with the condom for maximum protection. Shake the can approximately 20 times before use. Insert foam just prior to intercourse, as its effectiveness diminishes after 30 minutes. Repeat applications as needed.

Contraceptive Sponge

The contraceptive sponge is made from polyurethane foam with spermicide added to it. It works both through its spermicidal action and by absorption of sperm into the sponge matrix.

The sponge can be left in for up to 24 hours, and during this time it provides continuous protection regardless of the frequency of intercourse. It doesn't require use of additional spermicidal jellies or creams. It doesn't require fitting. One size fits all, and for this reason the sponge is available over the counter. It comes with step-by-step instructions, which you should learn before departure and follow precisely.

There are some disadvantages to consider. There may be a problem with removal of the sponge. Pulling too hard on the connecting loop can tear the sponge to pieces, and long nails may have the same effect. At present the sponge is not available outside the U.S. except in a few European countries and Singapore. It may therefore only be appropriate for short trips until it becomes more widely available.

Birth Control Pills

Pills are a good form of contraception for travel. Side effects are usually minor. When present, they can often be eliminated by adjustments in the dosage, formulation, and hour taken. These adjustments should be made with the help of a medical practitioner prior to travel.

In developing countries you can usually purchase birth control pills at pharmacies without a prescription. However, your particular pill may not be available locally. Another problem is that brand names change from one country to the next, making identification difficult. If possible, always take enough birth control pills for an entire trip. Remember that any barrier method is a good backup if pills are lost, unavailable for refill, or cause unexpected problems.

Problems with Birth Control Pills

Certain medical conditions can affect use of the pill. If during travel you develop severe diarrhea, use a backup form of birth control until after your next menstrual period. This is necessary because diarrhea decreases absorption, and may have the same effect as missing one or more pills. If you develop hepatitis or become pregnant, birth control pills should be discontinued for the duration. If while traveling medical attention is required for any reason, be sure to inform the physician that you are taking birth control pills.

Complications

Though uncommon, significant complications may occur from use of birth control pills. If any of the following symptoms develop, **stop** taking the pills. Seek medical help immediately for a thorough evaluation.

1. Severe headache;
2. severe abdominal pain, especially in right upper quadrant of abdomen;
3. chest pain which doesn't stop and/or shortness of breath;
4. eye problems, such as blurred vision, flashing lights, or blindness;
5. severe leg pain, especially in the calf or thigh.

Fertility Awareness

Monitoring fertility cycles can be a very effective form of birth control. Unfortunately, this is difficult to do while traveling. It's not recommended due to the normal stress which accompanies changes in climate, altitude, daily routines, eating patterns, diurnal rhythms, and other travel conditions. All of these can disrupt a normal menstrual cycle.

Vaginal Suppositories/Withdrawal

Neither of these are recommended as contraceptive techniques, as both have a high risk of pregnancy. Try something else.

The IUD, or Intrauterine Device

There are many types of IUD's. Availability varies widely from one country to another, and the replacement interval varies depending on the type. This interval can be from one year to several. The Progestasert, for example, is replaced yearly. If the 1 year period is due to expire during your travels, seriously consider instituting another form of birth control prior to departure.

Copper IUD's can usually be left in place for 3–4 years, and some of the newer products can be left in even longer. If the replacement interval is due to expire while traveling, either replace it before departure or use an alternate birth control method. The Lippes Loop and Safety Coil are usually left in place indefinitely as long as there are no complications.

IUD's may cause minor side effects such as an increase in menstrual flow, cramping, backache, and spotting between periods. **But they can also cause major, even life-threatening complications.**

Complications of IUD Use

Women traveling with an IUD in place *must* be aware of the signs of possible complications. These can be quite serious. Pelvic pain or lower abdominal pain, severe cramping, and unusual vaginal bleeding or discharge may all be signs of infection or other problems. These can occur with or without fever, and require immediate medical evaluation.

If untreated for even a short time, pelvic infections (PID) may lead to permanent sterility from infection and scarring. Unfortunately, recent studies have confirmed a significant increase in sterility from IUD's, with sterility rates that run 2-3 times that of nonusers. Besides sterility, pelvic infections can also cause death (see Chapter 14, "Sexually Transmitted Diseases, Gynecology," pp. 229–230).

Pregnancy can occur even with an IUD in place. This is another complication and requires immediate removal of the IUD. There is an approximately 25% chance of miscarriage when this is done, against a 50% chance of spontaneous abortion if the IUD is not removed.

When pregnancy occurs with the IUD in place, there is a greatly increased chance of ectopic pregnancy (pregnancy outside the uterus). This is a life-threatening emergency and surgery is mandatory. Because of this possibility, missing a period with an IUD in place calls for an immediate pregnancy test and examination.

Summary of IUD danger signs requiring immediate medical evaluation:

1. missed period;
2. lower abdominal pain, whether alone or accompanied by an elevated temperature or chills;
3. vaginal discharge with a foul odor, alone or with fever, chills, or abdominal pain;
4. abnormal uterine bleeding between periods.

Recommendation

From the above discussion, it should be apparent that an IUD is far from an ideal choice for travelers. Besides the danger of sterility, the possibility of serious complications from infection or pregnancy requires prompt access to reliable clinic and hospital care. For extended travel, only women who have had their families, and have a history of satisfactory use of an IUD without complications should consider IUDs.

Glasses and Contacts

Glasses

If you wear prescription glasses, it's a good idea to carry a spare set. Write the lens prescription down and put it in a safe place, such as a money belt or on your yellow *International Vaccination* card. Optometry services are available in major cities or most countries. New lenses can be made if yours are lost of stolen.

Contact Lenses

Contact users should carry lens prescriptions for both contacts and glasses. New contacts can usually be made in a day in any major city worldwide. However, replacements bought in a foreign country are not always satisfactory. We know of one trip to South America which was aborted in Mexico for this reason. Take a backup pair of glasses. These will save the day in case of an eye infection, lost contact, inadequate replacement, or inability to find cleaning and rinsing solutions.

Whether you're using hard, soft (including extended wear), or gas permeable contacts, carry enough cleaning and rinsing solution for the entire trip. These solutions may be difficult or impossible to find during travel, especially outside major cities.

Heat sterilizers

Carry the appropriate electrical conversion unit (adapter) for the countries you're visiting. Carry cold sterilization solutions as a backup in case of current incompatibility or electrical failure or absence. Make sure you're not allergic to the sterilization solution prior to travel.

Infection precautions

Use of contacts increases the risk of bacterial or parasitic eye infections when exposed to contaminated water. Avoid swimming with contacts in place in swimming pools, lakes, rivers, or the ocean.

When rinsing contacts, it pays to be cautious. We know one optometrist who carries plastic containers of sterile normal saline solution and tubing on backpacking trips for this purpose. Whether or not you use sterile normal saline, use only a pure water source. Never use tap water or saliva. Use boiled water, or bottled water if the producer's seal on the container is intact. Water purified with iodine can be used on hard or gas permeable contacts, but is not recommended for soft contacts. It may permanently discolor them.

Air travel

When traveling by air, consider wearing glasses instead of contacts. The low humidity is very drying. Alternatively, take along artificial tears.

Preparations for Extended Travel

3

For trips exceeding 3–4 weeks, you may need more than just a vaccination or two to be adequately prepared. Take care of all medical and dental needs before departure. It could make the difference between a successful or disastrous trip.

Medical Preparation

Obtain a complete physical exam if there are any underlying medical conditions such as diabetes or chronic heart or respiratory problems. This is the time to have other health maintenance measures done if needed, such as a Pap smear, mammogram, EKG, or breast, genital, or rectal exam. Besides routine matters such as vaccinations, antimalarial medications, and a first aid kit, we recommend:

1. blood typing; **and** 2. a TB skin test.

With your practioner, determine if any of the medications suggested in this book are contraindicated, particularly if you have known drug allergies or a chronic medical condition. Have the practitioner recommend alternative medications if possible.

Travel Clinics

Whether or not you have a personal physician, consider making medical preparations for travel through a travel clinic. Travel clinics are most likely to be on top of changing health conditions worldwide and to know the latest Centers for Disease Control of the Public Health Service (CDC) recommendations for travelers. Travel clinics can tailor their recommendations according to your health status, itinerary, duration of travel, and anticipated activities. They're also a good place to go for a post-trip medical evaluation, if needed. Appendix C is a list of travel clinics.

Blood Typing

All travelers should consider having their blood typed. Carry this information in the yellow international certificate of vaccination and on your person. It could save your life in an emergency.

Unfortunately, blood banks in developing countries often lack the resources to screen thoroughly for contaminated blood. Hepatitis, malaria, and HIV, the virus that causes AIDS, can all be spread by infected, transfused blood. If you're traveling for an extended time with a large group of people, it may be possible to suggest that group members voluntarily have their blood typed and HIV status ascertained. If a blood transfusion is needed, you may then be able to obtain it from within the group, with low risk of contamination.

Tuberculosis Skin Tests

Travelers who visit developing nations for more than 3–4 weeks should consider a TB skin test (PPD) before and after their trip. These tests will determine whether or not exposure to TB has occured while traveling.

Skip the skin test if you have been treated for TB in the past, or if you have previously had a positive TB skin test. Instead, get a chest X-ray upon completion of the trip. Unless you have previously had a positive TB skin test, obtain the skin test even if you have had BCG vaccine. BCG is a tuberculosis vaccine not routinely used in the U.S. or Europe, but which has been widely used in Asia and elsewhere. It may cause a positive PPD test result.

It takes 3–10 weeks for skin tests to turn positive following exposure to TB. If you've been out of the country for more than 6 months, get tested at your convenience upon returning home. For shorter trips, wait 2–3 months before testing. Record all TB tests and their results in the yellow vaccination certificate. For more information on TB see Chapter 7, "Infectious Diseases," pp. 167–168.

Dental Preparation

Travelers face an increased risk of gum and tooth disease. Changes in diet, increased sugar consumption (soft drinks used as a safe water source, etc.), and potential nutritional deficiencies all contribute to the likelihood of dental problems. For these reasons we strongly recommend a thorough dental exam and completion of pending dental work before extended travel.

If nothing else, have your teeth cleaned and checked. One of life's more unendurable experiences under any circumstances is suffering from the pain of a relentless toothache. Imagine it striking on the way to an elegant banquet, or three days out backpacking in the Andes!

Buy dental floss and use it daily. Both flossing and brushing are required to thoroughly remove plaque. If needed, review flossing and brushing techniques with a dentist. Individual concerns, including potential dental emergencies, should also be discussed before travel.

For extended travel in rural areas, add oil of cloves, CAVIT, and possibly I.R.M. to the first aid kit. The first is a dental anesthetic, the latter are temporary filling materials available at dental supply stores. If the need arises, Part II of this book contains instructions on how and when to use them. Also consider taking along .4% sodium flouride gel, which has proven effective in slowing cavity formation in adults. Not sold over the counter, it's available in the U.S. from dentists. It's difficult to find while traveling.

Self-Examination Skills

There's at least one aspect of a routine physical exam that everyone should probably do themselves — which is even more important during extended travel. This is a testicular examination for men, and a breast examination for women.

The earliest possible detection of abnormalities greatly increases the chance of survival should any changes turn out to be cancerous. Self-examination is a vital skill, especially for anyone living in a remote area, or traveling for an extended period of time without routine medical care.

Testicular Self-examination

Although relatively rare, testicular cancer is the most common form of cancer in men 20–35 years of age. Its rapid ability to spread makes early detection the best chance for survival.

Make a habit of regularly examining your testicles at least once a month for lumps or masses. These may indicate the possibility of cancer and should be examined immediately by a medical practitioner. A good time to examine yourself is while in the shower or lying in bed.

Examine the testicles one at a time starting at the top and feeling very carefully all around. Work your way to the bottom of the testicle. Then feel throughout the scrotum. If a lump, mass or anything unfamiliar is noted, have it checked immediately.

Breast Self-examination

This is an important self-care skill for women. If you're not already doing a monthly breast exam, learn how before traveling. A medical provider can show you how to examine your breasts during your next physical or gynecological exam.

Breast cancer kills more women than any other form of cancer except lung cancer. More importantly, 80 to 90 percent of all lumps, bumps, and breast changes are found through self-examination. The earlier the detection, the better the chances for successful treatment and cure.

Breast exams should be done once a month just after your period. At this time the breasts should neither be swollen nor tender. If using birth control pills, do the exam when opening a new package. After menopause or during pregnancy, the breast exam can be done on the first day of each month, or any other day that is easy to remember.

How To Examine Your Breasts

Visual inspection

This is done to become familiar with the normal appearance of the breasts and to detect abnormalities. Visual inspection is done from the following four positions, standing before a mirror.

1. Standing straight, arms down at your sides;

2. Leaning forward;

3. Hands clasped behind the head, elbows out to the sides;

4. Hands on hips and pressed firmly down to flex the chest muscles.

Note the shape and size of the breasts. They should be approximately symmetrical with no dimpling or swelling. The nipples should both point in approximately the same direction. Neither one should appear retracted (pulled inward).

Get medical evaluation if any of the following are present:

1. a rash;

2. unusual dimpling, swelling, or asymmetry in the shape of the breasts;

3. a retracted nipple, or one which angles differently from the other.

Palpation (feeling the breast tissue)

This is the second part of the exam. It's best done while lying down with a pillow or folded towel placed under the right shoulder.

Raise the right arm above and behind your head. This distributes breast tissue more evenly over the chest. Using the fingertips of the left hand, feel for lumps or tissue changes by gently pressing the breast tissue, using a rocking motion with your fingertips. Start in a circle around the nipple and continue in expanding circles covering the entire breast. Be sure to include the area under the arm.

Reverse the process and palpate the left breast. Finally, squeeze both nipples gently between thumb and forefinger to make sure there is no bleeding or discharge.

Get medical evaluation for any of the following:

1. bleeding or other discharge from the nipples;
2. new lumps or other swollen tissue;
3. breast tissue which feels different from the previous exam;
4. any other abnormal changes.

Summary

Know the normal look and feel of your breasts so that changes can be detected early. Do a breast exam regularly each month without fail.

Foreign Cultures and Culture Shock

Learning to live in a foreign culture can be exciting, rewarding, and a great deal of fun. It can also be very frustrating and demanding. Adopting a new lifestyle, learning the language and customs, changing one's expectations to fit a new reality — all this can require much effort and energy.

Coping with the physical environment, including the health-related challenges, is only one of the problems. Most of us have inherent difficulties adapting to a foreign culture. One of these is our ethnocentrism — a widely shared and deeply ingrained assumption that the way our own culture does things is the way things ought to be done. This unconscious prejudice against other cultures is a major obstacle with which to contend.

Communication is another demanding challenge. Language may be a large part of this, but it is only a part. Whether you know the language or not, the problems of cross-cultural communication can be stressful and disorienting. Various symptoms associated with "culture shock" are frequently the result.

Adapting To a Foreign Culture

We offer the following suggestions. Some are obvious, not all will be practical or necessary for everyone, and none are altogether easy.

1. Approach the people and their culture openly. Avoid the trap of looking at foreigners as "underdeveloped" Americans or Europeans.

2. Extend a nonjudgmental attitude not only to native individuals, but to yourself as well. It takes considerable time to develop expectations about peoples' performance — including your own — which are realistic in terms of the new culture.

3. Be patient. Learning about a foreign culture takes time. The meaning of what you observe and experience will not always be readily apparent, but often emerges gradually.

4. Learn the language. If you don't have a working knowledge, this is a top priority. Many countries have language programs which allow you to live and board with a native family. This is an excellent approach.

5. Talk with the people — storekeepers, market vendors, neighbors, waiters, bank tellers — whoever you come in contact with. It is good language practice, and the interactions may help you learn many of the nonverbal cues and gestures used in communication.

6. Research the culture. Learning the cultural history can be invaluable. In addition, the last 30 years have seen a lot of published information on different aspects of cross-cultural communication. Much locally relevant material is floating around in foreign countries, especially in the capitals. American and European private or government agencies, especially those concerned with economic development, might be of some help. Another place to look are the foreign campuses of American and European universities.

7. Before departure, talk with people who have been there. Once there, talk with foreign residents who have lived there a year or more. They may have insights or interesting anecdotes to share from their experiences.

Culture Shock

Culture shock is an emotional reaction to the experience of being unable to accurately convey or decipher many environmental and behavioral cues. These cues are primarily nonverbal, and normally operate *beyond conscious awareness*. For the foreigner plopped down in another culture, it is as if someone changed the rules — but no one can say what they are.

Culture shock doesn't appear overnight, but brews slowly over several months. It results from an accumulation of disconcerting experiences *which cannot yet be understood*, because the cultural context has not been learned.

Not everyone experiences culture shock. When it does occur, symptoms range from mild to overwhelming. Employment which requires working extensively and effectively with the native people is a good bet to produce at least some of the symptoms.

Symptoms of Culture Shock

Typically, there is a mounting sense of frustration with no tangible cause. Persons working with native citizens may feel discouraged and ineffective. The apparently sourceless frustration is often accompanied by confusion, anxiety, depression, or anger.

Behavior is often defensive. It's common at this juncture to hear criticism or condemnation of the foreign country, its citizens, its institutions, *ad. nauseum*. All aspects of the culture are apt to be vehemently disparaged, excepting possibly the beer. One's organization or employer may also be scapegoated.

Feelings can also run to intense depression and loneliness, with a sense of profound isolation. It's not uncommon to question one's motives for being abroad. Falling ill may elicit or intensify all of these feelings.

Severe culture shock can be a personal crisis — an opportunity for growth — but not without pitfalls. For one thing, it compounds the difficulty of adapting to the new environment. It may permanently sour one's attitude toward foreign countries, not to mention living abroad. One possible outcome is a quick trip home to familiar and comfortable territory.

Surviving the actual experience of culture shock may depend in part on helpful support at the time. The insights and experiences of fellow citizens who have "been there," or who may be having similar experiences, shouldn't be overlooked. The positive resolution of culture shock requires patience, openness to change, and time to accumulate and digest further experience. As the cultural context is gradually learned, adjustments are made.

Culture shock itself can be a strong motivation to understand the new culture and learn to work effectively within it. Like a mirror, the new culture may open up a different view of one's own. In the experience of culture shock also lies a germinal perception of the powerful role culture plays in determining the meaning and significance of our experience.

The Silent Language (1959), by Edward T. Hall, is still probably the best place to start an investigation of problems in cross-cultural communication. We highly recommend it.

Preventive
Health Measures

4

The key to successful travel outside western, industrialized countries is adherence to preventive health guidelines. Preventing illness isn't difficult. Increased public health risks, real enough in many places, are largely a threat to people who ignore the problems.

It's easy to make recommendations that will minimize health risks from the environment. The incentives for a traveler to follow them, however, will vary. This is a risk versus gain area. Such factors as length of stay, inconvenience of illness, the availability of health care, and personal traveling styles affect one's decisions.

For maximum safety, adhere strictly to the guidelines summarized in the Nutshell™ Guide at the end of this chapter. In our own experiences, when illness occurred, it usually followed some conscious decision to disregard normal precautions. While it's sometimes appropriate for guidelines to be modified, this can be done safely only when based on knowledge of the potential risks and local health conditions.

The most important preventive health measures pertain to food and water, but there are other sources of infection to consider. Chief among these are skin exposure to contaminated soil or water, and the bites of various insects, especially mosquitoes.

Food and Water Precautions

The Risks

Contaminated food and water are the most common source of illness among travelers. Disorders range from diarrhea to food poisoning, hepatitis to typhoid, cholera to a virtual rogue's gallery of disgusting little (sometimes not so little) parasites. If there's ever any doubt about the safety of the food or water you're using, err on the side of caution. Avoid it.

Contaminated Water

> "Water, water, everywhere
> Nor any drop to drink" — Coleridge

Tap Water

Because water delivery systems are unreliable, don't assume that tap water is safe — ever. *Assume that all tap water is unsafe*, no matter who says it's OK to drink. There are good reasons for this assumption.

Most major cities worldwide have potable water systems. In general they do an adequate job of purifying water much of the time. Unfortunately, the delivery of safe water to the tap cannot be assured *all* the time.

Even where chlorination and water treatment facilities exist, pure water cannot be guaranteed. Routine disinfection of water may not kill certain disease-producing protozoa, particularly giardia and amoebic cysts. Furthermore, contamination can occur at any point in the delivery system between the treatment plant and the tap. This is a problem wherever sewage is inadequately controlled. It's also a problem whenever water service is temporarily disrupted. When water pressure drops, the likelihood of outside contamination increases dramatically.

Another problem in many areas is the onset of the rainy season. Months of accumulated waste can be swept up and delivered to water intake and storage facilities all at once. This flood of garbage and sewage frequently overwhelms treatment and delivery systems. An increase in hepatitis A, typhoid fever, and dysentery commonly occurs at this time, all from tap water that may previously have been safe. This problem can occur during *any* heavy rainfall.

As you can see, there are many reasons not to trust tap water. Wise travelers don't even ask the question, "Is the water OK to drink?"

Rivers, Lakes, and Wells

In rural areas, local water supplies from lakes, rivers, and wells are also suspect. They are often contaminated with human and animal wastes. This is almost assured around small towns, villages, and farms. Even camping in isolated areas can have its surprises. One of the authors discovered he was sharing his source of water for morning coffee with a dead cow, as it came lazily floating by the riverbank. Do you know who your neighbors are upstream?

Ice and Frozen Confections

The rule is, "If you can't trust the water, don't trust the ice." This is a difficult rule for North Americans (not so much Europeans) to observe to the letter on hot, humid, tropical days and nights.

Interestingly, there's a study (JAMA, June 7, 1985) that sheds some light on the survival of bacteria in iced drinks. It showed that freezing did not completely eliminate any of the bacteria studied. However, freezing for more than 24 hours did significantly reduce the bacterial count.

Bacterial counts were further reduced when melting ice was exposed to high-proof alcohol, specifically scotch and tequila. By contrast, ice cubes melting in cola, soda water, or plain water showed little or no reduction in bacterial numbers. Finally, the longer ice sat in a drink melting, the higher the bacterial counts became.

One conclusion to be drawn from this study is that enough shigella or other bacteria can survive freezing to cause infection. Another is that if you do put ice in your drinks, they should be consumed quickly — using, of course, high-proof alcohol ("To your health, then! Bottom's up!"). This conclusion is of dubious merit.

Whatever can be said about ice cubes goes for sno-cones and confections made from shaved ice. We also urge avoidance of those mouthwatering, succulent popsicles made with fresh frozen fruit (such as strawberries) and water. They are irresistible on hot, muggy days in the tropics, but can be lethal. They cost one of the authors five miserable dysenteric days in Mexico City (guess which flavor).

Airline Water

Over the years, a number of travelers have successfully avoided illness abroad only to fall prey to traveler's diarrhea upon returning home. As a consequence the water served by international air carriers on the return flight has fallen under a degree of suspicion.

Some airlines make special efforts to test the water that goes into the airplane holding tank. Water in the holding tank is usually replenished at stopovers on the plane's route, by topping off at major destinations. As we have previously seen, the problem with this water is that it can not be counted on 100% of the time. Even conscientious spot inspections may fail to reveal a potential source of impure water.

It makes sense to avoid both the drinking water and ice cubes routinely served on flights originating from or with stopovers in Third World countries. Either request bottled mineral water from the steward or stewardess, or take your own bottled or purified water with you on board.

Other Sources of Contaminated Water

Avoid drinks such as smoothies or fresh squeezed juices if tap water has been added. Avoid using tap water for brushing your teeth or rinsing your mouth. Make sure that glasses, plates, and utensils are dry before using — not wet from washing. Note also that the comments regarding tap water and ice cubes apply to all classes of restaurants and hotels, even the top rated, most expensive tourist facilities. Don't be overly reassured by prestige and high prices. Travelers have reported to us that a prestigious hotel in Nepal bares the nickname "Diarrhea Alley."

At this point your reaction might well be "What's left but thirst and despair?" You need not cancel your trip. There are many ways of ensuring that your water and other beverages are safe.

Safe Water and Other Drinks

Bottled Beverages

Canned or bottled beverages are normally OK to drink. They need to be wiped clean and dry before consuming. Internationally known brands of carbonated beverages are usually considered the safest.

Avoid local brands of bottled soft drinks. Local bottlers may use contaminated or unpurified water for their drinks. If so, the high sugar content can promote bacterial growth.

In restaurants, an excellent way to avoid tap water as well as sugar and caffeine overload is to order soda water or mineral water. For variety, these can be flavored with limes or other citrus. The acidity from carbonation discourages bacterial growth.

Other safe beverages include beer and wine, and other alcoholic drinks (with tonic or soda water but not tap water). Tea and coffee are safe if made from boiled water.

Purified Bottled Water

Purified bottled water is also safe. However, problems arise because, for a variety of reasons, tap water is often misrepresented as bottled water. It's not unknown for delivery truck drivers to fill their bottles with tap water and pocket the proceeds, unbeknownst to the company. We suggest you distrust bottled water unless you break the producer's seal from the bottle yourself.

Methods of Water Purification

There are three main ways of purifying water: boiling, chemicals, and special filters. Prior to using *any* of these methods, cloudy or dirty water should first be coarsely filtered. For this purpose an inexpensive commercial filter, clean cloth, or coffee filter is usually adequate. If none of these are available, the water can be poured after allowing the sediment to settle.

Boiling

Boiling is by far the most reliable way to ensure that water is safe to drink. Water boiling at 212°F (100°C) will kill all dangerous bacteria, viruses, and parasites. Their protein structures begin to denature at about 170°F (76°C). A small electrical coil heater is a quick and practical way to boil water wherever electricity is available. Make sure the heater you buy is compatible with available current.

Bring the water to a vigorous boil. Allow it to cool before drinking. If you are at high altitudes, remember that the boiling point of water decreases by 2°F (1.1°C) for every 1,000 feet (305 meters) above sea level. Boil the water for one additional minute for every 3,000 feet (1,000 meters) of elevation.

If you have no available means of water purification it makes sense to use hot rather than cold water out of the tap. Allow it to cool to room temperature. Remember, this water may still be contaminated and should not be used regularly as a source of drinking water.

Chemical Water Treatment

Either iodine or chlorine can be used to treat water of uncertain potability. Iodine is always preferable; chlorine should be used only as a last resort. Chlorine can not be counted on to kill parasites such as amoebas or giardia, or certain viruses that attack the intestinal tract. Both chlorine and iodine alter the taste of the water, which initially may seem unpleasant.

Iodine should not be used by individuals who are hyperthyroid or have iodine allergies. It can be used safely during pregnancy for a maximum of 3 weeks. It's otherwise easy, safe, and effective.

There are 3 available forms — 2% tincture of iodine, iodine crystals, and tablets. Crystals and tablets carry directions on the bottle. Simply add the specified amount of iodine to the desired quantity of water, and let sit. For clear water at room temperature the manufacturer's recommended length of contact time is 30 minutes. For cold or cloudy water, the amount of iodine is usually doubled and the time increased. It's best to allow very cold water to come to room temperature prior to treatment.

Recent information shows that iodine tablets and crystals are only about 90% effective against giardia after 30 minutes of contact, and 2% tincture somewhat less than that. After 8 hours, however, all 3 are virtually 100% effective. If you mix your iodine and water at night, you'll be all set to go the following morning.

For extended trips crystals are preferable to tablets as their potency does not decrease with exposure to heat, air, moisture, and time. A bottle of "Polar Pure" iodine crystals makes about 2,000 quarts of purified water. The chemical name for the tablets is tetraglycine hydroperiodide; some brand names are *Globaline*, *Potable Agua,* and *Coghlans.* Both crystals and tablets are available at sporting goods stores and pharmacies in the U.S. They may be difficult or impossible to find while traveling.

Tincture of iodine (2%) is widely available. One disadvantage is that it will stain anything it touches if the container is spilled or broken. To purify water, add 5 drops per quart or liter of clear water, or 10 drops if the water is cloudy or cold. Let the solution stand for 8 hours before drinking.

A 10% providone iodine solution (Betadine) has been used for *emergency* water purification by the militaries of some countries. This use has **not** been approved by the Food and Drug Administration (FDA) in the United States. The suggested dose is 8 drops per quart of clear water, 16 drops per quart of cold or cloudy water. Wait 30 minutes before drinking, or up to 8 hours for increased protection from giardia.

Chlorine — Don't use chlorine if water can be boiled or treated with iodine. If these alternatives are unavailable, use either Halazone tablets or standard liquid laundry bleach. Be sure to check the percentage of liquid bleach on the label. Use the following chart to determine the number of drops to be added to each quart or liter of water.

Determining How Much Chlorine To Use

percent chlorine solution	Drops per quart or liter of:	
	clear water	cloudy water
1%	10	20
4-6%	2	4
7-10%	1	2
unknown	10	20

Mix thoroughly and let stand for 30 minutes. A slight chlorine odor should be detectable in the water. If not, repeat the process and let stand for an additional 15–20 minutes.

Filters

Micropore filters may be the ultimate convenience in water purification for travelers. Most filters, though, have one drawback. They cannot filter out viruses, so they will not protect you against waterborne viral infections. These include hepatitis A, polio, and the viral causes of traveler's diarrhea.

Filters with a sufficiently small pore size will protect you against all bacterial and parasitic infections transmitted through water. Disease-producing bacteria average around .5 microns in diameter, and none are smaller than .2 microns. Protozoa such as giardia and amoebas and the eggs of other parasites are even larger, ranging from 5 to 20 microns or more. Therefore any filter with a pore size of .2 microns or smaller is more than adequate.

The most appropriate micropore water filters for Third World travel are those with an additional iodine contact system, which kills viruses. The best of these filters is the "PUR." Well designed, it is easy to use and to clean, and adds little iodine taste to the water. Another is the "Water Tech Purifier." For increased protection against giardia when using the "Water Tech," let the water sit for 30 minutes or longer after filtering. Reliable noniodine water filters are the "First Need" and the "Katadyn." The "H20K" filter is only 90% effective in stopping giardia. Avoid the "Pocket Purifier," as it's not effective against giardia.

Some filters on the market have an additional chemical element utilizing chlorine or activated charcoal. They have only fair track records. Their effectiveness depends on a host of variables, such as water temperature, acidity, sediment, and loss of potency over time.

When using a micropore filter, let cloudy water settle out or prefilter the water with a course filter. If the filter contains a chemical element, heat cold water or allow it to come to room temperature before filtering.

Use the filter on water from all potentially contaminated sources, such as rivers, lakes, and wells. Use it on tap water for drinking or for brushing your teeth. But remember that unless the filter has an iodine element, it will not protect against viral infections.

More Sources Of Pure Water

With some imagination and preparation, it's possible to travel almost anywhere and still ensure a safe supply of drinking water. One woman we met, a Bahai missionary in Honduras, traveled frequently to remote Indian villages by mule. She made a habit of picking fresh lemon grass outside of town. Upon visiting in the Indian homes, she would offer the lemon grass with instructions to boil the leaves for at least 5 minutes. Stick cinnamon or any other herbal tea could be used the same way, thus ensuring a supply of water purified by boiling.

A wide variety of drinks are prepared by natives of local cultures, especially during regional fairs and festivals. If the drinks are boiled and served hot, they are usually safe depending on how hygienically the utensils or containers are handled. Again, this is a risk/reward area that requires individual judgement. The process of exploring a culture and getting to know its people sometimes requires a relaxation of customary precautions.

Food

Contaminated food is a major source of illness among travelers. Because impure water used to wash or prepare food is a source of contamination, most of the waterborne diseases already discussed can be passed along in food. Food handlers are another primary cause of contamination. Whenever handwashing is inadequate and intestinal disease widespread, the people involved in harvesting, transporting, preparing, and serving food are all potential sources of infection.

Contamination also occurs from irrigation water or fertilizer which may contain human and animal wastes. In markets and restaurants, flies or other insects may spread disease organisms to food.

In developed countries refrigeration is taken for granted in all aspects of food transportation, storage, and preparation. In the Third World this is often a luxury. Unrefrigerated, food spoils rapidly and even slight contamination can result in rapid bacterial growth, especially in warm or tropical climates.

Safe and Unsafe Foods

Some foods can be eaten safely without cooking or special treatment, such as foods with intact skins that you peel yourself. This includes most fruits (but not berries) and vegetables such as onions or cucumbers. The same foods peeled by others in restaurants can't be considered free of risk.

Cooked Foods

Boiled vegetables served hot (not reheated) are safe. Steaming, however, isn't as reliable a cooking method as boiling. Not all surfaces are reached by the steam so parasite eggs may not be killed. Beans, rice, and other cooked grains and legumes are safe to eat.

Beef, pork, lamb, and fish are safe — if well-cooked (medium-well to well done) — and served hot. Avoid ordering meats "rare" or "medium-rare." In addition to bacterial illnesses, raw or insufficiently cooked beef, pork, and other meats, as well as freshwater fish, are a source of parasitic infections. Eating raw shellfish such as oysters also entails a risk of hepatitis and cholera. It's best to avoid all raw or insufficiently cooked meat and fish, including shellfish.

Menu items which use sauces for meat, fish, and vegetable dishes are best avoided as they can contaminate easily. The sauces are also sometimes used to disguise spoilage. Dishes prepared with mayonnaise, like potato salad, are a good medium for bacterial growth. The same is true of such high protein foods as chicken or eggs, including custard. If these dishes are likely to have been prepared well in advance of serving, such as at party or picnic buffets, they should be avoided.

If you do your own cooking, consider investing in a pressure cooker. Not only will it save on fuel, but it's an excellent way to make sure food is thoroughly cooked and safe to eat.

Ciguatera fish poisoning — Some tropical reef fish, even when cooked, pose a hazard of ciguatera fish poisoning. Red snapper, grouper, barracuda, amberjack, sea bass, and other tropical reef predators can accumulate the toxin. Though infrequent, the potential for ciguatera poisoning exists in all subtropical and tropical areas of the West Indies, Pacific, and Indian oceans (see p. 255).

Canned foods
Canned foods are usually safe. Avoid cans with rust or swollen ends or sides. Once opened they should be consumed, refrigerated, or discarded.

Bread and baked goods
These are usually safe, but avoid pastries filled with cream or custard.

Milk and dairy products
Unless pasteurized, milk and all of its derivative products carry a risk of typhoid fever, tuberculosis, brucellosis, traveler's diarrhea, and other bacterial infections. Canned evaporated milk, condensed milk, or powdered milk are good milk substitutes if pasteurized milk cannot be obtained. In preparing powdered milk be sure to use purified water.

Raw milk can also be pasteurized by heating to 143°F (62°C) for 30 minutes. An alternative is to scald or "flash" heat almost to boiling for just under a minute.

Salads and green leafy vegetables
Fresh green leafy vegetables, radishes, and other ground crops used in salads are a problem. The water and fertilizers used to grow them are often contaminated, making them a source of disease. Yet green leafy vegetables are a major source of iron and B vitamins. One strategy often used is to soak leafy vegetables in chlorine or iodine solutions. The concentration can be slightly higher than that used for water purification. Unfortunately, this procedure is less than 100% effective, even using iodine.

Thorough scrubbing and dipping in hot or boiling water is also unlikely to be completely effective.

Travelers who don't give up salads should probably use some combination of the above measures to clean their unpeelable vegetables. Use iodine rather than chlorine as a chemical disinfectant. Better yet, substitute cabbage for spinach or lettuce in homemade salads and throw away the outer layer of leaves. By peeling cabbage, onions, cucumbers, tomatoes, and the like, it's possible to minimize the health risk from fresh, uncooked vegetables.

Restaurants, Street Vendors, and the Market Place

Restaurants catering to foreign travelers may be more attentive to food preparation and handling. Certainly the very expensive tourist hotels and restaurants, and the international chains, have an interest in maintaining high standards. What about other places? It may not always be wise to assume the safety of a restaurant, just because it caters to the tourist trade.

To some degree, whatever risks exist may be shared equally by all local establishments. In many cities and villages, especially the smaller ones, restaurants share the same market sources for their meats and produce. They share the same water supply. Contamination by food-handlers may be as likely in one place as another.

However, an inaccessible kitchen may well be more lax in general health practices than a kitchen under public scrutiny. It's easier to throw the food you dropped on the floor back in the pot and to tolerate a horde of flies when the customers aren't watching.

Logic argues that it may be safer to eat where the kitchen is open to inspection. Where the cooking is accessible, it's possible to verify for yourself that there are no flies, that dishes are well-cooked and kept hot. You can point to the food you want, rather than select blindly from a menu. An inspection of prospective eating places will many times yield a market stall or smaller restaurant that has appetizing food and an acceptable standard of cleanliness. The prices are often cheaper and there may be a wider variety of native foods than the usual tourist menu provides.

When it comes to street vendors, food can be found that is obviously safe. Fresh corn-on-the-cob pulled from boiling water is a good example.

Certain street foods, no matter how tempting, must be avoided. Sliced fruit such as watermelon and pineapple is frequently kept moist by periodic dowsing from a bucket of obviously questionable water. Look for it and you'll find it. Also glasses, dishes, and other serving containers may be used by more than one customer without washing. Or, they may be washed on the spot in sleazy-looking water. The point is that in selecting food from either restaurants or street vendors, your own observations can serve as a guide to what is or isn't safe. This is simply not possible in most other establishments, including those that cater to tourists.

The same principle applies to the marketplace. Observing the market scene before buying, you can usually pick up enough clues to eat safely. A word of caution, though — things are not always what they seem. Friends of ours were forced to live in Morocco for an extended period of time after their van broke down. They quickly learned to buy the meat in the marketplace that was covered with flies. The flyless meat got that way by repeated applications of insecticide, which many merchants kept handily accessible under the counter.

The sacrifices made to adhere to food and water precautions may seem like a lot of trouble, but they will help you avoid the most common sources of illness. That's a significant accomplishment.

Contact with Contaminated Soil

Hookworms are found in all Third World countries. Hookworm eggs are passed in human feces and the hatched larvae enter the body through skin contact. They then migrate to the intestines where they attach to the intestinal wall and feed on blood and other substances. Major hookworm infestations result in a loss of blood and protein and can cause anemia. Hookworms passed in the feces of domestic cats and dogs don't cause intestinal infection, but can cause a skin rash called "creeping eruption" (cutaneous larva migrans, pp. 115–116).

Prevention

Avoid going barefoot wherever there is a chance of soil contamination with human or animal feces. Avoid laying on beaches where cats and dogs roam. As a general rule, don't go barefoot outdoors in either rural or urban areas of developing countries.

Contact with Contaminated Water

Bacterial eye, ear, and skin infections can all be transmitted by skin contact with contaminated fresh or salt water. Don't swim or bath near sewage outlets in oceans or bays, lakes, streams, or rivers. Another important infection caused by skin contact with contaminated fresh water is schistosomiasis, also known as bilharziasis.

Schistosomiasis (Bilharziasis)

An unpleasant parasitic infection, schistosomiasis is potentially quite dangerous. The parasite's eggs are passed in urine and feces, but require an intermediate host for survival. The host is a fresh water snail found throughout tropical and subtropical regions. After leaving the snail, a microscopic free-swimming form of the parasite penetrates human skin on contact. It migrates to the intestines and bladder, completing the life cycle.

Wherever this disease is prevalent (see map in Appendix B, p. 315), all sources of fresh water should be considered potentially contaminated. This includes lakes, streams, rivers, and even irrigation canals. Since there is no practical way for the traveler to distinguish between infected and noninfected water, all sources of fresh water in regions with schistosomiasis should be viewed as potentially infectious, and avoided.

The disease is very widespread. Risk is particularly high in Africa, Egypt and the Middle East, India, Indonesia, Celebes, Laos, Thailand, the Philippines, and parts of China. In the Americas, areas of high risk include the northern two-thirds of South America, and some Caribbean islands including Puerto Rico, Santo Domingo, and Santa Lucia.

Prevention

Obviously, avoid swimming, washing, and bathing in fresh water in these areas. Stagnant or slowly moving water is especially risky. Wear high protective waterproof boots if skin contact is unavoidable, as when fording streams or rivers. Apply rubbing alcohol to areas of skin exposed to water and then dry throroughly. If rubbing alcohol isn't available, immediate and vigorous towel drying will reduce the risk of infection.

Drinking contaminated water can also result in schistosomiasis infection. Purify fresh water for drinking or bathing by boiling, filtering, or by treating with iodine or chlorine as previously recommended. Water for bathing can be made safe by letting it stand in a container for at least 72 hours.

Insects

See "Mosquito and Tick Precautions," pp. 38–40 in Chapter 1.

Sexually Transmitted Diseases

International travelers may be at increased risk of contracting sexually transmitted diseases (STD's). For various reasons, travelers out of their normal environments are sometimes more sexually active.

To decrease the risk of STD's, avoid casual sexual encounters. Having multiple contacts with different partners is dangerous behavior. Especially risky are contacts with prostitutes, intravenous drug users, bisexual or homosexual men, or a person who has or had multiple partners.

Be cautious with any new sexual partner. Be curious about their past sexual history and their current state of sexual health. Inquire about the presence of warts, lesions, or rashes in the genital area, a genital discharge, or symptoms of burning with urination. Check out your partner during foreplay. Be observant. Itching, for example, may indicate crabs or scabies.

There is no way to protect yourself totally from the potential threat of a new liaison or sexual relationship, and these measures may sound impossibly clinical. The best they can do is help to weed out a potentially risky contact. But in an age of epidemic and now fatal STD's, you owe it to yourself to be exceedingly cautious.

All condoms will help protect both men and women from bacterial infections such as gonorrhea and chlamlydia. Only condoms made from *latex* will also protect against herpes, AIDS, and other viral infections. Make sure the product says "latex" on the package when you make your purchase.

It's unrealistic, however, to count on a condom for absolute protection. On occasion they may leak, break, or unknowingly slip off. In fact, condoms manufactured in Third World countries have a higher failure rate than those produced in industrialized nations. It may be best therefore to take a supply of condoms with you. Keep some in your first aid kit.

Other barrier methods of birth control for women offer some safety. Use of a diaphragm or cervical cap in conjunction with spermicide, for example, provides protection from many sexually transmitted diseases.

It goes without saying that certain sexual practices, especially involving the anus or rectum, spread infectious organisms. Avoid any such behavior.

AIDS and the Traveler

AIDS (Acquired Immune Deficiency Syndrome) or HIV (human immunodeficiency virus) infection has spread throughout the world. AIDS has been reported from more than 100 countries. The risk to Third World travelers is determined less by their destination or itinerary than by their individual behavior. As frightening as AIDS is, it's a preventable disease.

There is no documented evidence of HIV transmission through non-sexual casual contacts, air, food, water, contact with inanimate objects, or through mosquitos or other insects. Travelers are at increased risk for acquiring HIV infection if they engage in the following behaviors:

1. sexual intercourse (heterosexual or homosexual) with an infected person;
2. use of unsterilized syringes or needles for any injections (intravenous drugs, tattooing, acupuncture, or medical/dental procedures);
3. treatment with blood, blood components, or clotting factor concentrates in countries that don't screen donated plasma or blood for HIV antibodies.

Travelers should avoid sexual encounters with anyone in a high-risk category for HIV infection. This includes IV drug users, prostitutes (male or female) or others with a history of multiple sexual partners, homosexual or bisexual men, and hemophiliacs. Latex condoms may decrease but not entirely eliminate the transmission risk of HIV. Use of a latex condom is encouraged for any new sexual encounter, whether the contact is vaginal, oral, or anal. Diaphragms in combination with spermicide may provide additional protection.

In many Third World countries there is inadequate testing of blood or blood products for HIV infection. Avoid locally produced blood clotting factors, immune globulin, and blood products for transfusion. Needles used to draw blood or administer injections should be sterile and disposable. Diabetics or others who require frequent injections should carry a supply of syringes and needles sufficient to last their entire stay abroad. Make an exception only when a foreign supply of sterile supplies has been confirmed in advance of travel. Carry a prescription and a letter from your physician detailing the medical need for these items.

High, Deep, and Dark Places

As Richard Halliburton discovered, new environments can lure us to exotic challenges as well as dangers. Unlike him, few of us will feel compelled by our first view of Mt. Fuji to improvise an immediate ascent — alone, and in the middle of winter! Yet few of us can resist the view from "just over there. . . ." New places tempt us, begging to be experienced, explored, and occasionally surmounted. This section covers the special hazards and requirements of high elevations, underwater environments (Scuba diving), and caves.

High Places: Safety at High Altitudes

There are increasing risks in activity as you ascend above 6,000-8,000 feet (1,800-2,400 meters). This is just as true for young, healthy travelers as for the old or infirm, although certain chronic medical conditions may require special precautions.

Chronic Health Conditions

Travel above 6,000 feet (3,660 meters) may aggravate some medical conditions. Prior medical consultation and consent is strongly recommended for travelers with:

1. chronic lung conditions such as asthma, emphysema, COPD, or a history of a collapsed lung (spontaneous pneumothorax);
2. severe anemia, recent or chronic, including sickle cell anemia;
3. a recent heart attack, history of angina, or other heart problems.

For any of these conditions, check the elevation of stopovers on your scheduled itinerary. Every year a few travelers are literally stunned to learn that La Paz, Bolivia, sits at 12,000 feet (3,660 meters) above sea level. A few have required continuous hospitalization from arrival at the airport until their departing flight.

Prevention of High Altitude Illness

Acclimatization

Acclimatization is the gradual normalizing adjustment the body makes to higher altitudes where less oxygen is available. To get high without getting sick, allow your body to adjust by making a slow ascent. A 2-4 day rest is recommended at 6,000-8,000 feet (1,800-2,400 meters) and again at 10,000-12,000 feet (3,050-3,660 meters). Changes due to acclimatization are lost after staying at lower elevations for 10 or more days (de-acclimatization).

If rest days are not possible at higher elevations, the following measures will help prevent or minimize altitude sickness:

1. Make a slow ascent — 2,000 feet/day (610 meters/day) between 5,000 and 10,000 feet (1,526-3,050 meters) and 1000 feet/day (305 meters/day) from 10,000 to 15,000 feet (3,050-4,575 meters).
2. "Climb high, sleep low." Make the final and highest parts of a climb quickly and early in the day. Get down off the mountain to minimize exposure.
3. Drink plenty of nonalcoholic fluids to avoid dehydration. Fluid loss increases with altitude.

4. Avoid alcohol, cigarettes, and hypnotic medications.

Physical conditioning at sea level does not reduce the need for acclimatization.

Diamox is prescribed to help prevent symptoms of acute mountain sickness. Diamox may have significant side effects (see Part III). It should be taken only on the advice of a medical practioner. It's prescribed for travel above 8,000 feet (2,400 meters) or for rates of ascent greater than 2,000 feet/day (610 meters/day). For a quick one day ascent/descent, a single 500 mg. sustained release dose is taken the day before the climb. Otherwise take 250 mg. 3 times a day, starting 24–48 hours before the ascent and during each day of the climb. The last dose of Diamox should be taken at the highest point of the climb. Then discontinue the medication upon descent.

Don't take Diamox if you're allergic to sulfa drugs. Diamox causes fluid loss and dehydration must be prevented by drinking increased amounts of fluids. Don't take Diamox with sedatives such as Halcion (triazolam) or barbiturates.

High altitude and the unacclimatized traveler.

Above 8,000 feet (2,400 meters) there is an increasing risk of altitude sickness among physically active but unacclimatized people. This frequently happens on trekking, hiking, skiing, or backpacking trips planned on a tight schedule. The incidence and severity of illness is increased by higher and/or more rapid ascents and by greater physical exertion.

Acute mountain sickness (AMS) — This term refers to the mildest and most common symptoms. Headache, weakness, fatigue, and a rapid pulse are characteristic. Of these, headache is the most severe and disabling symptom. There may be nausea, vomiting, loss of appetite, insomnia, shortness of breath, even hallucinations. These usually begin within 6–48 hours of ascent to high altitude but may occur later.

Treatment — Either descend or halt the ascent. Symptoms usually subside in 1–7 days as acclimatization occurs. You can gradually resume activity, including further ascent at a slower rate. Drink plenty of fluids to avoid dehydration. For headache, take 1 or 2 Tylenol every 4–6 hours as needed. Don't take aspirin. Don't attempt to climb to higher altitudes until the signs of AMS completely disappear. If not taking Diamox, you can treat AMS with 250 mg. of Diamox at bedtime. In the Andes, mate de coca (a tea made from the coca plant) is available in markets and restaurants. It's been reported to help relieve mild symptoms.

Other minor forms of high altitude illness.

Rapid ascents above 8,000 feet (2,400 meters) sometimes cause a progressive swelling (edema) of the face and eyelids, hands, ankles, and legs. This occurs within 2–4 days of arrival at elevation. Women are more commonly affected than men. Further ascent should not be attempted.

Unless disabling, however, the condition does not require medical attention or descent to a lower altitude. Decreased salt intake or the use of Diamox will reduce symptoms. Avoid treatment with diuretics (water pills) other than Diamox as they can cause dehydration or salt imbalance.

Flatus, or the uncontrolled passage of gas, occurs more commonly at high altitudes. It's of no medical consequence. If symptoms are bothersome, reduce them by avoiding foods that cause gas, such as beans, chili, onions, and cucumbers. Use of an antacid which contains simethicone may also be helpful.

Around 14,000 feet (4,270 meters), heavy exertion may cause bleeding from vessels behind the eye (retinal hemorrhage). "Floaters," blind spots, or blurred vision may result. *If visual disturbances occur, further ascent should be halted.* Although permanent damage is rare, it does sometimes follow the development of blind spots. Above 18,000 feet (5,490 meters) retinal hemorrhages are common, especially with rapid ascent and strenous exertion. These usually resolve within 7–10 days.

High Altitude Sickness: Emergencies

Occasionally, high altitude exposure can lead to fluid accumulation in the lungs (high altitude pulmonary edema, or "HAPE"). This is a potentially life-threatening condition. It's associated with heavy exertion, usually above 12,000 feet (3,660 meters) but occasionally at elevations down to 8,000 feet (2,440 meters). It's more frequent in young adults under 21 and recently deacclimatized persons. Recurrent episodes are common.

Symptoms begin 1-3 days after arrival at higher elevation. They are worse at night. Early symptoms are fatigue, shortness of breath, an aching chest, a dry, unrelenting cough, and difficulty sleeping. Respirations may become rapid, shallow, and gurgling. A low fever up to 101°F (38.3°C), an increase in pulse rate, and mental confusion, may accompany these symtpoms. In later stages sputum becomes frothy, pink, and tinged with blood. **Coma and death may follow.**

Treatment

At the earliest sign of HAPE, descend immediately to below 8,000 feet (2,440 meters). Give supplementary oxygen at a rate of 6-12 liters a minute if available. Get to the nearest treatment center as quickly as possible for ongoing medical care.

Deep Places: Diving and Underwater Safety

Scuba diving requires mastery of special skills and knowledge to be done safely. Certification by trained instructors is an absolute prerequisite. Be wary of outfits that offer to "show you the ropes" in an hour and then strap a tank on your back. Certified divers should observe the following precautions for safe diving:

1. Never dive when ill. Increased barometric pressure during a dive can make an infection worse. Allergies or infections involving the sinuses, ears, nose, throat, or lungs are especially hazardous. They may trap air, causing pain or injury during descent or ascent.

2. For chronic conditions involving the sinuses, ears, or nose, see an ear, nose, and throat (ENT) or diving medicine specialist prior to diving.

3. The only medications approved for use during a dive are decongestants, specifically the oral decongestant pseudo-ephedrine and the long-acting nasal sprays with oxymetazoline such as Afrin. The use of any other medication may be hazardous, and a diving medicine specialist should be consulted. Even the use of nasal sprays must be restricted, as use for more than 3 consecutive days can cause rebound congestion. This could be disastrous during a dive.

4. To prevent chilling use an insulating suit when the water temperature is 75°F (24°C) or less. If shivering occurs, stop diving. It's an indication of excessive heat loss.

5. Have a dental checkup every 6 months. Cavities subjected to pressure changes can be excruciating. Avoid diving after dental extractions or surgery.

6. Decompression sickness (the "bends") is primarily a hazard of repetitive dives. However, there are other contributing factors that should be avoided. These include alcohol consumption, dehydration, exposure to cold, and physical injuries (such as a sprain). Avoid airline flights or other high altitude exposure for 24–48 hours following repetitive dives.

7. Some environments require advanced training. These include caves, wrecks, cold water or ice, and rapidly flowing water. Diving at altitudes above 1,000 ft. (305 meters) elevation, or to water depths greater than 100 feet (30.5 meters), requires additional certification.

8. Avoid diving completely throughout pregnancy.
9. Knowledge of CPR, especially mouth-to-mouth resuscitation, is recommended. Information on how to cope with wounds, injuries, seasickness, sunburn, and marine animal hazards is in Part II of this book.

Dark Places: Caves, Tunnels, and Mines

In these places, unlike diving, it doesn't take a lot of specialized training, skill, and equipment to get into trouble. Curiosity and a flashlight often suffice. To be explored safely, however, caves do require special knowledge, skills, equipment, physical conditioning, and 1 more essential: the company of an experienced guide already familiar with the area to be explored.

Be aware of potential health hazards from places inhabited by bats. There is a risk of rabies and other diseases from inhaling aerosolized bat droppings.

Poisonous Plants and Recreational Drugs

Item. *Several years ago a small group led by an experienced easterner were rafting on a river in the western United States. Making camp one evening, their leader prepared a salad from foraged plants similar to ones with which he was familiar. He died, and the rest of the group spent several days stranded, too sick to go for help, wondering which of them might be next. One of the foraged plants was water hemlock.*

Item. *Periodically along the west coast of the U.S., both Southeast Asian and Latin immigrants are hospitalized, suffering irreversible liver damage or dying from foraged wild mushrooms. These almost always turn out to be one of several deadly Amanita species.*

Misidentification is the major cause of accidental plant poisoning. The above incidents illustrate the hazards of plant foraging in new environments. They suggest that prior experience may actually increase the danger.

These examples lead to a general rule for travelers. In a new environment, NEVER eat or taste any wild mushroom, fruit, leaf, root, seed, or berry — *especially* if it appears similar to one you already know.

A case of poisoning that occurred in Peru involved one of the authors. His fellow hikers decided to pick some berries identical to ones they had seen for sale in an Indian market that morning. As they later discovered, the berries were indeed identical — only the plant leaf varied. The misidentification resulted in 4 cases of belladonna alkaloid poisoning. The local indian name for the berries was "Dog Killer." A foreign visitor had died from eating them a few months earlier.

Belladonna Alkaloid Poisoning

As in the above incident, the majority of accidental plant poisonings occur from belladonna alkaloids (anticholinergics). Small doses produce only a slowing of the pulse and a dry mouth. Larger doses may cause dilated pupils and blurred vision, red hot dry skin, nausea, thirst, fever, a fast pulse, headache, inability to urinate, agitation, and disorientation. The classic description is "hot as a hare, blind as a bat, dry as a bone, red as a beet, and mad as a hatter."

The stomach and intestinal tract are often paralyzed. As a result, it's useful to induce vomiting up to 36 hours after ingestion. Fatalities are rare, but the symptoms are most unpleasant.

Other Plant Poisons

Less frequently, poisonings occur from plants that can affect the nervous system, heart, and lungs, as well as the gastrointestinal tract. Many of these are quite common, such as oleander, foxglove, azaleas, rhododendrons, philodendrons, diffenbachia, holly, and mistletoe.

Emergency Treatment of Plant Poisoning

While there are a variety of poisons, emergency treatment is in most cases the same for victims who are conscious and alert.

1. Induce vomiting if not already present. Syrup of Ipecac is ideal for this purpose. The adult dose is 30 ml. (one ounce or 2 tablespoons), along with 8–16 ounces of water. Ipecac produces vomiting within about 15 minutes.
2. Obtain medical help as soon as possible.

Note: vomiting should not be induced in unconscious victims, or when poisoning is due to caustic agents (strongly acidic or alkaline substances), petroleum distillates, theophylline, tricyclic antidepressants, camphor, or Kwell.

Ipecac should be given as soon after poisoning has occurred as possible. Don't use salt water to induce vomiting.

Mushroom Poisoning

Like plants, mushrooms are powerful chemical factories that may

The Nutshell™ Guide To Healthy Traveling

Observe the following precautions in Third World countries:

Beverages — Don't drink:
- drink tap water, or use it for rinsing your mouth or brushing your teeth;
- consume drinks prepared with unpurified water (such as smoothies);
- use ice cubes, or eat frozen confections such as popsicles or snow cones prepared from unpurified water;
- drink local brands of sweetened bottled beverages;
- drink unpasturized milk;
- drink water served in hotels or restaurants;
- drink from a glass that is wet from washing.

Beverages — Do drink:
- purified bottled water;
- water purified by boiling. If unavailable, treat water with iodine ;
- internationally recognized brands of soft drinks;
- bottled carbonated water or bottled mineral water;
- tea or coffee made with boiling water;
- bottled or canned juices, canned milk, bottled or canned beer or wine.

Food — Don't eat:
- raw fruits that you cannot peel yourself, or with broken skins;
- raw vegetables that you cannot peel yourself, including salads;
- foods likely prepared far in advance of eating, especially with chicken, eggs, or mayonnaise;
- custards and cream or custard-filled pastries or other deserts;
- raw or rare meats, poultry, fish, or shellfish;
- with silverware or plates that are wet from washing.

Food — Do eat:
- raw fruits and vegetables with intact skins you can peel yourself;
- well-cooked vegetables, meats, poultry, fish, or shellfish served hot;
- canned or packaged foods;
- freshly cooked beans, rice, or other grains;
- bread and other baked goods.

Milk Products — Don't:
- consume unpasteurized milk or dairy products.

Milk Products — Do:

- use pasteurized milk products. Raw milk can be pasteurized by heating to 143°F. (62°C.) for 30 minutes, or by "flash" heating almost to boiling for just under a minute.
- substitute powdered milk, mixed with purified water, if pasteurized milk isn't available.

Other Guidelines

Don't go barefoot outdoors.

Don't swim, bathe, or wash in contaminated fresh or salt water. Avoid fresh water streams, rivers, or lakes where schistosomiasis is a potential hazard.

Do take precautions against biting insects. Use insect repellent containing DEET. Wear appropriate clothing and use a permethrin clothing spray. Use mosquito netting when necessary.

Do take precautions against sexually transmitted diseases.

Do protect yourself from sunburn with clothing, sunscreen, lip balm and sunglasses.

---

produce a variety of toxins. A few are destroyed by heat but most are not. Some are toxic only in combination with alcohol.

In general, reactions that occur within minutes up to 2–4 hours after eating are not cause for undue alarm in healthy adults. Reactions that occur from 6–24 hours after consumption are very worrisome, and require immediate medical evaluation and care.

The safe collection of mushrooms depends on the ability to identify not only edible varieties, but all known poisonous ones as well. Remember the precautions at the beginning of this chapter. Experience may *increase* the chance of accidental poisoning, especially in a new environment.

Alcohol and "Recreational" Drug Use

While the medical consequences of substance use and abuse don't change from place to place, the social and legal consequences most certainly do. In some places, travelers may be especially vulnerable to punishment and exploitation from infractions of local customs or laws. In July of 1986, for example, an Australian and a British citizen were executed by hanging in Malaysia for drug possession (heroin). Use common sense and consider the consequences of any behavior *within the context of local law and culture.*

Part II

Diagnosis and Treatment of Medical Disorders

In spite of precautions, illness and injury may occur. Part II will help you with the interpretation of symptoms and identification of commonly encountered illnesses. Use the table of contents and the index to locate specific information quickly. To identify possible causes and find relevant information when you know only the symptoms, consult the Quick Reference guides in each chapter. A guide to identification of a mysterious rash, for example, will be found at the end of Chapter 5. There are guidelines to help you determine when medical evaluation is mandatory.

We provide treatment schedules in Part II for use when medical care isn't available. Also use this information to ensure that when care is available, the medications prescribed for you are appropriate and safe.

Preventing and Treating Skin Problems

5

There are literally hundreds of kinds of skin problems. Some are common and easy to recognize. Others are difficult to identify without considerable experience. Unfortunately, the more you travel, the greater the chance of acquiring some unfamiliar, uncomfortable, possibly scary, skin problem. This is especially true in tropical countries. Warmth and moisture are ideally suited to fungal, viral, bacterial, and parasitic skin infections. Wounds that would heal without treatment at home may inevitably become infected in the tropics.

Some disorders affect only the skin surface, such as fungal rashes, scabies, crabs or warts. Others are a result of an internal viral infection like measles or chicken pox. Still others may have environmental causes, such as food and drug allergies. And occasionally, a rash can signify a serious disease such as lupus, syphilis, or leprosy.

We cover only the most common and easily treatable skin disorders. See a doctor, preferably a dermatologist, if you have a rash that:

1. cannot be identified;

2. becomes worse — with or without treatment;

3. looks as if it's found a permanent home.

Minor Skin Wounds

Wound Care

Many wounds are minor and you can treat them yourself. Whether minor or major, the steps involved in treating all wounds are:

1. stop the bleeding;
2. clean the wound;
3. bandage the wound to help prevent infection.

Tetanus Boosters

For any deep and/or dirty wound, especially puncture wounds, obtain a tetanus shot if it's been more than 5 years since the previous booster.

Wounds Requiring Medical Attention

Get immediate medical help for:

1. bleeding not controlled by simple pressure;
2. injuries in individuals with increased susceptibility to infection (diabetics, young children, the elderly);
3. foreign bodies which cannot be easily removed;
4. loss of sensation or function (mobility) in an affected area.

Care of Minor Skin Wounds

Minor cuts, scrapes, and abrasions that don't cause severe bleeding you can generally treat yourself. The goal is to prevent wound infection, and the key to this is proper cleaning and care until the wound is healed.

As soon as possible, wash the wound with soap and clean water. Scrub dirt out of abrasions. Rinse with hydrogen peroxide, then apply a topical antibacterial ointment. If necessary, cover with a sterile bandage and obtain a tetanus shot. During all procedures, avoid coughing or breathing on the wound or dressing.

Topical antibacterial ointments

Using a topical antibacterial ointment will often help prevent wound infection. Almost any of the available products will do. These include:

Polysporin ointment	Betadine (providone-iodine) ointment
Neosporin ointment	Triple antibiotic ointment
Bacitracin ointment	

Unless specified, any of these or an equivalent medication can be used when "topical antibacterial ointments" are referred to in this chapter.

However, be alert to the possibility of allergic reaction, indicated by the sudden onset of itching with redness. Some products may contain either neomycin or iodine, both of which can produce an allergic response. If a reaction occurs, switch to a product without the offending ingredient.

Regardless of the medication used, watch carefully for signs of secondary bacterial infection following any break in the skin.

Wound bandaging

Most abrasions and lacerations heal faster if you cover them. Cover other wounds to protect them from irritation from shoes or clothing, or from dirt or other contamination. A Band-Aid or other sterile dressing can be used. Don't use cotton — the fibers are difficult to remove from the wound.

Dressings should be kept dry and changed daily until the skin is healing and clean. If sterile dressings are not available, use clean fabric. This can be either ironed, scorched with a flame, heated in an oven, or washed and dried outdoors in the sun. Fabric boiled for at least 5 minutes also makes a good sterile covering.

Use of steri-strips and butterfly bandages — Some cuts, especially lacerations, may need suturing (stitches) or other measures to bring the edges together to promote healing. Steri-strips or butterfly bandages are available commercially and can be used for small, deep cuts. They can also be used on larger or more extensive lacerations when you're traveling in isolated areas where suturing is not available.

To use steri-strips, you must first prepare the skin so that the strips will adhere. Using a Q-tip, paint tincture of benzoin on both sides of the cut. Avoid getting any on the wound as it will sting. Allow the benzoin to dry so that it feels sticky. Starting from one side, put down one end of the steri-strip and gently pull it across the laceration. Bring the edges of the wound closely together and press the strip down on the other side. Repeat the procedure, placing the strips next to each other so that the entire wound is closed.

Butterfly bandages are applied the same way, except that you don't need to prepare the skin with benzoin. If butterfly bandages are not available, they can be made from Band-Aids. Cut away both edges of the padded area with sterilized scissors, leaving a narrow padded central strip.

Other Skin Wounds and Injuries

Bruises (Contusions)

A bruise is a common injury, usually from contact with a blunt object, n which the skin remains intact. The skin is often discolored from small broken blood vessels beneath the surface. Bruises usually look purple, or 'black and blue."

It's normal for some people to get small bruises on their legs from minor bumps and scrapes which they may not notice at the time. As a rule, though, **if bruising occurs spontaneously — without known injury — it requires immediate medical evaluation.**

Treatment

Apply cold compresses for 10–15 minutes several times during the first 24–48 hours. Then switch to hot soaks, 2–3 times a day. Take 1 or 2 acetaminophen (Tylenol) or aspirin for pain every 4–6 hours. Tetanus shots are not necessary if the skin is unbroken.

Puncture Wounds

A puncture wound is caused by a sharp penetrating object, such as a splinter or nail. These rarely bleed much but are very prone to infection and difficult to clean.

Treatment

Remove small, accessible foreign particles with tweezers. The tweezer ends should be sterilized first with rubbing alcohol or a match flame. Clean the site well with soap and water, then rinse thoroughly with hydrogen peroxide. This is especially important with puncture wounds. Obtain a tetanus booster if needed.

Indications for Medical Assistance

If the penetrating object is long or very deep, don't attempt to remove it. Obtain medical help instead. Medical assistance should also be obtained for penetrating injuries to the chest, abdomen, or eye.

Deep Cuts (Lacerations)

A laceration is a deep cutting wound through the tissues beneath the skin, into the fat or muscle. These usually require suturing.

Treatment

First, apply direct pressure to the wound to stop the bleeding. Then clean the cut thoroughly with soap and water. **Don't use hydrogen peroxide on deep lacerations involving muscle tissue,** as it will damage the tissue. These cuts are best cleaned in a medical setting using a sterile normal saline solution. Sterile normal saline is simply a dilute (.9%)

solution of salt in sterile water. When not available, you can make your own. Add 1 teaspoon of salt to a pint of water, boil for 5 minutes, and let it cool. Don't apply any ointment to deep cuts.

Suturing is usually done within 6–8 hours of the injury to be most effective. If medical care cannot be obtained within that time, bring the edges of the wound together and tape them in place with steri-strips or a butterfly bandage as previously described. Scalp wounds can be closed by tying hairs together across the wound. Cover all wounds with a sterile dressing, tape the dressing in place, and get medical care as soon as possible.

Gouging Wounds (Avulsions)

An avulsion is a cutting or gouging injury in which a piece of the skin is dug out. If the wound is very wide or deep, it may need suturing or other professional care. Otherwise treat it in the same manner as a minor cut or abrasion.

Bacterial Skin Infections

The bacteria most often responsible for skin infections are "staph" (Staphylococcus aureus) or "strep" (Streptococcus), both of which normally reside on the skin. Treatment usually requires a topical antibacterial ointment and may require oral antibiotics as well. In isolated areas when medical attention isn't available and antibiotics are indicated, you can treat cellulitis, folliculitis, boils, impetigo, and secondary bacterial infections with one of the following antibiotics. They're listed in order of preference:

1. dicloxacillin 250–500 mg. orally, 4 times a day for 10 days (don't use dicloxacillin if you're allergic to penicillin); **or**

2. erythromycin 250 mg. orally, 4 times a day for 10 days; **or**

3. Keflex or Velocef 250–500 mg. orally, 4 times a day for 10 days; **or**

4. ciprofloxacin 500 mg. orally, twice a day for 10 days.

More severe infections require the higher dosages. After starting antibiotics, medical attention should be obtained if there is no improvement within 48–72 hours.

Secondary Bacterial Infections

Any wound can become infected with bacteria, especially if not taken care of properly. This is called "secondary" bacterial infection because it follows rather than causes the original injury. The injury could be from a cut, scrape, abrasion, puncture wound, insect bite, rash, burn, or frostbite.

Symptoms

Secondary infections are characterized by redness and swelling, increasing tenderness or pain, red streaks running up the skin, or pus forming at the wound site. Fever may also be present.

Treatment

Treat a small infection with hot soaks for 10–15 minutes, 3 times a day. Change the dressing and reapply antibiotic ointment after each soak. If unable to do soaks, change the dressing and reapply ointment at least twice a day.

Add oral antibiotics to the above measures if the infection grows worse or fails to improve after 2–3 days. Any of the following indicate a worsening infection:

1. increase in swelling, tenderness, and discharge of pus, or enlarging red area of inflammation;

2. fever greater than 101°F (38.3°C);

3. red streaks running up an extremity from the site of infection.

Cellulitis

Cellulitis is a secondary bacterial infection which fails to be localized or confined to a small area. Instead, infection spreads outward through connective tissue beneath the skin, producing an expanding area of inflammation.

Symptoms

The reddened, inflamed area of cellulitis doesn't have a clearly demarked edge or border. The skin is red, warm, swollen, and tender to touch. As the area enlarges, fever is common and there may be swollen lymph nodes or red lines running up the skin. This indicates infection of the lymph channels. Untreated, infection may reach the blood stream causing a systemic infection. In the event of spreading cellulitis, medical attention must be obtained as soon as possible.

Treatment

Cellulitis must be treated with oral antibiotics. In addition, apply hot soaks to the affected area for 10–15 minutes 3 times a day.

Barber's Itch (Folliculitis)

Hair follicles sometimes become infected, commonly by "staph" bacteria. Infection causes itching or burning, with discomfort or pain if the hair follicle is touched. The base of the follicle is red and contains pus. The infection looks exactly like a pimple with a hair follicle in the center. Folliculitis can appear anywhere on the body, most commonly under the arms, on the face or neck from shaving, or on the buttocks, thighs, or groin. Tight jeans, wet trunks, or wet suits increase heat, moisture, and skin irritation and contribute to folliculitis.

Although these infections frequently go away on their own, it is best to treat them aggressively to avoid complications. This is particularly true in the tropics where bacteria thrive and are prone to spread. Infected follicles which don't heal, with or without treatment, often develop into boils.

Treatment

Apply warm soaks or compresses to the affected area for 15 minutes, 3 times a day. Keep the area clean and dry. Apply a thin layer of topical antibiotic ointment after each soak, or at least twice a day. If the beard is affected, skip shaving for a few days. If you do shave, avoid shaving closely, and use Hibiclens antiseptic soap before and after. Change the razor blades daily until the infection clears.

Indications for Medical Attention

Increasing pus, redness, swelling, and tenderness indicate a progressing infection — get medical attention. Treat infections near or around the eyes in the same manner, **except**

medical attention is mandatory and you must obtain it as quickly as possible. The presence of a spreading infection or inflammation near the eye is a medical emergency.

Boils (Furuncles)

An abscess of an infected hair follicle is a furuncle or boil. Infection of the follicle extends below the skin, forming a pus sac beneath it. Boils are red, warm, painful and tender when touched. They may cause fever or swelling of local lymph nodes.

Small boils may heal by themselves or they may quickly enlarge and cause the formation of additional boils. These can pop up in areas such as the hands, face, back, buttocks, or legs. Frequently boils enlarge, forming pus pockets which soften and open spontaneously. These may drain pus for a few days to a week or more. Occasionally several adjacent boils join, forming a conglomerate mess with several points of drainage.

Treatment

Any skin infection which becomes abscessed should receive medical attention. Large or persistent boils usually need to be surgically opened, drained, and packed. The infected area must be washed and kept clean and dry. Hot soaks for 10–15 minutes, 3 times a day, are essential. Oral antibiotics are usually required.

Indications for Immediate Medical Attention

Boils that develop on the face or in the rectal area require **immediate** medical care. These can have potentially dangerous complications, including scar formation.

Impetigo

Impetigo is a superficial skin infection, caused by "staph" or "strep" bacteria usually found on the chin or around the nose. It's characterized by multiple, separate sores (lesions), pea size or larger. The lesions are raised and have a red base. They sometimes appear as circular red patches and may resemble ringworm.

The lesions form sacs or blisters, occasionally filling with fluid or pus. These break open, dry, and form a honey-colored crust. If the crust is removed the underlying skin is red. The lesions can spread to other parts of the face or to other areas of exposed skin. The lesions are both itchy and contagious. Infection is easily spread via wash cloths or towels.

Treatment

Apply warm soaks to the affected area for 15–20 minutes, 3–4 times a day. Spread a thin layer of antibiotic ointment to each lesion twice a day or after each soak. This may be sufficient to cure the infection. If there is no improvement in 3 days, or if the infection becomes worse, oral antibiotics may be required. Obtain medical attention.

Infections of the Nail or Nail Margin (Paronychial Infections)

The most common causes of nail margin (cuticle) infections are bacteria and yeast. Prolonged contact with water often makes the nail margins prone to infection. Such exposure, frequently occupational, must be reduced when it's implicated as a cause of infection.

Nail margin infections which are red, tender, and swollen with pus are treated with hot soaks for 15–20 minutes, 3–4 times a day. Apply an antibiotic ointment twice a day or after each soak. Open a pus pocket carefully with a sterile knife blade, inserted and inscribed in an arc under the infected skin along the nail edge. Cover with a Band-Aid and keep the area clean. Get medical attention if there is no improvement in 3–4 days.

If no pus is present, treat with one of the topical antifungal ointments or creams listed on p. 111.

Care of the Feet

Except for diabetics, foot problems are rarely serious in healthy adults. For the traveler with limited time in a foreign city, however, a minor problem like a hangnail or blisters is a major annoyance. It may even spell disaster for someone hiking in a remote area. Because they're potentially disabling, foot problems must be prevented if at all possible.

Preventing Infection

Travelers should avoid going barefoot in developing nations. Infection is always a possibility following any cut, scrape, or other break in the skin. In addition to bacterial infections, there is a risk of acquiring hookworm and other parasitic infections from going barefoot.

Many cities, towns, and rural villages throughout the world lack adequate sewage treatment facilities. Local water supplies are frequently contaminated as a result. This is also often true of rivers, lakes, and coastal areas. Water reaching the ocean or even the ocean itself can be contaminated. Cuts from coral, shells, rocks, glass, or metal hidden along banks or beaches commonly become infected.

In Salvador, Brazil, one of the authors was disabled for a week with a severe foot infection after stepping in contaminated water that flowed across a beach. This occurred in spite of the fact that he had no known open cuts or breaks in the skin.

Treatment of Minor Cuts and Wounds

Feet require the same conscientious care recommended for any wound, only more so. Thoroughly remove all splinters, glass, or other foreign bodies. Clean the wound carefully as previously described. Watch for development of secondary bacterial infection or cellulitis and treat as required. If these develop, pain can be quite excruciating when pressure is applied to the foot. In addition to antibiotics and hot soaks, keep the affected leg elevated. Take 1 or 2 aspirin up to 4 times a day for pain or fever.

Hangnails

In addition to being painful, hangnails are a potential site of infection. They're largely preventable. Usually they're a result of improper nailcutting or shoes that don't fit. Accumulation of debris under the nail, prolonged exposure to moisture in damp climates, or injury to the nail or toe are other contributing factors.

Hangnails cause pain with redness and swelling around the nail bed, sometimes with bleeding. Secondary bacterial infection with pus formation may follow.

Prevention and Treatment

To avoid hangnails, toenails should never be cut very short. Leave the edges square, not rounded. If dampness or sweating is a problem, wear socks made of cotton rather than synthetic materials. Change them often.

It's also important to wear well-fitting, comfortable shoes that allow the feet to breathe. Avoid high-top boots which cause more dampness to accumulate. Open-toed shoes are preferrable or wear 2 or more pairs of shoes in rotation, allowing each pair to dry out between use. Antifungal powders (Tinactin, Zeasorb, Desenex, etc.) will help decrease dampness. If redness and swelling occur without infection, place several layers of thin, twisted cotton fibers (from a cotton ball or swab) between the toe and nail, near the sides of the nail. Tamp them gently but firmly into place with something thin and blunt so as not to cut the skin. The cotton will buffer the skin and elevate the nail, allowing it to grow out without causing further injury.

If infection occurs, hangnails can become very painful. Use warm soaks, topical antibacterial ointment, dressing changes, and oral antibiotics as described for secondary bacterial infection. Obtain medical help to have the hangnail removed in severe infections, or if no improvement is noted in 2–3 days.

Blisters

Whether hiking in remote mountains or exploring a new city, a blister may be calamitous if you're unable to walk without pain or discomfort. Friction against the skin from poorly fitting shoes or socks and/or excessive moisture buildup is the usual cause of blistering.

Prevention and Treatment

A good pair of walking shoes or hiking boots, with support and cushioning, is essential. Always break in new shoes *prior to travel*. When hiking, wear 2 pairs of socks. The inner pair should be a wicking sock that carries moisture away from the feet. Carry extra socks to change into if needed to keep your feet dry.

Immediately stop walking and take care of any developing blister. Dry your feet well and pack around the sore or blister with a doughnut-shaped ring of moleskin or gauze and tape. Leave the blister intact if possible to prevent infection. If no padding is available, or if the blister interferes with walking or is likely to break from further rubbing, use a sterile needle to puncture it at the edge. The needle can be sterilized with a match flame until red hot, then allowed to cool. After the blister is pierced and drained, cover it with a thin layer of topical antibiotic ointment and a Band-Aid 2–3 times a day or as needed to keep it clean and dry. If the blister becomes infected, treat as indicated for secondary bacterial infection, described earlier in this chapter.

Superficial Fungal Skin Infections

Superficial fungal infections, like athlete's foot, jock itch, and ringworm, are relatively common. They thrive on moisture and can pop up like mushrooms almost overnight. Both prevention and cure require keeping the affected area as dry as possible.

These infections are usually itchy and annoying. They sometimes lead to secondary bacterial infection, especially athlete's foot. Avoid scratching to prevent secondary infection.

Use of Antifungal Medications

In addition to other measures, you usually require antifungal medications to speed relief from athlete's foot, ringworm, or jock itch. Use any of the antifungal preparations listed below twice a day. Wash the affected areas beforehand with soap and water, and dry thoroughly before applying medication.

These preparations come in different formulations, such as creams, lotions, solutions, or powders. They may also be designated for specific infections, such as "jock itch" or "athlete's foot." Use whatever is available and/or works. If there is no relief after 7-10 days of treatment, seek medical attention.

1. clotrimazole (Mycelex 1% cream or solution, Lotrimin 1% cream, lotion, or solution);
2. tolnaftate (Tinactin cream, solution, or powder);
3. undecylenate (Desenex cream, ointment, liquid, or powder);
4. miconazole (Monistat Derm cream);
5. mycostatin (Nystatin cream, ointment, or powder);
6. ketaconazole (Nizoral cream);
7. miconazole (Micatin cream or ointment).

Athlete's Foot (Tinea Pedis)

This common rash usually starts between the toes. It may spread to the sides, tops, or soles of the feet. The affected skin feels itchy or burning, and appears cracked and peeling. Clear, fluid-filled blisters may form. These are subject to secondary bacterial infection when they break.

Occasionally the hands or groin are also affected. Once established, athlete's foot may be impossible to eliminate without reducing sweaty activity or relocating to a drier climate.

Prevention and Treatment

Preventing the spread of athlete's foot requires diligent attention. Sandals, thongs, and open-toed shoes are the preferred footwear for everyday use provided they don't irritate the feet. It's also a good idea to wear thongs or sandals in a public or community shower to prevent acquiring or spreading infection.

Carefully dry between the toes after showering or swimming. A hair dryer works wonders. Socks, if worn, should be made of cotton rather than nylon or other synthetics. Liberally anoint their interiors with an antifungal powder. Change socks as often as necessary to keep the feet dry.

Use a topical antifungal cream, lotion, or ointment to control athlete's foot not responsive to the above measures. Severe infections may require the placement of small wads of cotton between the toes at night.

Ringworm of the Body (Tinea Corporis)

This infection is characterized by one or more ring-shaped lesions that usually appear on areas of exposed skin or the torso. The ring develops as the fungus grows outward in an enlarging circle while dying in the center. The "rings" are usually itchy and scaly, with small raised, possibly fluid-filled lesions appearing on the well defined outer border. The central area is flat and scaly to clear or clearing. Cats or puppies may be the source of infection.

Treatment

Treat with any of the topical antifungal medications.

Jock Itch (Tinea Crusis)

"Jock itch" is an extremely itchy, red, raised, slightly scaly rash of the groin and inner thighs. It sometimes extends to the edges of the buttocks. The rash has a sharply defined border which may have clear central areas. There may be small fluid-filled blisters along the outer edge.

The rash spreads quickly with small red, raised spots (satellite lesions) frequently occurring adjacent to the central rash. Tinea crusis commonly affects men. It can occur in women, often associated with a vaginal yeast infection (see p. 213 for vaginal yeast infections).

Treatment

Keep the area dry (hair dryers work well) and clean. Avoid overbathing and irritation. A drying antifungal powder should be dusted on 2–3 times a day. Don't use underwear or pants made of synthetic or rough materials. Wear shorts to allow air to reach the groin. Men may need to wear an athletic supporter to decrease irritation.

Tinea Versicolor

This fungal infection is usually noticed because of skin discoloration. Rashes appear white, pink, or tan, often as spots or patches on the back, chest, or arms. They can cover large areas, extending to the abdomen, neck, and occasionally the face. Itching is absent or minimal. Scales can be obtained by scraping with a fingernail.

Recurrences are common even after treatment. The rash causes no harm and isn't very contagious. With treatment the scaling will stop, although the discolored areas remain until either tanned or until the surrounding tan fades.

Treatment

Scrub the lesions with a stiff brush after bathing, then apply Selsun solution (selenium sulfide) to all areas of the body with discoloration. Avoid the eyes and genitals. Wash the medication off after 15 minutes. Repeat treatments daily for 2 weeks.

If an allergic reaction occurs, discontinue use. Try one of the following topical antifungal preparations:

1. tolnaftate (Tinactin) solution; **or**
2. miconazole (Monistat Derm Cream); **or**
3. clotrimazole (Mycelex 1% cream or solution, Lotrimin 1% cream, lotion, or solution)

Allergic and Hypersensitivity Reactions

Changes in the skin, usually some form of rash, often reveal allergies. The reaction may be localized — confined to a small area of affected skin — as in contact dermatitis. It can also be systemic, affecting the whole body and producing generalized symptoms such as itching or wheezing.

Systemic Hypersensitivity Reactions

Systemic reactions may occur from medications, food, insect stings, animal dander, pollen, cold temperature, and other causes. Rashes due to systemic reactions are usually either red and flat, or red and raised in the form of welts (hives). They're frequently symmetrical, affecting right and left sides of the body equally. The skin may also appear flushed. There may be moderate to severe itching.

Rashes due to systemic reactions are sometimes, though not always, accompanied by other signs of allergic response. These can include sneezing, runny nose, nausea, vomiting, diarrhea, fever or headache, lethargy, and a tickling or lump in the throat which cannot be cleared by coughing.

Occasionally, systemic reactions result in respiratory symptoms.

Wheezing or labored breathing indicates a potential emergency, requiring immediate medical help, possibly including injectable epinephrine from an allergy or medical kit if available.

Drug Reactions

When a skin rash or any other symptom of allergy follows use of a medication, stop taking the medication immediately.

Treatment

For skin rashes or other mild allergic reactions, the usual treatment is either:

1. Benadryl (diphenhydramine HCl) 25–50 mg. orally, every 4–6 hours;

or

2. Atarax (hydroxyzine HCl) 10–25 mg. orally, every 4–6 hours. Take these until the rash and itching subside.

Hives (Urticaria)

Hives are large, red, raised round areas of skin (welts) which itch moderately to severely. They're usually an allergic response to some environmental factor and develop very quickly. Factors that may induce hives during travel include extreme changes in temperature and humidity, insect bites, medications, and new foods, especially fruits. Parasites and hepatitis are other possible causes.

Hives disappear on their own schedule once the cause is removed— in as little as 2–3 hours from some food and drug allergies or up to several days or even weeks. If you started a new medicine or ate a new food, discontinue it immediately. If diarrhea or abdominal cramps accompany hives, take a stool sample to the nearest medical laboratory to check for parasites. If there's yellowing of the skin (jaundice) or right upper abdominal pain just below the rib cage, then hives may be due to hepatitis.

Treatment

Treat itching with Benadryl or Atarax as indicated above for mild allergic reactions. Cool compresses, showers, or baths will help. One cup of cornstarch (Aveeno powder) or Domeboro's solution added to bathwater twice a day will also help to relieve symptoms. When swelling occurs around the eyes and/or mouth, obtain medical evaluation and treatment. Steroid injections may be necessary.

Contact Dermatitis (Localized Allergic Reaction)

Hypersensitive skin reactions can follow direct contact with chemicals or other irritants, such as the oils from certain plants. The resulting rash is usually red, flat or raised, and may be blistery with clear fluid (vesicular). Rashes from plants often follow lines where the plant has brushed against the skin.

Severe itching, burning, or stinging frequently accompany skin lesions. The area may be hot and swollen, and sometimes appears crusty after blisters break open.

Prevention

The key, of course, is to avoid exposure or re-exposure to the irritating substance. If you have sensitive skin or known allergies to certain products such as soaps or perfumes, carry enough of your own non-allergenic supplies with you. Soaps made in Third World countries are often particularly harsh and irritating.

When the cause is unknown, a rash's location often provides a clue. A new shampoo, soap, hair spray, dye, or other hair product may cause rashes of the scalp. Soap, cleansers, moisturizers, suntan lotion, or shaving cream are possible causes of a facial rash. For rashes on the hands or wrists, consider rings, bracelets, soap or other chemicals. Sometimes protective gloves or other covering can be used to avoid contact, especially in work situations.

Treatment

For relief of itching, use Atarax or Benadryl as described for mild systemic reactions. Hydrocortisone 1% cream applied sparingly on the rash twice daily is also helpful. However, **if a rash becomes infected, don't apply hydrocortisone or other steroid ointments.** Treat as indicated for secondary bacterial infection.

Indications for Medical Attention

Obtain prompt medical attention for any of the following:

1. wheezing, shortness of breath, or other respiratory difficulty;

2. symptoms unimproved after 4–5 days, with or without treatment;

3. large areas of swelling, especially of the face, eyes, neck, or genitals;

4. swelling with itching or pain unrelieved by antihistamines.

Medical treatment for these symptoms may include oral or intramuscular steroids, which should be taken only under medical supervision.

Creature Discomforts:
Scabies, Lice, And Other Pests

Rashes Caused by Parasites

Creeping eruption (cutaneous larva migrans)

Larvae of hookworms that infest dogs and cats cause this rash. Infection is spread by contact with the feces of infected animals. There is a high risk of infection in moist, sandy areas, especially for several days following a rainfall. Though the larvae don't cause hookworm in humans, they do produce a rash. On contact, larvae penetrate areas of exposed human skin, usually the feet, legs, buttocks, or hands.

The larvae burrow through the top layer of skin. This leaves a winding, threadlike red trail of inflamed tissue, visible just under the skin. The trails can look quite bizarre. Itching is moderate to severe and secondary bacterial infection is common. When the rash appears on the buttocks or around the anus it may be caused by another parasite called strongyloides (see "Common Intestinal Parasites," p. 147).

Prevention
Don't go barefoot in tropical and subtropical countries. In sandy areas, avoid skin contact. Wear gloves for digging and use a blanket or other groundcover when sitting or lying down.

Treatment
For itching take Benadryl 25–50 mg., or Atarax 10–25 mg., orally 3–4 times a day. The drug of choice for treatment is topical thiabendazole. Oral medication is used only when the topical preparation is unavailable.

1. *Topically* — apply the preparation to the affected skin areas 4 times a day. This decreases the itching within 24–48 hours. The larvae are killed after 7–14 days of treatment.

2. *Orally* — take thiabendazole twice a day for 2 days. Each dose is computed at 22 mg. per kg. of body weight, not to exceed a total of 1.5 grams per dose. If active lesions are still present two days after the end of therapy, the treatment is repeated.

Scabies
Scabies is a mite that produces red, raised lesions, occasionally with small clear fluid-filled blisters. These lesions sometimes appear as straight lines. They're usually found in the webs between fingers, or on the wrists, elbows, beltline, ankles, legs, breasts, or genital region. They're very itchy, especially at night.

Travelers are most likely to encounter scabies in cheap hotels from contaminated beds, sheets, or blankets. Scabies can also be acquired from sleeping bags or from intimate contact with an infected individual.

Treatment (except during pregnancy)
Use Elimite (5% permethrin) cream. Thoroughly massage into the skin from the neck down to the soles of the feet. Leave on for 8–14 hours, then wash off.

Kwell Lotion (lindane) is an alternative treatment. Apply in the same manner, avoiding contact with eyes and mucous membranes. Wash off after 8 hours. Kwell is related to the pesticide DDT and is toxic if used more frequently. Kwell can also cause rashes or allergic reactions (contact dermatitis), in which case discontinue it and thoroughly wash it off.

During the first 8 hours of treatment, wash in hot water all recently used sheets, clothing, or other fabrics that have been in contact with your skin, and use a clothes dryer if available. If washing by hand, use gloves and the hottest water tolerable. Alternatively, boil clothes and dry with direct exposure to sunlight. Sleeping bags should be dry-cleaned if possible, or bagged in plastic and left for 48–72 hours.

After treatment, itching may persist for up to 2 weeks. Treat itching with Benadryl 25–50 mg. or Atarax 25 mg. 3–4 times a day as needed. Repeat treatment after 7 days, but only if new lesions are noted at that time.

Treat close traveling companions even if they show no symptoms of infection. While this sounds simple, under travel conditions it can be a major hassle. One of the authors and a friend were obliged to spend an entire day in a Quito, Ecuador hotel room in undergarments after entrusting all of their other clothing to the single washing machine and dryer located across town. Two more days were spent patiently anticipating the demise of scabies larvae in their sleeping bags which had been isolated by bagging and sealing in plastic.

Treatment in Pregnancy

Don't use Elimite or Kwell during pregnancy. Use Eurax (crotamiton) instead. Apply to the entire body from the neck down. Repeat the application in 48 hours. Wash off thoroughly 48 hours after the second application.

Head and Body Lice

These lice look similar. Head lice can be found in the hair, along with their small, white egg nits which are attached to the hair shafts. You can distinguish nits from dandruff because they can't be pulled off the hair with fingers. Dandruff is easy to remove.

Body lice are somewhat harder to find, frequently hiding in clothing seams. Their nits are also found on body hairs, including the eye lashes. Itching from both head and body lice is intense.

Treatment

For head lice, use 1–2 ounces of Kwell shampoo before showering, with special attention to head and facial hair. Leave on for 4 minutes, then rinse thoroughly. A capful of Kwell in a sink of warm water is sufficient for sterilizing combs and brushes. Let them soak for about 2 hours, then rinse well.

Nits are easy to remove after using Kwell. Hair should first be soaked for 30 minutes in a solution of hot water and white vinegar. Then comb thoroughly with a fine-tooth comb. Eyebrows or lashes can be treated with petroleum jelly or an occlusive eye ointment twice a day for 10 days. **Don't** use Kwell around the eyes. **Don't** use Kwell during pregnancy.

For body lice, use Kwell lotion and treat clothing as indicated for scabies. To control itching, take Benadryl 25–50 mg. or Atarax 25mg., orally 3–4 times a day. As an alternative to Kwell, use:

1. **for head lice** — permethrin 1% cream rinse ("Nix"), applied to all affected areas and washed off after 10 minutes; or

2. **for head or body lice** — pyrethium and piperonyl butoxide ("RID" or "R and C Shampoo"), applied to all affected areas and washed off after 10 minutes.

Crabs

These critters can take up anonymous, quiet residence in private places, causing barely an itch before their offspring overrun the entire neighborhood. The presence of white nits (eggs) on the hair shafts is a clue to keep looking. As we said earlier, nits can be distinguished from dandruff because they resist being pulled from the hair.

If you find black spots at the base of the hair, they may scamper away on little legs if you watch carefully. Pick one up with tweezers to examine closely if you are feeling brave. Personally, we have always felt that if you held a mirror to your groin, the crabs would probably commit mass suicide upon seeing their true appearance.

Treatment

Use 1–2 ounces of Kwell shampoo before showering. Lather and leave on for 4 minutes, then rinse thoroughly. Pay special attention to all hairy places below the neck, although beard and head are occasionally involved. If shampoo is unavailable, substitute lotion. It must be left on for 8 hours. Don't use Kwell during pregnancy. Another medication which should not be used during pregnancy is 6% precipitated sulfur in petrolatum. This is a medication some pharmacists might prepare for treating crabs.

Treat clothing and bedding as for scabies. Repeat Kwell after 7 days, but only if new crabs are seen. The nits will eventually fall off, or can be pulled or combed out with a fine tooth comb dipped in white vinegar and water. Clean combs and brushes as for head lice. As an alternative to Kwell, use either Nix, RID, or R and C Shampoo (see above).

Fleas

Fleas are often encountered in older hotels, from old or dirty mattresses, bedding, or carpeting. They may also be found in grassy areas around campgrounds where pets or other animals are present.

Bites result in small, red, raised, itchy lesions, especially on the arms, legs, feet, and ankles. For severe itching, apply 1% hydrocortisone cream twice a day or use "Itch Balm Plus".

It's sometimes difficult to identify the source of bites. If you put on white socks, fleas show up easily against the white background. If a suspected flea bite doesn't get better, but instead spreads and gets very itchy, especially at night, consider the possibility of scabies.

Ticks

You can acquire ticks by brushing against vegetation while walking or hiking. On rare occasions, they cause a paralysis of an arm or leg which slowly ascends the limb, and which disappears when you remove the tick.

If symptoms of illness arise following tick exposure, be sure to mention this fact when seeking medical evaluation.

Prevention

Wear protective clothing. Treat clothing if necessary with tick repellent chemicals such as permethrin (see "Mosquito and Tick Precautions," pp. 38–40).

Treatment

Remove ticks with blunt tweezers, or with your fingers protected by a rubber glove, paper towel, or Kleenex. Grasp the tick as close to the skin as possible and pull straight back gently but steadily. If necessary lift the tick upward and pull parallel to the skin until the tick is freed. Don't yank or twist, as this risks leaving the head imbedded in the skin. Wash the wound with soap and water or hydrogen peroxide, then apply antibacterial ointment to prevent secondary infection.

Don't apply gasoline, rubbing alcohol, ether, nail polish, or the hot end of a match or needle to the tick! These methods don't work well and can cause pain or skin damage.

Baby ticks can attack in great numbers — several hundred to a thousand, all at once. This befell one of the authors at the Mayan ruins of Palenque, Mexico. Freshly hatched and ravenous, they rapidly ascended under both pantlegs.

There was nothing to but strip on the spot and brush them off as quickly as possible. A nearby pool provided a chance to try drowning the 40 or 50 that remained, and those still lurking in the jeans. The attempt was totally ineffective, but felt good anyway. Back in the hotel room there was ample opportunity to practice every known method of tick removal, and invent a few more (tequila doesn't work). In an ongoing debate between the authors over the usefulness of underwear, score one or more points for the "pro" side, depending on your degree of modesty.

Personal experience attests that itching can be intense, lasting up to 2 weeks. Use 1% hydrocortisone cream, Calamine lotion, cool wet compresses, or "Itch Balm Plus" to relieve symptoms. Treat for secondary bacterial infection if necessary.

Viral Skin Infections

Venereal Warts

Venereal warts can occur on the external or internal genital or rectal areas in both men and women. Like other warts, a virus causes them. However, these are spread through sexual contact. There may be 1 or more warts. They're soft, raised, flesh-colored in appearance, with either a smooth or cauliflower-like top.

Diagnosis

You must obtain medical attention to distinguish venereal warts from Molluscum or other venereal diseases, including secondary syphilis. A syphilis blood test should always be done. Women should have a vaginal exam and Pap smear at the time warts are diagnosed. They should be aware that there is a higher rate of cervical cancer in women with venereal warts. For homosexual men, the medical workup should include anoscopic examination.

Once diagnosed, treat warts vigorously. Left untreated they will grow and gleefully spread like weeds.

Treatment

There are several alternative treatments. None work perfectly, and most require the care of a doctor. Medical attention is essential when warts are present inside the urethra, rectum, vagina, or on or near any mucous membrane.

Venereal warts are usually frozen off with liquid nitrogen. An alternative is to apply a chemical acid, either Podophyllin or trichlorocetic acid (TCA), directly to the wart. Treatments are repeated until the warts are gone. With both methods, secondary bacterial infection is common. Use a topical antibiotic ointment twice daily on the affected area until treatment is completed and the area healed. Podophyllin should not be used during pregnancy.

During treatment, abstain from sex or use a condom. Sexual partners should also be evaluated medically and treated if necessary.

Genital Herpes

The herpes simplex virus, similar to the one that causes cold sores, causes genital herpes. Normally, herpes lesions go away by themselves without treatment. However, they can be quite painful and mortifying.

Genital herpes may be your first encounter with a sexually transmitted disease. It doesn't help to know that no cure has yet been found. This has led one wag to ask, "What is the difference between herpes and true love?" Answer: "Herpes is forever." Although a first attack of genital herpes may feel like the end of the world — the end of innocence, sex, and perhaps mobility — it is in fact not cause for despair.

Herpes sores appear first as raised, pimple-like lesions (small vesicles) with white tops and a red base. They're usually grouped together. The lesions break open, releasing clear fluid. They then form small ulcers which crust over.

The first occurrence of herpes is frequently very painful. Women, in particular, can find it incapacitating. An initial attack may last 1–2 weeks. Recurrences are less frequent, of shorter duration, and produce much less discomfort.

After an initial attack there may never be a recurrence. If there is, it may be due to stress, exposure to heat or sunlight, trauma, or minor infection.

The herpes virus is usually contagious only while a lesion is present. Avoid sex during this time. Likewise if you have oral herpes, avoid kissing or sharing drinks, glasses, or cigarettes.

While most herpes infections have no harmful or lasting consequences, women should be aware of 2 facts about genital herpes. As with venereal warts, once you contract it, herpes is associated with an increased risk of cervical cancer. It's thus prudent to have a yearly Pap smear. An open herpes lesion is also potentially very dangerous to a baby during delivery. If you become pregnant, inform your medical provider that you have had herpes. If herpes occurs for the first time during pregnancy, consult your medical provider.

Treatment

Acyclovir speeds the rate of healing and decreases pain with first occurrences of genital herpes. The oral form of the medication works much better than the topical ointment. Both are expensive and may be hard to find outside of major cities while traveling. If prone to outbreaks due to stress, take Acyclovir with you. Even on vacations, travel can be stressful.

Oral Acyclovir is used for all initial outbreaks except in pregnancy. The usual dose is 400 mg. 3 times a day for 7–10 days. Or, use 200 mg. 5 times a day for 7–10 days. During pregnancy use Acyclovir ointment instead. Apply to the lesions 5-6 times a day for 7–10 days.

For frequent recurrences, obtain medical evaluation. Most recurrences don't benefit from Acyclovir. If used, the dose is 200 mg. 5 times a day for 5 days or 800 mg. twice a day for 5 days. The drug can also be used to suppress attacks, but only under medical supervision.

If Acyclovir isn't available, try 1,000 mg. (1 gram) of L-lysine, an amino acid, as a daily dietary supplement. This dose can be doubled to 2,000 mg during herpes outbreaks. This regime, in conjunction with a low arginine (an amino acid) diet, has been an effective preventive measure for some people.

For discomfort during an acute attack of genital herpes, try shallow cool baths with baking soda applied to the genital area. Avoid warm water, as heat activates the virus. Cool water applied during urination (or urinating in a bath tub) helps to alleviate burning.

The lesions should be washed with soap and cool water 3 times a day to help keep the affected area dry. If tight underwear must be worn, apply talcum powder or cornstarch to the area. Women, especially, may benefit from the drying effect of a blow dryer (air only, no heat), or exposure to light (but not a heat lamp) several times daily.

Indications for medical attention — Anyone with an active herpes lesion who develops an eye infection should seek medical help immediately.

Other Skin Problems

Sunburn

Sunburn occurs very quickly at tropical latitudes, higher elevations, and near reflective surfaces. Preventive measures are important (see Chapter 1, pp. 31–34). Minimizing sun exposure also helps retard the skin's aging process and reduces the risk of other problems such as skin cancer.

Treatment of Sunburn

For sunburn, take 2 aspirin tablets up to 4 times a day as necessary for discomfort. Apply cool wet compresses to the worst areas. Plain water is best, as vinegar and other home remedies may be irritating. Skin lotions may sound soothing, but oils can increase discomfort by trapping heat. Some people swear by the aloe vera plant as a means of soothing sunburns.

Don't use anesthetic sprays or ointments. These may sensitize the skin to allergic reaction. If blisters occur, don't break them. Avoid re-exposure to sunlight, and watch for secondary infection.

Skin Cancer

Repeated exposure to sunlight can lead to dangerous skin changes, including the uncontrolled growth of abnormal cells (skin cancer). Of these, malignant melanoma is the most life-threatening.

Skin cancers are largely avoidable by reducing sun exposure, using sunscreens, and preventing sunburn. They're also curable. Even melanomas, if detected and treated early, are completely curable.

Risk Factors

People with fair skin, light hair and eye color, or who sunburn easily, are typically more prone to skin cancer. A family history of skin cancer, or a prior occurrence of melanoma, are also considered risk factors.

Danger Signs

Melanomas, in particular, often appear around existing moles, birthmarks, or skin lesions. Examine your skin monthly for any changes. Note particularly the following "ABCDs":

Asymmetry — when one half of the mole doesn't look like the other half.

Border — irregularity. Edges may be ragged, notched or blurred.

Color — pigmentation that is not uniform. Shades of tan, brown, and black may be present. In some cases red, white, or blue discoloring add to the mottled appearance.

Diameter — greater than 6 millimeters (about the size of a pencil eraser). Any growth in size of a mole or increase in number is cause for concern.

Additional warning signs include changes in the surface of a mole — scaliness, oozing, bleeding, or the appearance of a bump or nodule; spread of pigment from the border into surrounding skin; change in sensation including itchiness, tenderness, or pain. If any of these changes are noted, **obtain medical evaluation as soon as possible.** Protection from excessive sun exposure and early detection and treatment of any abnormal skin lesion could be life-saving.

Heat Rash (Prickly Heat)

This is a rash that occurs in hot moist regions, usually in the tropics or subtropics. Obese people are most affected. The cause is blockage of the skin pores (sweat glands). The use of skin ointments or powders, or sweat mixed with dirt or sand, increases the risk of developing a prickly heat rash.

The rash is red, with slightly raised blisters. It most often occurs on covered rather than exposed parts of the body. Burning and itching may be present. The heat and reduced sweating associated with this rash are conducive to other symptoms of heat exposure. Dehydration (see pp. 132–134) must be avoided to prevent complications such as fever and heat prostration.

Prevention and Treatment

Gradual exposure to sunlight will reduce the risk of both sunburn and prickly heat rash. Reduce sweating by wearing cool loose-fitting clothing made from nonsynthetic material, preferably cotton. Avoid greasy skin ointments or powders. Take advantage of air conditioning when available, and bathe frequently.

Cooling lotions, with menthol, phenol, glycerin, or alcohol, will reduce itching and can be used 2–4 times a day. If needed, a topical steroid cream can be applied to the rash. Use either 1% Hydrocortisone cream or Valisone 1% hydrocortisone (HC) twice a day.

If none of these measures are effective, it may be necessary to relocate to a cooler, dryer climate.

Chafing

Chafing occurs most often in hot, moist climates. When adjacent skin surfaces rub against each other, the result is an irritated rash. The area affected is red, slightly tender and itchy, and flat, not raised.

Prevention and Treatment

Wear cool, loose clothing. Men may need to wear an athletic supporter to reduce chafing in the groin area. A thin coat of ointment such as petroleum jelly may also help reduce friction in this area.

Otherwise, chafed areas should be gently washed and kept dry with corn starch or talcum powder. These can be applied at bedtime. For tenderness or itching, try applying 1% cortisone cream or lotion sparingly to the affected area, twice a day.

Itching (Pruritis)

Dry skin is the most frequent cause of flaking or itching. This is sometimes due simply to climate changes. However, overbathing, by depleting the natural oils, is often the root of the problem.

Prevention of Itching Due to Dry Skin

Reduce bathing. Take a sponge bath every other day, only in the areas needed. Use tepid or lukewarm water. This is less drying than hot water.

Plain soaps may be less drying and irritating than those with added perfume or deodorant. It's not advisable to use an antibacterial soap, such as Betadine or Hibiclens, for general skin care unless prescribed medically for a specific condition.

Bath oils can be very helpful to prevent drying if added towards the end of the bath. Skin moisturizers and creams are most effective when used immediately after a bath or shower. They help keep in moisture, but add little or none of their own.

Hydrating baths may be helpful in very dry climates. Add 1/2 to 1 cup of salt to a tub of cool to lukewarm water. Soak for 25–30 minutes. Blot dry and apply a bath oil or other moisturizing skin cream or lotion immediately after bathing.

Other Causes of Itching

There are other causes of itching, and related sensations of burning or crawling of the skin. These include diabetes, stress, insect bites, contact dermatitis, drug or other hypersensitivity reactions, hepatitis, and parasites including scabies, crabs, and lice. Treat the causes of itching whenever possible.

Symptomatic treatment of itching

Light stroking of an itchy area is sometimes effective without aggravating the itchy sensation. For local itching, try Calamine lotion or 1% hydrocortisone cream, lightly applied to the affected area twice a day. For severe itching, take 25–50 mg. of Benadryl or 10–25 mg. of Atarax 2 or 3 times a day and at night for sleep.

For intense localized itching (from insect bites, etc.), try direct application of a cold water compress, ice bag, Domeboro's solution, or Itch Balm Plus. The latter is an over-the-counter medication containing hydrocortisone, benadryl, and tetracaine. It works well for relief of mild itching and skin irritation from insect bites, sunburn, contact dermatitis, and stings from some marine animals. One home remedy that works for insect bites is to rub lime juice on the bite. This stings initially but is followed by relief of the itching.

If there is no improvement, or if the cause is unknown, symptoms of itching require medical evaluation. When itching is accompanied by a rash, the rash must be identified and treated appropriately.

Jaundice or yellow skin — see hepatitis

 Quick Reference

Bacterial Skin Infections and Other Lesions

Signs, symptoms, location	Possible cause
Mild to moderate pain or discomfort:	
small red or purplish inflamed area surrounding a hair follicle, occasionally with pus; may affect chin, scalp, armpit, groin, or any other area with hair	folliculitis
pea-sized blistering lesion which opens, drains, and forms a honey-colored crust; often on the chin or around the nose	impetigo
red swollen tender area around nail margin, sometimes infection with pus	nail margin (paronychial)
previously broken skin (scratch, cut, bite, etc.) that becomes red, tender, warm to the touch; possibly with swelling, pus, or red streaks up the skin	secondary bacterial infection
flat, spreading red area, hot and tender to the touch	cellulitis
small to large sac-like area below skin, red, swollen and tender when touched; if opened will drain pus	abscess or boil (furuncle)
blistery lesion(s) in genital area that form small ulcers and then crust over; pain may be intense, especially in women	herpes
Nonpainful skin lesions:	
groin: small raised cauliflower-like lesion(s) in genital area	warts
mole, scar, birth mark, or other skin feature that changes color, shape, texture, or size	possible melanoma

---

✓ Quick Reference

Common Causes of Itching and/or a Rash

Signs, symptoms, location	Possible cause
Itching *without* a rash:	
rectal area, increased itching at night	pinworms
rectally, with painful bowel movements and blood on toilet paper	hemorrhoids
rectally, after recent episode of diarrhea	normal reaction, usually lasting 1-2 days
dark urine, light-colored stools, nausea, yellow eyes or skin	hepatitis
flaking skin	excessively dry skin
generalized, worse at night, especially wrists, finger webs, waist, or breasts	early scabies
genital area, male	crabs
genital area, female	vaginal infection or crabs
Itching *with* a rash:	
on feet, toe webs, with cracked, peeling area between the toes	athlete's foot
small to large red, raised, welt-like lesions anywhere on the body	hives (urticaria)
small groups of blistering (vesicular), lesions sometimes linear with adjacent flat, red areas; anywhere on body but frequently on arms and hands	contact dermatitis
on scalp with small white particles resembling dandruff at base of hair follicle which cannot be pulled off	head lice
one or more red raised lesions frequently on feet or or ankles	flea bites
small red, raised lesions in webs of fingers, waist, breasts, groin, and/or thigh; itching worse at night	scabies
groin: with white particles like dandruff that don't pull off hairs, black spots at the base of hairs	crabs

Signs, symptoms, location	Possible cause
groin: flat red lesion affecting labia or scrotum, spreading to adjacent skin; well-defined border with small red spots adjacent to central rash	fungal infection (jock itch or jock rash)
occasionally itchy, with flat, discolored (usually whitish) patches on the back, chest, and arms	tinea versicolor
occasionally itchy, circular lesion or lesions with red, raised, well-defined outer border; scaly or clearing in the center	ringworm
on feet or buttocks with red, thread-like winding trails	strongyloides or cutaneous larva migrans

 Quick Reference

Symptomatic Treatment of Itching with or without a Rash

If a rash is present, it needs to be identified and treated. For specific causes of itching without a rash, such as heat or dryness, see recommendations in this chapter.

1. Severe, localized itching (from insect bites, etc.): Use direct application of a cold water compress, ice bag, or Domeboro's solution. Topical hydrocortisone cream or "Itch Balm Plus" can be used when the cause is not bacterial or viral.

2. Generalized itching: Take a cool bath with 1-2 cups of baking soda or mulled oatmeal added to the water.

For severe itching, systemic treatment with oral antihistamines may be needed, especially for sleep. Use one of the following:

1. Benadryl 25-50 mg. orally, 3-4 times a day; or
2. Atarax 10-25 mg. orally, 3-4 times a day; or
3. Periactin 4 mg. orally, 3 times a day.

 **Quick Reference**

Guidelines for Treating Unidentified Rashes

Indications for medical evaluation

Obtain medical evaluation and treatment for:

1. Any ulcerated lesion.

2. Any generalized body rash, especially one that involves the palms of the hands or soles of the feet (possible secondary syphilis).

3. Any persistent rash that worsens with or fails to respond to treatment.

Unless medical treatment is indicated, unidentified rashes can be treated temporarily using the following guidelines:

1. Rashes which are *not infected* (they may be red, swollen, itchy, and dry or weeping clear fluid, but don't contain pus) — treat with cool moist compresses or baths for 15–20 minutes, 2–3 times a day. Rashes due to allergic or hypersensitivity reactions respond to hydrocortisone cream and antihistamines. *Don't use antibiotics.*

2. Rashes which are *infected* (hot, painful, producing pus or whitish, yellow, or greenish matter) — treat with warm compresses for 15–20 minutes 3 times a day. In addition, bacterial infections will usually require topical or oral antibiotics. *Don't use hydrocortisone or other steroid cream.*

3. Lesions which are dry, keep moist. If applying a topical preparation, ointments are preferable to creams or lotions.

4. Lesions which are *moist* — keep dry. If you're using a topical preparation, avoid ointments. Creams are considered slightly drying; powders may be best.

5. Topical hydrocortisone cream may be used on rashes due to contact dermatitis or other allergic reaction. Don't use on fungal rashes, primary or secondary bacterial infections, scabies, or rashes due to viral infections.

6. Apply all topical ointments very thinly and sparingly.

7. If unsure whether a rash is due to heat or fungal infection, try applying Vioform 1% Hydrocortisone (iodochlorhydroxyquin and 1% hydrocortisone) topically twice a day. Or, try alternating a topical antifungal cream or ointment with topical hydrocortisone at 4-6 hour intervals.

Stomach and Intestinal Disorders

6

I am poured out like water . . .
my heart like wax is melted in
the midst of my bowels.
                    Psalms 22:14

To some travelers, midnight vigils in the water closet might seem as commonplace as passport visa applications. The price of an adventuresome spirit sometimes seems to be extracted in literal pounds of flesh. As one veteran traveler put it, "nausea and abdominal cramping should be dues enough . . . losses from diarrhea and vomiting aren't even tax deductible."

With a few exceptions these symptoms, although occasionally dire, are of minor consequence. Remember, however, that the gastro-intestinal or GI tract is a meandering pathway through organs of the chest and abdomen. Almost any of these organs can cause related symptoms.

At the end of this chapter there's a chart of abdominal disorders that may cause nausea, vomiting, diarrhea, or abdominal pain. Use this to help quickly locate relevant information in the text.

Nausea, Vomiting, and Diarrhea

Although they often occur together, nausea, vomiting, and diarrhea are distinct entities. Each has many possible causes. For example, anxiety, pregnancy, and even head injury can cause vomiting. We'll discuss only the infectious causes which concern most travelers — bacteria, viruses, and parasites.

In otherwise healthy travelers, these symptoms often serve a protective function. They help rid the body of potentially harmful organisms or substances. It's worth noting that the physical stress of travel sometimes causes mild diarrhea or other minor GI disturbances. Jet lag, fatigue, new foods (especially fruits), caffeine, and alcohol may contribute to symptoms.

Most viral or bacterial causes of these symptoms are "self-limiting." Allow them to run their course and they go away with no harmful effects — *provided your fluid intake is adequate*. In general, it's wise not to treat symptoms when they first appear. However, dehydration is always a potential danger when nausea, vomiting, and/or diarrhea occur. You must completely replace lost fluids. **If vigorous oral fluid replacement can't prevent dehydration, medical care is mandatory.**

Nausea, vomiting, and appetite loss are related, but can occur separately. When there's a self-limiting cause, symptoms rarely last more than 24–48 hours. In cases of nausea alone, or mild nausea and vomiting in which adequate oral fluid intake is maintained, no treatment is necessary.

Treatment

Nausea and vomiting without diarrhea should never be treated with antibiotics. Obtain medical treatment for the following conditions:

1. Severe nausea and/or vomiting if oral fluids can't be taken or kept down. Dehydration must be prevented, or treated if present.

2. Symptoms of nausea and/or vomiting persisting more than 48 hours.

3. Vomiting which follows a head injury (may be accompanied by lethargy and disorientation). **This is a medical emergency.**

Treatment of Nausea and Vomiting Due to Pregnancy

Vitamin B_6 supplements may help symptoms of nausea due to pregnancy. Take 50 mg. in the morning and 100 mg. at night. Discontinue these when symptoms diminish. Eating snacks at 2-hour intervals and having crackers available at the bedside in the morning can help. The "Sea Band," described on p. 30 as a treatment for motion sickness, may also be of benefit. If there's no improvement, or if symptoms are severe enough to cause dehydration, obtain medical help.

Treatment of Vomiting in Isolated Areas

Medications to stop vomiting (antiemetics) may be needed if medical help is not accessible and sufficient fluids can't be taken orally to prevent dehydration. Use these medications to stop nausea and vomiting so that fluids can be replaced. This is an interim measure only, to be used until medical help can be found.

To prevent vomiting, take Tigan 250 mg. or Compazine 10 mg. orally, up to 3 times a day. When unable to keep oral medications down, use a Tigan 200 mg. rectal suppository 3–4 times a day or a Compazine 25 mg. rectal suppository twice a day, as needed. When symptoms are due to hepatitis use Tigan, not Compazine. See Part III (p. 283) before taking either medication. *Don't* use these or other antiemetics during pregnancy.

Dehydration and Rehydration

Whenever nausea, vomiting, and diarrhea occur, dehydration is a potential threat. With nausea and vomiting, fluid intake is often minimal. With severe or prolonged diarrhea, fluid loss may be substantial.

Uncorrected, dehydration can lead to internal damage, shock, and death. **Dehydration must be prevented by drinking a sufficient quantity of liquids to replace all lost fluids. When dehydration can't be prevented by vigorous oral fluid replacement, medical attention must be obtained quickly. Intravenous fluids are required.**

Symptoms of dehydration

Decreasing urine output is one of the earliest indications of dehydration. Urine becomes very concentrated, usually dark yellow or amber in color. The mouth is often dry. As the condition progresses, there may be fatigue and light-headedness or dizziness when standing. Later signs include extreme weakness, a loss of skin elasticity (turgor), sunken eyes, and weight loss. It's this progression of symptoms which must be avoided or reversed by vigorous oral fluid replacement. If this can't be accomplished, intravenous fluids are mandatory.

Treatment of Dehydration:
Rehydration (Oral Fluid Replacement)

Measure for measure, you must replace the total volume of fluid lost from vomiting, diarrhea, sweating, and urine. You must also replace body electrolytes (sodium, potassium, chloride, and bicarbonate). It's best to drink small amounts every few minutes at a rate of about one quart or liter per hour. Drink fluids from an uncontaminated or purified source (see pp. 80-84).

Treatment of Minor Fluid Losses

For fluid losses from mild diarrhea or vomiting, ordinary carbonated soft drinks (preferrably without caffeine), teas, broth, fruit juice, and purified water are adequate sources of fluid replacement.

Treatment of Moderate Fluid Losses

Take clear fluids for 24–48 hours. These include purified water, broth, Gatorade, caffeine-free soft drinks such as 7-UP, chamomile or other soothing teas without caffeine, and bottled mineral water, perhaps with a squeeze of lemon or lime juice.

When vomiting is present, make sure drinks contain sodium and chloride, or add 1/4 teaspoon table salt to each 8 oz. of liquid. You can also try nibbling on salted crackers. When diarrhea is present, add 1/4 tsp. baking soda to 8 ounces of water. See "rehydration formulas" on the next page.

When you're feeling better, take bland easily digested foods such as soups, cola drinks, jello, or fruit juices (orange, apple, etc.) for a day or two. Slowly add bananas and other soft foods (rice, baked potatoes). Avoid dairy products, fatty or spicy foods, red meats, vegetables, caffeine, alcohol, and other fruits until fully recuperated.

Treatment of Severe Fluid Losses

For severe vomiting and/or diarrhea, use one of the rehydration formulas or products listed below. If unavailable, use any source of pure fluid to prevent dehydration. If you can't prevent dehydration, there's no choice but to seek medical help for intravenous fluids.

Fluid replacement when pure fluids aren't available

If required to prevent or correct dehydration, use whatever water source is available. Tap water, preferrably from the hot tap, or water from a river, lake, or well, even if possibly contaminated, is justified when there are no alternatives. Progressively worsening dehydration with ongoing fluid losses is a medical emergency.

Rehydration Formulas

Some commercial products, such as Gatorade, are available to help replace electrolytes lost along with water. Powders which can be added to water include Hydra-lyte, Infalyte, and WHO (World Health Organization) Oral Rehydration Salts. Packets of this formula ("Dialite") are available from IAMAT (see p. 44). In many tropical countries equivalent rehydration formulas are available commercially in small packets which are added to a quart of pure water. Another product is Pedialyte RS, a ready-to-use fluid replacement for children which works fine for adults.

You can make your own electrolyte replacement drinks with the following formulas from the U.S. Public Health Service. Sip alternately from each glass until you quench your thirst:

Glass #1	Glass #2
	8 ounces pure water
8 ounces orange, apple, or other pure water	1/4 teaspoon baking soda (sodium bicarbonate)
fruit juice (potassium source)	
1/2 teaspoon honey or corn syrup (glucose, which is necessary for absorption of salts)	
1/4 teaspoon table salt (sodium and chloride)	

If fruit juice is unavailable or can't be tolerated, cream of tartar is an alternative source of potassium which you can use as follows:

>   1 quart water with 1 teaspoon baking soda, 1 tablespoon corn syrup, and 4 teaspoons cream of tartar

These recipes haven't won any international tasting competitions, but they do the job.

Traveler's Diarrhea

By any name ("New Delhi Belli," "Montezuma's Revenge," "Greek Gallop," "Turkey Trots," "Casablanca Crud," "Rangoon Runs," "Hong Kong Hop," etc.) the results are identical and all too familiar. The illness is usually caused by the bacteria *E. Coli.*, but may also be due to viruses, parasites, or other bacteria.

The source of infection is usually contaminated food, water, or beverages. High risk items include raw, unpeeled fruits and vegetables, uncooked or poorly heated meat, raw seafood, tap water, ice cubes, and unpasteurized dairy products. Your destination, and the precautions you take (or fail to take) against traveler's diarrhea, largely determine your risk of acquiring it. See Chapter 4, "Preventive Health Measures — Food and Water Precautions," pp. 77–87.

Adherence to preventive measures may require some determination. You'll have to endure the braggard testimonials of those who "ate and drank everything and never got sick." Yet even the best precautions do not confer immunity.

Symptoms

Traveler's diarrhea usually develops during the first week of travel, but may occur at any time during travel or shortly after returning home. The onset of symptoms is usually sudden. There's abdominal cramping, relieved by episodic bouts of diarrhea which are frequently accompanied by a sense of urgency. These occur about 4–5 times a day. There may also be nausea, vomiting, fever, bloating, and weakness. Symptoms usually don't last more than 3–5 days even if untreated, but occasionally persist up to a week or more.

The presence of blood, pus, or mucus in the stool, or a high fever above 102°F (38.8°C)., signals a more serious infection by organisms which cause dysentery. **These are indications for prompt medical attention.**

Treatment

Avoid dehydration! The most important measure for treating diarrhea is the replacement of lost fluids and electrolytes (see rehydration on preceding pages).

For rapid relief of symptoms use a combination of antibiotics and antimotility drugs. At the onset of diarrhea take one antibiotic tablet and one or two antimotility tablets. Continue taking one antibiotic tablet every twelve hours (twice a day) for 3 days. If bloody diarrhea or diarrhea with fever is present after three days of antibiotics, continue the antibiotic for two more days (a total of 5 days). The antimotility medications are only taken after each loose stool and for no more then two days. **Don't** take antimotility medications if diarrhea is bloody or accompanied by fever.

Antibiotics

The drugs of choice are:

1. ciprofloxacin 500 mg. orally, twice a day for 3–5 days; **or**

2. norfloxacin 400 mg. orally, 2 or 3 times a day for 3–5 days; **or**

3. ofloxacin 200 mg. orally, twice a day for 3–5 days; **or**

4. Bactrim DS or Septra DS, one tablet orally twice a day for 3–5 days (only recommended for travelers to Mexico outside the Caribbean coast, due to increasing bacterial resistance).

If diarrhea lasts more than 3–5 days after starting antibiotics, stop taking them. Obtain medical evaluation. To identify the cause and determine the appropriate treatment requires stool tests for bacteria and parasites .

In considering antibiotic use, it's important to remember that the indiscriminate use of an antibiotic can have serious side effects. It may produce strains of bacteria resistant to the antibiotic. It can also open the door to infections from organisms not affected by the antibiotic.

Antimotility Medications

Use either Imodium, the drug of choice, or Lomotil. These reduce movement of food through the intestinal tract. The dosages are:

1. *Imodium AD* — 4 mg. initially (2 capsules or 4 teaspoons), then 2 mg. after each loose stool. *Don't* exceed 16 mg. per day (8 capsules or 16 teaspoons). Don't use for more than two days.

2. *Lomotil* — 1 or 2 tablets orally as needed every 4–6 hours up to 4 times a day, for a maximum of 2 days. Lomotil should be used cautiously by elderly individuals due to possible side effects including urinary retention and dry mouth.

If Imodium AD and Lomotil aren't available, paregoric, tincture of opium, or codeine may be used. These will reduce bowel cramping and the number of bowel movements. All antimotility medications must be used cautiously as excesses are often constipating.

Some situations confronting travelers have their own compelling arguments for the use of antimotility medications. If there's a Murphy's Law of Foreign Transportation, it undoubtedly reads: "Lengthy travel on any vehicle lacking toilet facilities will inevitably induce diarrhea." Travel through remote areas by horseback, mule, or camel, or rafting down the Amazon, are examples of other activities that may require the use of antimotility medications if diarrhea occurs.

Alternative treatment

Pepto-Bismol can be used as an alternative to antibiotics and antimotility medications. Expect the number of stools to be reduced by half. When diarrhea starts the dosage for Pepto-Bismol is 1 ounce (2 tablespoons) every half hour for 8 doses (one 8–ounce bottle). Tablets can also be used — 4 tablets 4 times a day for 1 or 2 days. Don't exceed this dosage if symptoms persist.

Tongue and stools may appear black from this medication, and mild constipation may occur. Don't use Pepto-Bismol during pregnancy. It's contraindicated for travelers with kidney impairment and for those taking

Coumadin or salicylates (aspirin) regularly for other medical conditions. It shouldn't be used by travelers who have been directed not to take aspirin.

Use of Prescribed and Unprescribed Medications

It's not unusual for useless or potentially dangerous medications to be recommended for gastro-intestinal tract disturbances in some countries. Use this book to check medications for appropriateness, contraindications, warnings, and side effects. For your own protection, this should be done for all medications prescribed during travel.

Useless medications

Kaopectate (kaolin plus pectin), traditionally given for diarrhea, is of no therapeutic value. It doesn't shorten the course of illness or diminish diarrhea. It doesn't alleviate abdominal cramps. It gives stools a little more consistency — that's all.

A lactobacillus preparation (yogurt or acidophilus) won't help most of the conditions which cause diarrhea among travelers. It won't, for example, help symptoms of traveler's diarrhea. It may be of benefit if diarrhea occurs as a side effect of antibiotic use.

Dangerous prescriptions

Avoid certain drugs altogether. **Don't** take *Enterovioform, MexaForm, Intestopan, chloramphenicol (Chloromycetin* and other brands), *clioquinol,* or *iodoquinol,* for undiagnosed disorders. These drugs are dangerous, with potentially serious side effects. They are popular in some countries for treating and preventing various gastro-intestinal, respiratory, or other disorders. If prescribed, ask for something else. There are safer and more effective alternatives.

Don't take Lomotil or other antimotility medications if they are combined in a single medication with neomycin, sulfa drugs, aminapyrine, butazolidin, or any other medicine or antibiotic. Don't combine antibiotics, or take medications which combine antibiotics, unless prescribed by a doctor for a diagnosed condition.

See the Quick Reference guides on the following pages.

Specific Infectious Causes of Diarrhea

Viral gastroenteritis ("stomach flu")

One or more viruses are capable of causing mild symptoms of diarrhea, nausea, and vomiting. These are often accompanied by muscle aches, a slight fever under 101°F (38.3°C) or abdominal cramping. Symptoms usually disappear in one to three days, but may persist up to a week.

Treatment

For headache, muscle aches, or mild fever, take 1–2 aspirin up to 3–4 times a day as needed. Symptoms of vomiting and diarrhea should be treated as required to prevent dehydration. Antibiotics are of no benefit in viral illnesses.

Shigella

Flies as well as food handlers are sometimes to blame for the contaminated food or utensils through which this bacterial infection is spread. Shigella is highly contagious and good handwashing is essential to prevent spreading the disease.

Following exposure, illness develops within 1–4 days. In adults most cases of Shigella are mild and resolve on their own in 4–8 days.

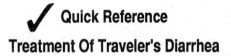

✔ Quick Reference

Treatment Of Traveler's Diarrhea

For initial treatment of diarrhea:

1. prevent dehydration by replacing lost fluids (see pp. 132–134). If you are unable to keep fluids down or keep hydrated then obtain medical evaluation immediately.

For rapid relief of symptoms:

1. use a combination of antibiotics and antimotility medication (see pp. 135–136) or use Pepto-Bismol as an alternative treatment (see p. 136).

2. Don't take antimotility medications if diarrhea is accompanied by blood or pus in the stools, fever above 102°F (38.8°C), or abdominal pain unrelieved by the passage of stools or gas. Instead, obtain medical evaluation.

3. After 3–5 days of antibiotics if diarrhea persists, stop taking the antibiotics and obtain medical evaluation.

Note: a particular form of diarrhea (pseudomembranous colitis) may occur following treatment with some antibiotics, especially clindamycin and cephalosporins. If diarrhea develops after beginning antibiotics and persists after antibiotics have been discontinued, medical evaluation is required.

 **Quick Reference**

Nausea, Vomiting, And Diarrhea: Conditions Requiring Immediate Medical Attention

When nausea, vomiting or diarrhea are accompanied by any of the following conditions, get medical help quickly:

1. severe or progressive dehydration when adequate oral fluid replacement isn't possible;
2. weight loss greater than 5% of body weight;
3. chest pain;
4. vomiting which lasts more than 48 hours;
5. projectile vomiting or vomiting which follows a head injury (often accompanied by lethargy or disorientation);
6. bright red blood or "coffee ground" material from vomiting;
7. acute abdominal pain not relieved by the passage of stool or gas;
8. diarrhea, treated or untreated, which lasts longer than 3–5 days;
9. a fever with gradual daily elevations (possible typhoid);
10. bloody stools, either bright red (unless due to hemorrhoids) or black and tarry (unless color is due to iron tablets or Pepto-Bismol).

Symptoms

The earliest symptom is often painful, colicky cramping relieved with passage of stool. Sensations of urgency may accompany these episodes. They become more frequent and severe with increasing diarrhea. Later, blood and pus are often seen in the stool.

High fevers, up to 104°F (40.0°C), follow the onset of diarrhea. Chills, headache, and loss of appetite may accompany these. Nausea and vomiting are absent or minimal.

Treatment

Dehydration can be a dangerous complication and may develop quickly. *Oral fluid replacement must be vigorous.* Relieve abdominal cramping with a hot water bottle or other source of heat. Apply it locally. Antibiotics aren't usually necessary.

Antimotility medications such as Lomotil, Imodium, or paregoric must never be used for Shigella infections. Their use will prolong infection. It may also result in severe intestinal damage or infection that spreads throughout the body (septicemia). Codeine and other constipating medications should be used only under medical supervision.

Treatment in isolated areas when medical help isn't available

In isolated areas, the occurrence of bloody diarrhea or a fever above 102°F (38.8°C) warrants the use of antibiotics as directed for traveler's diarrhea (see pp. 135-137).

Conditions requiring immediate medical treatment

The following require prompt medical intervention:

1. dehydration;
2. severe abdominal pain unrelieved by the passage of stool or gas or by applications of heat (and not related to menstruation);
3. any severe or continuous bleeding;
4. symptoms that fail to improve within 4–8 days;

Cholera

Travelers rarely encounter this bacterial illness. It's transmitted through contaminated food and water. Vaccination isn't very effective and isn't routinely recommended. Avoid cholera by following the food and water precautions recommended in Part I, pp. 67–77. With adequate replacement of lost fluids, infection is usually mild and self-limiting. Even in severe cases, cholera is completely curable in otherwise healthy adults if treated early. Nevertheless, severe untreated cases, especially in children and the elderly, can have high death rates.

Symptoms

Symptoms are often confined to a mild episode of diarrhea which doesn't need treatment, except for fluid replacement. Severe cases, however, are capable of producing massive water loss and dehydration. There may be frequent episodes of severe, painless, watery gray diarrhea, described as "rice water" stools. These are odorless and *don't* contain blood or pus. In severe cases, symptoms are usually of abrupt onset and may be accompanied by vomiting.

The huge amount of water lost results in intense thirst. Oral fluid replacement must be extremely vigorous. Early signs of inadequate fluid intake include a diminished output of dark colored urine. There may be fatigue, muscle cramps, and light-headedness or dizziness when standing. Later signs of dehydration are loss of skin tone, sunken eyes, extreme weakness, and weight loss. **In such cases hospitalization with intravenous (IV) fluid replacement is required.**

Treatment

In areas where cholera is known to exist or an epidemic occurs, these symptoms require immediate medical evaluation. A stool culture and sensitivity should be done prior to starting antibiotics, whenever possible. In addition to antibiotics, treat diarrhea with oral fluids. The rule of thumb is to take in at least as much fluid as is lost. (See "Dehydration and Rehydration," pp. 132–134.) If these measures can't prevent dehydration, intravenous fluids are necessary.

Treatment in isolated areas

If you suspect cholera and medical evaluation is unavailable, start tetracycline. The usual dose is 500 mg. orally every 6 hours for 3–5 days. In many areas of the world cholera is now resistant to tetracycline. Obtain medical help if tetracycline doesn't reduce symptoms dramatically. It's essential to drink lots of fluids, even when taking antibiotics.

Food Poisoning

"Food poisoning" isn't a precise term. We use it here to refer to certain bacterial causes of acute nausea, vomiting, and diarrhea. Illness follows ingestion of contaminated food, usually when it's left unrefrigerated for long periods. This allows the growth of bacteria and/or the accumulation of bacterial toxins. These conditions don't normally require antibiotics.

"Staph" Food Poisoning

Staphylococcal bacteria are present on the skin. They cause common infections like pimples and boils. When spread to foods such as fish, processed meats, milk, custard, and cream-filled pastries, especially when unrefrigerated, they can produce a potent toxin.

Soon after eating (usually within an hour or two) there's an abrupt onset of intense, violent vomiting. This lasts for several hours, rarely more than 6 or 8. Abdominal cramping may occur; fever and diarrhea don't. The experience is awful but recovery is rapid and complete. No treatment is usually necessary.

Salmonella Food Poisoning (Non-typhoid)

Foods high in protein are the usual source of salmonella infection.

These include chicken, fish, meat, eggs, and dairy products.

There's an abrupt onset of mild to severe nausea, vomiting, and diarrhea, usually 8 to 48 hours after eating. Abdominal cramps, fever, and chills may be present. Bloody stools are rare.

The severe vomiting and diarrhea are characteristic of salmonella poisoning. They don't often occur together in other bacterial infections of the intestinal tract. The intense symptoms are usually self-limiting, though they may persist for a while in milder form.

Treatment

Keep hydrated by drinking plenty of fluids. Except for rare occasions under medical supervision, avoid antibiotics. Obtain medical attention for:

1. dehydration;

2. fever persisting more than 36 hours;

3. localized abdominal pain.

Following is a list of potential laboratory findings *after stools have been sent for culture and sensitivity,* along with the indicated treatment. "Supportive" refers to treatment of symptoms, rather than the underlying cause.

Note: a stool culture and sensitivity test will only reveal bacterial causes of diarrhea. Intestinal parasites may also be a cause of persistant ongoing symptoms. Other tests are required to identify parasites.

Intestinal Parasites

Intestinal parasites are common in regions with inadequate sewage treatment, water purification, and personal hygiene. Most are transmitted through fecally contaminated food and water, from food handlers and other sources. They're largely avoidable (see Chapter 4, "Food and Water Precautions", pp. 77–87).

An occasional parasite isn't cause for undue alarm. Problems usually arise from prolonged or massive infections. However, some parasites can be dangerous if they escape the digestive tract to other parts of the body. To avoid potential problems, always treat parasites promptly.

Parasites are often comparatively shy. They may signal their presence, if at all, through vague, fleeting symptoms. These are frequently recurrent. They include:

1. mild constipation or diarrhea, sometimes alternating;

2. abnormally foul stools or gas;

Quick Reference

Treatment of Bacterial Causes of Diarrhea

Stool Cultures: Reference Chart for Treating Bacterial Causes of Diarrhea

The indicated treatment for diarrhea from most bacterial causes is rest and rehydration (R&R). Sometimes, antibiotics are necessary for specific cases, when symptoms persist beyond the normal duration of illness.

Organism	Normal duration of illness	Treat if symptoms persist beyond	Indicated treatment (unless organism shows resistance on stool C&S)
E. coli	3-7 days	2 weeks	Bactrim (Septra) DS, 1 tablet twice a day for 3–5 days; **or** one of the following: ciprofloxacin 500 mg., norfloxacin 400 mg., or ofloxacin 200 mg., orally twice a day for 3–5 days
Shigella	3-7 days	1 week	Bactrim (Septra), 2 tablets orally twice a day for 5 days; **or** ciprofloxacin 500 mg. orally twice a day for 5-7 days.
Staphylococcus	less than 24 hours	NA	supportive treatment only
Salmonella typhii	1-4 weeks	NA	usually, supportive treatment only. For very severe symptoms, antibiotics may be required under medical supervision
Salmonella (all except S. typhii)	3-7 days	NA	supportive treatment only; antibiotics may be required for severe symptoms
Clostridium perfringens	12-24 hours	NA	supportive treatment only
Campylobacter jejuni	3-7 days	1 week	erythromycin 500 mg. 4 times a day for 7 days; **or** ciprofloxacin 500 mg. orally for 7 days; **or** doxycycline 100 mg. orally twice a day for 7 days
Yersina enterocolica	2-14 days	NA	supportive measures only; severe cases require hospitalization for antibiotics (Septra DS one tablet orally once a day for 7 days)
Bacillus cereus	variable	NA	supportive treatment only
Vibrio cholerae	3-5 days	5 days, or acute cases resulting in dehydration	tetracycline, 500 mg. 4 times a day for 5 days (check culture and sensitivity prior to starting antibiotics as the bacteria may be resistant); **or** erythromycin 500 mg. orally 4 times a day for 2-3 days
Vibrio para-hemolyticus	1-7 days	1 week	severe cases only — tetracycline, 500 mg. 4 times a day for 5 days.

3. decreased appetite;
4. abnormal sensations of fullness or bloating;
5. occasionally, nausea and vomiting.

Over the course of weeks or even months you may finally identify the faint signals of an E.T. (Extra-inTestinal) trying to phone home.

Even without symptoms, a parasite may be passed in the stool. For this reason, many travelers make a habit of visual inspection. If a parasite is found, save it in a jar or other container and take it to a laboratory for identification.

Guidelines for Identifying and Treating Suspected Parasites

When symptoms suggest parasites, there are several options. One is to see a doctor. A single stool sample is ordered for "culture and sensitivities," to check for bacteria. At the same time, 3 separate samples are ordered for "ova and parasites" (for parasites and their eggs). These should be as fresh as possible.

In cities of most developing nations, money can be saved by going directly to a medical laboratory for these tests. While awaiting lab results, certain home remedies such as chamomile tea or garlic cloves may help reduce intestinal symptoms. They won't, however, eliminate the parasites.

Once a parasite is identified, further information and treatment schedules can be found in this section. With the lab results, you can obtain appropriate medication from a local pharmacy. If symptoms persist and stool samples don't reveal parasites or bacteria, obtain medical evaluation.

Two weeks after completing treatment, repeat the stool exams. If parasites are still present, either repeat treatment, try an alternative medication, or see a doctor. If no parasites are found but symptoms persist or recur, obtain medical advice.

Common Intestinal Parasites

Roundworms

Ascaris or giant roundworm (Ascaris lumbricoides)

Giant roundworm infections are common among travelers, though seldom harmful. Minor infections are usually without symptoms. Suddenly encountering a fat, spaghetti-like adult worm in one's stool can nevertheless be quite traumatic.

Roundworms are spread through fecally contaminated food and water. Irrigated, low-growing vegetables such as lettuce are a frequent source of infection.

After ingestion, roundworm eggs hatch into larvae. These migrate from the intestines through the lymph and bloodstream to the lungs. In sufficient numbers they may cause fever, coughing with blood-tinged sputum, and hives or other allergic reactions.

The microscopic larvae ascend the respiratory tract in coughed secretions. Some are inevitably swallowed and grow to adult size in the small intestine.

Symptoms

When numerous, roundworms cause vague, generalized abdominal discomfort and cramping. There may also be nausea, vomiting, decreased appetite, weakness, and weight loss. Most commonly, though, symptoms are absent and the worms first appear in the stool.

On occasion, their size and migratory habits can make these worms particularly unsettling. One of the authors, admiring the spectacularly scenic Iguasu Falls between Brazil and Argentina, was startled to find an Ascaris disembarking from his pants cuff . . . presumably to get a better view.

Treatment

When lab results show the presence of other parasites in addition to Ascaris, always treat the Ascaris infection first. This is necessary to prevent the migration of these worms outside the intestines. The drug of choice, widely available, is mebendazole (Vermox). The adult dosage is 100 mg. orally twice a day for 3 days.

Alternative medication

There is one other drug which you can use — pyrantel pamoate — although the dosage is computed according to body weight measured in kilograms. First convert your weight in pounds to kilograms by using the conversion table in Appendix D or dividing your weight in pounds by 2.2. Take 11 mg. per kg. of body weight, taken as a single oral dose. The maximum dosage is 1 gram. This should not be exceeded by those weighing more than 90 kg. (198 pounds).

Whipworm (Trichuris trichiuria)

Whipworm is another common roundworm that causes symptoms only when numerous. Symptoms include abdominal pain, diarrhea, bloating, and gas. Nausea, vomiting, and weight loss occur only in very severe infections.

Treatment

The drug of choice is mebendazole (Vermox), 100 mg. orally twice a day for 3 days.

Pinworm (Enterobius vermicularis)

Pinworm infections occur throughout the world. Rectal itching, usually worse at night, is the main symptom. Itching may lead to insomnia, restlessness, and irritability. In severe cases there may be vague abdominal pain, nausea, vomiting or diarrhea, and decreased appetite. In women itching and inflammation can spread to the vagina.

Treatment

Treat pinworm infections with a single 100 mg. oral dose of mebendazole. Repeat this 2 weeks later. An alternative medication is pyrantel pamoate, 11 mg./kg. of body weight, up to a maximum of 1 gram. Take it in a single oral dose and repeat in 2 weeks.

Hookworm (Ancylostoma duodenale or Necator americanus)

Unlike other roundworm infections, hookworms are transmitted from skin contact with larvae in fecally contaminated soil. Infection is therefore most likely outdoors in areas that lack sewage and toilet facilities.

Hookworm larvae, microscopically small, burrow through the skin. This causes an itchy local rash, usually on the feet. Wear shoes! Don't go barefoot! Since the larvae are capable of wriggling through layers of cloth, care must also be taken when choosing a spot to sit down.

Once in the body, larvae reach the lungs in the same manner as *Ascaris*. There may be a cough, sore throat, and blood-tinged sputum in severe infections. Larva reach the digestive tract after being swallowed. They then hook into the intestinal lining in order to feed on blood and mucosal substances.

Blood is often detectable in stools. Other symptoms include abdominal discomfort or pain, increased gas, diarrhea, and weight loss. Weakness, fatigue, and anemia can occur after prolonged infection.

Treatment

Keep skin lesions clean, dry, and covered to prevent secondary infection. Treatment is indicated only after the worms are identified by microscopic examination. Lab reports positive for hookworm may read either "*Necator americanus*" or "*Ancylostoma duodenale.*"

The usual treatments, in order of preference, are:

1. mebendazole, 100 mg. orally twice a day for 3 days; **or**

2. pyrantel pamoate orally, 11 mg./kg. of body weight up to a maximum of 1 gram daily for 3 days.

Threadworm (Strongyloides stercoralis)

The life cycle of this threadworm closely resembles that of hookworm. The disease is widespread throughout the tropics, and is found in the same climatic and sanitary conditions that favor hookworm infections. A rash on the buttocks or anal area is one manifestation of infection.

Severe infection may cause stomach pain, just below the breastbone (sternum), as well as vomiting and diarrhea. Diagnosis is made from microscopic examination of stool. Prevention is the same as for hookworm.

Treatment

The usual treatment is thiabendazole, 25 mg. per kg. of body weight orally twice a day for 2 days. Don't exceed a total of 3 grams a day (1.5 grams per dose).

Protozoa

"Giardia" (Giardia lamblia)

Of all parasites which infect travelers, the protozoa giardia is the most common. Infection is known medically as "giardiasis" or "lambliasis." Giardia inhabit the small intestine just below the stomach, where they adeptly sabotage fat digestion and absorption. Initially stools may be watery and profuse. They then become characteristically foul-smelling, bulky, yellow, and frothy with undigested fats. This frequently causes them to float.

Bloating sensations are common. Giardia also cause burping that smells sulfurous, like rotten eggs. This is known among the initiated as the "Purple Burps."

Other possible symptoms include nausea, occasional vomiting, and pain in the right upper part of the abdomen. There may be cramping and intermittent diarrhea, sometimes alternating with constipation.

Indications for medical attention

Symptoms accompanied by the characteristic burping and digestive disturbances strongly suggest giardia infection. When fever, yellowing of the skin or eyes, or severe abdominal pain are also present, there may be another cause and **immediate medical evaluation is required.**

Treatment

The usual treatments for giardia in adults are:

1. quinacrine 100 mg. orally, 3 times a day for 7 days; **or**
2. Flagyl (metronidazole) 250 mg. orally, 3 times a day for 7 days; **or**
3. Fasigyn (tinidazole) 2 grams orally in a single dose.

Amoebas
Found worldwide, amoebas cause a potentially serious infection of the large intestine. Although rare, amoebas sometimes reach the liver or other organs where they can be very damaging. More likely is the development of a chronic carrier state, in which highly infective cysts are passed in the stool.

Symptoms
Amoebas produce symptoms slowly and gradually. Diarrhea occurs intermittently, worsening over several days, sometimes alternating with constipation. Stools may contain strands of mucus or blood. If there's a fever it's usually slight, less than 101°F (38.3°C). There may be lower abdominal pain or cramping, usually on the left side. All of these symptoms may disappear, only to recur at varying intervals.

Diagnosis
Diagnosis is made by examination of stool for ova and parasites. If taking Pepto-Bismol (bismuth subsalicylate), kaolin products, or castor oil, wait 3–4 days after stopping their use before submitting a stool specimen. These products make it difficult to find amoebas under microscopic examination. Start treatment if the lab report lists any of the following: "*Entamoeba histolytica*", "*Entamoeba dysenteriae*", "*Endamoeba histolytica*", or "*Endamoeba polecki*."

Treatment
The preferred treatment for amoebas is Flagyl, 750 mg. orally 3 times a day (every 8 hours) for 10 days. It's then followed by diiodohydroxyquin (same as iodoquinol), 650 mg. orally 3 times a day for 20 days. If one of these medications isn't available, taking the other alone may be sufficient treatment. Follow up with repeat stool tests 2 weeks after finishing treatment.

Other Parasitic Infections
You can acquire a variety of flukes, tapeworms, and other diseases from eating raw or undercooked beef, pork, or seafood. Another source of infection is contaminated water. These illnesses are preventable by avoiding raw or undercooked meat and seafood, and by boiling or purifying drinking water.

If lab reports indicate the presence of tapeworms or flukes, **obtain medical attention immediately.** See chart on p. 187 for reference.

Parasitic infections requiring immediate medical attention

If stool samples sent for examination (ova and parasites) show any of the following, get immediate medical evaluation and treatment.

1. all tapeworms;
2. all flukes;
3. all forms of schistosomiasis;
4. hookworms, Ascaris, and strongyloides if accompanied by respiratory symptoms (coughing, shortness of breath, coughing up blood);
5. strongyloides if accompanied by severe abdominal pain or bloody stools.

Noninfectious Abdominal Disorders

Ulcers, appendicitis, and minor gastrointestinal problems are discussed in the following pages. Moderate to severe abdominal pain unrelieved by the passage of stool or gas (and not related to menses), **requires immediate medical attention.** As the "Quick Reference Guide to GI and Abdominal Symptoms" indicates on pp. 156–157, there are many possible causes for these symptoms. Some are life-threatening. Only a qualified medical practitioner can provide a reliable diagnosis and adequate treatment for disorders with these symptoms.

Appendicitis

Appendicitis may develop very quickly. It's potentially life-threatening. When suspected, get immediate medical attention.

Symptoms

Pain often, but not always, begins near the navel or belly button. Usually, within 2–12 hours it moves toward the right lower abdomen where it settles and intensifies. **This progression of pain is important for early recognition of appendicitis. Don't take pain medications.**

Other possible symptoms include:

1. a slight fever (less than 101°F (38.3°C);
2. decreased appetite, nausea, and vomiting, usually mild when present;
3. constipation or diarrhea.

 **Quick Reference:**

Stool Exams for Protozoa, Amoeba, and Roundworm Ova and Parasites

Exam shows:	Treatment:
Protozoa	
Giardia lamblia	quinacrine 100 mg. 3 times a day for 7 days; or Flagyl 250 mg. 3 times a day for 7 days; or Fasigyn 2 grams orally as a single dose.
amoebas:	
Entamoeba histolytica Endamoeba histolytica Entamoeba dysenteriae Entamoeba polecki	For mild to moderate intestinal symptoms: Flagyl 750 mg. 3 times a day for 10 days, followed by iodoquinol (Yodoxin) 650 mg. 3 times a day for 20 days.
Dientamoeba fragilis or Balantidium coli	tetracycline, 500 mg. 4 times a day for 10 days; or iodoquinol (Yodoxin) 650 mg. 3 times a day for 20 days or Paromomycin 25-30 mg. per kg. a day in 3 divided doses for 7 days.
Isospora belli	Bactrim 4 times a day for 10 days, then 2 times a day for 3 weeks.
Blastocystis hominis	Flagyl 750 mg. 3 times a day for 10 days or iodoquinol (Yodoxin) 650 mg. 3 times a day for 20 days.
Roundworms	
Ascaris lumbricoides	mebendazole 100 mg. twice a day for 3 days; or pyrantel pamoate 11 mg. per kg. of body weight (maximum, 1 gram) as a single oral dose.
hookworm (Ancylostoma duodenale or Necator americanus)	mebendazole 100 mg. twice a day for 3 days; or pyrantel pamoate 11 mg. per kg. of body weight (maximum, 1 gram) daily for 3 days.
pinworm (Enterobius vermicularis)	mebendazole 100 mg. as a single oral dose – repeat in 2 weeks; or pyrantel pamoate 11 mg. per kg. of body weight (maximum, 1 gram) – repeat in 2 weeks.
whipworm (Trichuris trichiura)	mebendazole 100 mg. twice a day for 3 days.
Capillaria philippinensis	mebendazole, 200 mg. twice a day for 20 days; or thiabendazole, 12.5 mg./ kg. of body twice daily for 30 days (maximum: 3 grams per day).
Strongyloides stercoralis	thiabendazole 25 mg. per kg. of body weight twice daily for 2 days (maximum: 3 grams per day).

The following organisms are sometimes reported after a laboratory stool exam for ova and parasites. They don't cause disease and don't require treatment.
   Entamoeba coli, Entamoeba hartmani, Iodamoeba butschlii, Endolimas nana, and Chilomastix mesnili

Pain increased by coughing, jumping up and down, or releasing pressure after pressing on the abdomen ("rebound tenderness"), indicates severe inflammation and requires immediate medical evaluation.

Treatment

If constipation or diarrhea are present, these symptoms should not be treated. **Never take laxatives or antimotility medications when symptoms suggest appendicitis.** Avoid enemas, pain medications, food, and liquids.

Unfortunately, there's little else that can be done short of surgery. Appendicitis is one condition that requires ready access to modern surgical medicine. It's definitely a hazard, though probably a small one, for anyone living, hiking, or traveling in an isolated area.

Ulcers

Pain from ulcers is often described as burning, gnawing, or aching. It occurs in the area above and over the stomach. The pain is mild to moderate, occurring typically 45–60 minutes after eating.

Pain is decreased by taking food, crackers, or antacids. It's increased by coffee, tea, or other stimulants. Occasionally, other symptoms such as constipation, vomiting, or fatigue may be present. Stools are sometimes black and tarry, which may indicate the presence of blood.

If you suspect ulcers, **get medical help immediately**. With proper treatment complications are usually preventable. When ulcers progress unarrested they can cause severe or life-threatening damage.

Treatment in Isolated Areas

Start antacids, which are available over the counter. Take 1 ounce 1 hour and 3 hours after meals, and at bedtime. Avoid aspirin, Pepto-Bismol, iron, and the nonsteroidal anti-inflammatory agents such as Motrin or Indocin. If symptoms persist, seek medical treatment as soon as possible.

Minor Stomach and Intestinal Problems

Heartburn

"Heartburn" is a painful burning sensation felt just above the stomach, beneath the sternum or breastbone. It usually occurs between meals. The cause is irritation of the lower esophagus from stomach acids. Heartburn can be associated with consumption of hot spicy food, coffee, or tea. Pregnancy or a hiatal hernia are conditions which often contribute to symptoms.

Treatment

Reduce occurrences by eating more frequent, smaller meals. Avoid irritating food and drinks and evening snacks. Since the reclining position often intensifies symptoms, elevate the head of the bed. Antacids are also helpful. Relief should occur within fifteen minutes after taking antacids.

Indications for Medical Assistance

Obtain medical help immediately if heartburn is accompanied by any of the following:

1. pain radiating to the neck, arms, or jaw;

2. increasing pain and discomfort, especially with exertion;

3. pain unrelieved by antacids;

4. symptoms persisting more than 1 or 2 weeks;

5. shortness of breath;

6. evidence of blood loss, including black, tarry stools or vomited material which looks like coffee grounds.

Hiccups (Hiccoughs)

Irritation of the diaphragm, or of the nerve which controls it causes hiccups. There are many possible causes, including spicy foods or an "upset" stomach.

Treatment

Most hiccup cures do work at times. Some, such as breathing from a paper bag, may correct a physiological imbalance. Other techniques physically interrupt nerve impulses to the diaphragm. This can occur through abdominal stretching, or through movement, irritation, or numbing of the throat and esophagus. Techniques which do this include eating sugar, drinking ice water, sipping from the far edge of a glass, and holding your breath.

Psychological inputs can also interrupt hiccuping. A sudden startle or scare is traditional, though frequently difficult to improvise and rarely appreciated. Another method involves "paradoxical intention" — trying to hiccup. It was used successfully with one of the authors. A friend simply promised a credible and tempting reward on one condition — hiccup just one more time. With money on the line, the hiccups vanished instantly.

On rare occasions hiccups may be intractable, defying for days all efforts to abort them. This requires medical help, which must be obtained immediately if breathing becomes labored.

Flatulence (gas)

Excessive gas in the digestive tract can cause abdominal distension, sometimes with cramping. These conditions are relieved by passage of the gas.

One cause is swallowed air. Gum chewing and anxious sighing with deep respirations are possible causes. More commonly, air is swallowed during meals. This occurs either because of talking, eating hurriedly, or sloshing the food down with lots of liquids. Smaller, more slowly paced meals are helpful.

Another cause is the activity of digestion and intestinal bacteria on certain foods. Beans are of course the most notorious. Almost 2 decades ago, a wry, prematurely nostalgic obituary appeared in *Newsweek* entitled "A Farewell to Flatulence." It reported supposedly fruitful efforts to create a strain of gasless legume, a development the world still awaits with bated breath. Other implicated foods include dairy products, green peppers, broccoli, cabbage, cauliflower, onions, and radishes. Sensitive travelers can probably add many more. If symptoms warrant, remove implicated foods from the diet.

Treatment

Antacids with simethicone may provide temporary relief of symptoms. The usual dose is 1/2 ounce (15 ml. or one tablespoon) of liquid or 1–2 chewable tablets 30 minutes after eating. Be sure to check for parasites if:

1. gas unassociated with a particular food continues;
2. other symptoms develop, such as abdominal bloating, diarrhea, constipation, or sulfurous burps.

   Get medical evaluation if no parasites are found and:

1. symptoms continue;
2. vomiting, fever, or abdominal pain occur.

Constipation

Travelers are frequently subjected to the minor indignity of simple constipation (unaccompanied by pain, cramping, or other symptoms.) Changes in body rhythm, daily routine, diet, and fluid intake are contributing factors. Another is the use of antimotility medications, such as Lomotil, Imodium, or paregoric. These often cause excessive slowing of the bowel. Other medications that may be constipating are codeine and aluminum-based antacids.

Prevention and Treatment

If constipation becomes a problem, it can usually be resolved with these measures:

1. Additional dietary fiber or natural laxatives. Sources include vegetables, fruit, whole grain products (especially bran) and prune juice. A supplementary fiber, such as Metamucil (psyllium hydrophilic mucilloid), is also helpful.

2. Increased fluid intake. Excessively hard stools are often a result of dehydration.

3. A regular bowel habit. Reflex movement of the lower intestine often occurs after eating. This is a good time to establish a regular pattern if constipation is an ongoing problem.

4. Use of a mild bowel stimulant. Caffeine is often effective, especially after breakfast. A mild laxative, such as milk of magnesia, can be taken at bedtime.

Use enemas or stronger laxatives only as a last resort. Avoid straining as this frequently leads to hemorrhoids.

If constipation is accompanied by vague, recurrent abdominal symptoms, the cause may be parasites. Stool exams should be done, and treatment initiated if the results are positive. If exams don't reveal parasites but symptoms continue, obtain medical evaluation. Medical help should also be obtained if:

1. enemas or laxatives become routinely necessary;

2. there's nausea, vomiting, fever, or increasing abdominal tenderness, pain, or rigidity;

3. there's rectal bleeding (blood mixed in the stools or water). Blood appearing just on toilet paper and not in stools or water is probably due to hemorrhoids.

Hemorrhoids

Hemorrhoids are enlarged protruding veins of the rectum that cause itching and sometimes pain. This can be excruciating during the passage of hard stools. There may be some bleeding, with bright red blood usually appearing on toilet paper but not in the stool or water.

Hemorrhoids occur from a variety of causes including pregnancy, alcoholism, straining as a result of constipation, or from lifting heavy objects. Travel conditions may foster symptoms. Sitting for long periods, especially on bus rides over bad roads, often aggravates existing hemorrhoids.

Prevention and Treatment

Avoid straining, lifting, or other activities that increase lower abdominal pressure. To keep stools soft and easily passed, follow the measures previously described for preventing constipation. Avoid vigorous wiping with toilet paper, which increases uncomfortable symptoms.

For itching and discomfort, try warm soaks in a bathtub for 10–15 minutes 3–4 times a day. These are soothing and also help to shrink hemorrhoids. Hemorrhoidal suppositories such as Preparation H, Anusol, or Anusol with hydrocortisone can be used twice a day for 7–14 days. Medical help is necessary if the condition:

1. doesn't resolve with treatment;
2. becomes severe enough to interfere with normal activities.

If blood appears mixed in the stool or the water, medical evaluation is also required.

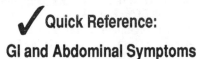

✓ Quick Reference:

GI and Abdominal Symptoms

The following chart is provided to help locate relevant information in this book. It can't be used to diagnose abdominal disorders.

Symptoms	Possible cause
Acute nausea and/or vomiting with NO diarrhea:	
tiredness, right upper quadrant pain, yellowing of the eyes and skin (jaundice), mild headache, whitish clay-colored stools, brown urine, cigarettes that suddenly taste bad, loss of appetite;	hepatitis
nausea and vomiting of sudden onset soon after eating; crampy abdominal pain, no fever;	"staph" food poisoning
recurrent symptoms, ear pain or ringing in the ears, room spinning	inner ear infection or too much aspirin
high fever, chills, headache, neck stiffness, photophobia (light sensitivity), vomiting (may be projectile) with or without nausea;	meningitis*
morning nausea, weight gain, breast tenderness or fullness, late or missed period;	pregnancy
tenderness, burning centered in upper abdomen; symptoms may be relieved by vomiting or with antacids	ulcer or gall bladder*

Vomiting blood — either red or black (blood altered by digestion resembles dark coffee grounds) — is a medical emergency. Get immediate medical attention.

Diarrhea:	
with nausea and vomiting, crampy abdominal pain, often fever and chills; onset 8 or more hours after eating; diarrhea lasting 1–5 days, stools may contain blood or mucus	food poisoning-Salmonella
abrupt onset of symptoms, fever up to 104°F (40°C), lower abdominal cramps, decreased appetite, blood and mucus present in stools;	shigella or campylobacter
mild diarrhea, lower abdominal cramping relieved with passage of stools or gas, no fever, no blood, pus, or mucus in stools;	traveler's diarrhea
recurrent diarrhea and/or constipation, vague abdominal discomfort, bloating, occasional foul-smelling stools or rotten-egg burps;	parasites (amoebas, giardia, etc.)

* Requires immediate medical attention

Symptoms	Possible cause
low fever, muscle aches, headache, mild abdominal pain, nausea or vomiting, fatigue;	viral gastroenteritis
massive fluid loss, "rice-water" stools, dehydration;	cholera
"pea-soup" diarrhea, step-ladder fatigue, flu-like symptoms	typhoid fever
diarrhea that develops after beginning antibiotics and persists after antibiotics have been discontinued, especially following use of clindamycin or cephalosporins	pseudomembranous colitis*

Note: other potential causes of diarrhea include medications (antibiotics like ampicillin, penicillin, tetracycline), toxic chemicals, mushroom or other natural poisons, and diet (alcohol, food allergies, changes in diet or eating habits).

Abdominal Pain

mild to moderate pain, gnawing or burning, located just below the breastbone; occurs 45-60 minutes after meals or at night, relieved with vomiting or antacids;	stomach ulcer*
sensation of pressure, squeezing to vice-like, across the chest; may move to the neck, jaw, or arms; often accompanied by shortness of breath, sweating, nausea, vomiting; symptoms increase with exertion;	heart attack*
pain beginning near the navel, moving and localizing in the right lower quadrant and intensifying;	appendicitis*
slight fever, mild nausea, vomiting; pain with bloating, diarrhea or constipation, increased burping, gas;	parasites

Abdominal pain unrelieved by the passage of stool or gas (other than routine menstrual cramping), requires medical evaluation.

Abdominal pain in women (additional symptoms which may indicate specifically female disorders):

dull to sharp lower abdominal pain on both sides and/or pain with intercourse; usually with vaginal discharge, bleeding, or spotting, a slight fever, nausea, vomiting;	pelvic inflamatory disease (PID)
lower abdominal pain or discomfort, sometimes radiating to the groin; *missed or irregular period* with irregular vaginal bleeding or spotting;	ectopic pregnancy, a life-threatening emegency
dull to sharp midline lower abdominal pain, burning with urination of frequent, small amounts; possible slight fever;	bladder infection
dull to sharp midline lower abdominal pain, with urination of frequent, small amounts; back pain, high fever, & nausea;	kidney infection
with missed period, increased breast tenderness, nausea usually in morning;	pregnancy
abdominal pain or bloating prior to or during period; with cramping that goes away on its own;	dysmenorrhea, PMS (premenstrual tension syndrome)

* Requires immediate medical attention

Infectious Diseases

7

Diseases Transmitted by Mosquitoes and Ticks

There are several mosquito-borne diseases of concern to travelers. Of these, malaria is by far the most important, although dengue fever is of increasing concern in many areas of the world (see Maps in Appendix B).

Malaria

The bite of a female Anopheles mosquito transmits malaria. The disease itself is caused by a parasite, Plasmodium, which infects red blood cells. Some forms of malaria are also harbored in the liver, which complicates treatment. There are four kinds of Plasmodium, and the recurring rhythm of malarial symptoms varies with the reproductive cycle of each.

Symptoms

The parasites reproduce within red blood cells. Chills lasting 15–60 minutes occur when they burst from the cell into the blood stream. Headache, nausea, vomiting, and fatigue may accompany the chills.

Entry of the parasite into new cells is associated with a fever which lasts several hours. It's followed by sweating and weakness. The particular Plasmodium species determines the duration of the cycle. Symptoms can recur every 72 hours, and occasionally every 48, but they may also be quite erratic.

The earliest appearance of malarial symptoms may be mistaken for the flu. There is often no identifiable pattern until the parasites are more firmly established.

Prevention

Medicines to prevent the establishment of Plasmodium infections are available. They're recommended for a stay of one or more days in a malarial area. The potential for exposure varies with both the season and elevation in a given region. See "Preventing Malaria — Mosquito and Tick Precautions," pp. 38–40.

Treatment

If malaria is suspected, **medical evaluation is required**. The choice of treatment depends on the type of malaria identified on a blood smear. For best results, have blood taken during the fever cycle.

Malaria treatment in isolated areas

Treatment should always be done under medical supervision. Use the following guidelines for treatment in isolated areas when medical care isn't available, and head immediately for the nearest medical care facility:

Treatment of acute, uncomplicated attacks in areas of nonchloroquine-resistant malaria — Take chloroquine phosphate (Aralen) 300 mg. base, 2 tablets orally. Take 1 tablet 6 hours later, and 1 tablet a day for the next 2 days. If using 150 mg. base tablets, take 4 tablets initially and 2 six hours later. Then take 2 daily for the next 2 days.

Treatment of chloroquine-resistant Plasmodium falciparum malaria or acute attacks of presumptive malaria in chloroquine-resistant areas — use one of the drug regimes listed below *if not using mefloquine for malaria prevention*:

1. Take quinine sulfate, 650 mg. orally 3 times a day for 3-7 days; **plus**
   Fansidar (pyrimethamine/sulfadoxine), 3 tablets in a single dose.

   Don't take fansidar if you're allergic to sulfa drugs.

   An *alternative* treatment is:

2. Take quinine sulfate 650 mg. orally, 3 times a day for 3 days; **plus either**

   a. tetracycline, 250 mg. orally 4 times a day for 7 days; **or**

   b. doxycycline, 100 mg. orally twice a day for 7 days.

The quinine and either tetracycline or doxycycline are taken concurrently. By the third day of quinine treatment, it's not uncommon to start feeling ill as a side effect.

If using mefloquine for malaria prevention:

If symptoms suggesting malaria occur while taking mefloquine preventively, obtain medical attention. Inform the physician you have been taking mefloquine. Quinine sulfate or other malarial medications may be contraindicated or require medical supervision.

Treatment of recurrent attacks of Plasmodium vivax or P. ovale — Take primaquine phosphate 15 mg. base, one tablet orally, once a day for 14 days.

A G_6PD blood test is required before taking primaquine. This drug regimen can also be used after treatment of P. vivax and P. ovale with chloroquine to prevent relapse. If treatment of recurrent P. ovale or P. vivax with this dose of primaquine fails, the dose can be doubled to 2 tablets daily for 14 days during a subsequent relapse. Treatment failure at this dosage requires renewed medical evaluation.

Dengue (Breakbone or Dandy Fever)

Dengue is a viral infection transmitted by urban Aedes mosquitoes. The incidence of disease is expanding rapidly in most tropical areas of the world. It can be found in Asia, Africa, Mexico, Central and South America, the Caribbean basin, and the South Pacific. See map in Appendix B. It often occurs in epidemics, and millions of cases occur each year. The disease is seldom fatal in adults.

Symptoms

Five to eight days after exposure, onset is sudden with high fever and chills. Joint and muscle pain, headache, and complete exhaustion accompany fever. Nausea and vomiting may also be present. Medical evaluation is necessary for diagnosis, as symptoms may be hard to distinguish from flu or hepatitis. In addition, malaria and Japanese B encephalitis can mimic dengue symptoms.

A rash appears 3–5 days after the onset of fever. It's red, flat or raised, and may spread from the torso to the arms, legs, and occasionally the face. Also after 3–4 days, the fever abruptly stops for 24–48 hours. It then recurs in slightly milder form.

Treatment

There is currently no vaccine or treatment available. Antibiotics are of no benefit. Recovery in otherwise healthy adults is usually complete, but may require an extended period of time. **For children under age 10 with dengue, medical care is mandatory.**

The most important supportive measure is to ensure good fluid intake. Dehydration must be avoided (see Dehydration and Rehydration, p. 132). In severe cases you may require hospitalization for rehydration with intravenous fluids. Treat fever and pain with 1 or 2 aspirin up to 4 times a day.

Prevention

The risk of acquiring dengue is low for most people unless their travels take them to an area where an epidemic is in progress. Risk can be reduced by following the insect precautions outlined in Part I (see Mosquito and Tick Precautions, pp. 38–40).

Mosquitoes that spread dengue are most frequently found in or near human habitations. Biting activity occurs chiefly in the morning for several hours after daybreak and in late afternoon for several hours before dark. The mosquitoes are more inclined to feed throughout the day when it's overcast, as well as indoors or outdoors in shady areas.

The mosquito larvae thrive in artificial water containers such as discarded tires, barrels, buckets, flower vases, cans, and cisterns. In dengue regions, keep the living area free of potential breeding places.

Yellow Fever

Yellow fever is a viral infection transmitted by mosquito bite. It 's preventable through vaccination. As with other viral infections, antibiotics are of no use in treatment.

Symptoms

Most cases of yellow fever produce mild symptoms which disappear in 3–5 days. Onset is sudden, with headache, fatigue, fever, nausea, vomiting, and constipation. More severe infections may also cause body aches and pain, especially in the neck, back, and legs. Bleeding can occur under the skin or from mucous membranes, and vomited material may be dark and look like coffee grounds. Jaundice or yellowing of the skin and eyes may also be present — hence, "yellow fever."

There is a high death rate in severe cases between the sixth and ninth day of illness. Otherwise, fever returns to normal within 7–8 days and recovery is usually complete.

Treatment

Mild cases may be difficult to distinguish from severe sinus attacks, the flu, or hepatitis. Symptoms severe enough to cause concern must be treated quickly with medical care and hospitalization for supportive treatment, including intravenous fluids.

Prevention

In endemic areas, the best protection against yellow fever is vaccination, combined with insect precautions. See Mosquito and Tick Precautions, pp. 38–40.

Japanese B Encephalitis

This viral disease is also spread by mosquitoes and is preventable by vaccination. It occurs both sporadically and in epidemics in the tropical and temperate zones of Asia with an increased risk from June through September (see Appendix A).

Symptoms

The incubation period is from 4 to 14 days. Many infections are mild enough to escape notice, but in severe cases there's an abrupt onset of fever and headache. Mild respiratory symptoms and gastrointestinal symptoms including poor appetite, nausea, vomiting, and abdominal pain may accompany this. Illness progresses with confusion, delirium, and other symptoms. In mild cases, fever resolves after 6 or 7 days and other symptoms after about 2 weeks. Severe cases may proceed to coma and death within 10 days of onset, or to a prolonged period of recovery.

Treatment

There's no cure. Severe cases may require supportive measures including hospitalization.

Prevention

Vaccination is recommended for travelers spending an extended period of time in endemic rural areas. The mosquitoes responsible for infection begin feeding outdoors at dusk and continue through the evening. Observe insect precautions (see Mosquito and Tick Precautions, pp. 38-40).

Relapsing Fever (Tick or Recurrent Fever)

This illness occurs in many parts of the world. In the Americas, Africa, Asia, and Europe it's most likely to be spread by tick bites. It may occasionally be spread by lice.

Symptoms

The incubation period is about one week. Onset is sudden, with fever, chills, an increased heart rate, nausea and vomiting, joint pain, and severe headache. These symptoms may be hard to distinguish from a severe case of the flu or hepatitis. Within 3–10 days all symptoms abruptly cease. Unless treated, however, they continue to recur in milder form every week or two.

Treatment

Remove ticks (see p. 119) or treat lice (see p. 117) as described in part II. Their presence should be noted mentally in case illness follows within the incubation period. **Medical evaluation is required for any recurring fever.** Relapsing fever can be cured with a single oral dose of 500 mg. of either erythromycin or tetracycline.

Other Infectious Diseases

Hepatitis

One of the diseases most feared by travelers is hepatitis. It's caused by a virus, usually spread through contaminated food or water or sexual contact. In simpler times, there was infectious hepatitis, now hepatitis A, and serum hepatitis, now hepatitis B. Two new categories have been established. For practical purposes "non-A non-B" hepatitis (of which hepatitis C is a subgroup) is similar to hepatitis B, and "enteric non- A non-B" hepatitis is similar to hepatitis A. Infection by any of these viruses can cause the liver to become swollen and inflamed. The liver is unable to efficiently process and eliminate harmful substances from the body. These include the normal waste products of metabolism, as well as alcohol and medications. **When you suspect hepatitis, obtain medical evaluation.** Although potentially dangerous, with proper care most people recover completely.

Hepatitis A

Hepatitis A is the one travelers are most likely to encounter. It's excreted in the stools of infected persons and transmitted through a fecal-oral route. Food handlers who don't wash their hands are a major source of infection. Other sources are contaminated water and food, especially raw shellfish such as oysters and clams. Traveling in areas with generally poor hygiene and inadequate water and sewage facilities increases the chance of encountering hepatitis A. Sex with oral-rectal contact also spreads infection.

Hepatitis A is infectious for 2–4 weeks before symptoms develop, and for a few days afterwards. Fortunately, hepatitis A is a mild and limited infection. Most people recover completely within 2–4 weeks.

Enteric Non-A Non-B Hepatitis

This form of hepatitis is transmitted in a manner similar to hepatitis A. Person to person transmission occurs, but it's primarily spread through contaminated water. This is most likely in areas without adequate sewage disposal after heavy rains. There have been large outbreaks in India, Nepal, Burma, Pakistan, the USSR, and Mexico. Prevention and treatment are the same as for hepatitis A.

Hepatitis B

Hepatitis B is less common than hepatitis A. It's a more severe and dangerous infection. It's spread through sexual contact, particularly between male homosexuals, or contaminated blood. All body secretions are potentially infectious — saliva, sweat, semen, vaginal secretions, and blood, including menstrual blood. If not sterile, dental instruments, needles used in medical facilities and pharmacies, needles shared by drug users, and even needles employed in acupuncture or tatooing are potential sources of infection.

Full recovery from hepatitis B usually takes about 3–6 months. It's infectious throughout this time, and for 4–6 weeks before symptoms develop.

Signs and symptoms

The symptoms of hepatitis A, B, and non-A non-B are very much alike. They can cause any combination of the following:

- headache, nausea, and possibly vomiting;
- decreased appetite;
- malaise or extreme tiredness;
- yellowing of the eyes and skin (jaundice);
- fever;
- abdominal pain.

When present, abdominal pain is usually felt on the right upper side just below the rib cage.

As the liver is progressively affected, the urine turns dark, the color of cola. Stools become a clay-like greyish white. The skin and eyes may turn yellow (jaundiced). Smokers often find that cigarettes acquire an unpleasant taste.

Symptoms resembling the flu may precede Hepatitis B. Joint pain or a hive-like rash (*urticaria*) can also accompany it.

Care and Treatment

Regardless of the type of hepatitis, the liver requires lots of tender loving care. **Don't** take aspirin, Tylenol (acetaminophen), alcohol, antibiotics, or **any** other drug or medication except under a doctor's order. Even after a quick recovery, it's wise to avoid such substances for a few weeks.

Women using birth control pills should stop taking them until they fully recover. To prevent spreading the virus, avoid all sexual contact until recovery is complete. If sexual contact does occur, by all means use another form of birth control.

Avoid exertion and dehydration. Get lots of rest and drink plenty of fluids. Fruit juices and light soup broths are usually well tolerated.

Eat whatever is appealing and stays down. If unable to eat because of prolonged vomiting or nausea, medication may help. Try a Tigan (trimethobenzamide HCl) 200 mg. rectal suppository once every 6–8 hours until symptoms diminish. If unavailable or further measures are needed to control nausea and vomiting, obtain medical evaluation. A dietary supplement of B-complex vitamins and vitamin C may be helpful.

Indications for Medical Assistance

In all cases of hepatitis, get medical help **immediately** for any of the following:

1. uncontrolled vomiting or dehydration;

2. spontaneous or easy bruising anywhere on the body;

3. spontaneous bleeding from the nose or gums;

4. presence of blood in the urine;

5. symptoms of hepatitis occuring any time during pregnancy.

Preventing the Spread of Illness

Observe the following measures to prevent spreading hepatitis A or enteric non-A non-B hepatitis:

1. Keep your own plates, cups, and utensils separate. Wash them well with soap and hot water.

2. Wash your hands thoroughly after using the bathroom. Avoid preparing food for other people.

3. Avoid sexual intercourse or other intimate contact.

4. Don't share drinks, cigarettes, or food with others.

5. In restaurants, advise the staff of your illness and request that your utensils be washed separately.

To avoid spreading hepatitis B:

1. Abstain from sexual contact.

2. If you require dental work, inform the dentist of your illness.

3. Don't donate blood.

4. Don't share needles for any purpose.

Coping with Extended Illness

Hospitalization is not usually required for hepatitis. It may be the only alternative if you are too sick to care for yourself and other assistance is not available. This is most likely when traveling alone. In such circumstances, hospitalization is reasonable and may be surprisingly inexpensive.

If there's someone to take care of you, a rented house or room will probably be cheaper than a hotel room for the length of time needed to fully recuperate. This is especially true for hepatitis B.

Treatment of Hepatitis A Exposure

Following exposure to a person with hepatitis A, an injection of immune globulin (formerly gamma globulin) may prevent illness. You must obtain it within 2 weeks of the last exposure to be effective. Don't take immune globulin if hepatitis symptoms are present, or if immune globulin was already obtained within the preceding 3 months. *Note the precautions in Appendix A before obtaining immune globulin in a Third World country* (see pp. 301–302). The dose for adults is 0.6 mg per kg. of body weight, given by intramuscular injection .

Vaccination for Hepatitis B

Travelers at risk for infection should consider vaccination against hepatitis B. This includes travelers residing abroad in high risk areas, such as Asia, especially if living with local families. Others at risk are health care workers with potential blood exposure, homosexual men, and IV drug users. There are 3 shots in the series, the second 4 weeks after the first and the third 5 months later.

Treatment of Hepatitis B Exposure

If you're exposed to hepatitis B while traveling, a 2-shot series of hepatitis B immune globulin is recommended. Be forewarned that this is an expensive medication (several hundred dollars) and may be hard to find. An alternative is to start the hepatitis B vaccine series, which is also quite expensive.

Sterile, disposable equipment must be used for any injection obtained while traveling.

Tuberculosis

Tuberculosis is not a highly contagious disease. Healthy adults rarely become ill with active TB. Those at risk are primarily children, the elderly, or immune compromised persons with extended exposure to an infected but untreated adult. Infection normally occurs from inhaling germs that are coughed or sneezed into the air. Tuberculosis is also spread from unpasteurized dairy products. Don't eat or drink unpasteurized dairy products.

Have a TB (PPD) skin test done before and after extended travel (see Chapter 3, p. 71). If the first test is negative and the second is positive, exposure to TB occurred during travel. Medical evaluation, a chest x-ray, and medication are required.

Symptoms of Active TB

Often, there are no symptoms of lung disease. When present, symptoms develop slowly. They may include weakness and fatigue, weight loss, decreased appetite, cough, fever and night sweats. Sputum is occasionally tinged with blood. If TB is suspected, get medical help immediately for a thorough evaluation. **The presence of blood in the sputum always requires immediate medical evaluation including a chest x-ray.**

Rabies

Rabies is a viral infection transmitted in saliva through the bites of infected mammals, mainly carnivores. These commonly include domestic dogs and cats, and wild foxes, bats, skunks, or raccoons. It's unusual for rabbits or rodents to be infected.

Take every precaution against rabies. Treatment is possible only between the time of the bite and the onset of symptoms. Once the symptoms appear, there's no cure, and the outcome is almost always death. Infection can occur from exposure of a mucous membrane or fresh skin abrasion to infected saliva, as well as from a bite.

In industrialized nations because of dog vaccinations, most cases of rabies since 1960 have been due to wild animals. In Third World countries domestic dogs, many really homeless urban scavengers, must be considered a potential threat. In some cultures, religious strictures against the killing of animals contributes to an increased incidence of rabies.

In many countries dog populations are periodically reduced by aggressive eradication of strays. Poisoned meat may be widely distributed on public streets in both urban and rural areas. Anyone traveling with their own pet should keep this in mind.

Unchecked, dog populations can become frightening. Some U.S. agencies operating in foreign countries have at times armed their employees with chemical aerosol weapons. These have been issued for protection against dog packs running at night through city streets, as well as against rabies. The risk of rabies to travelers is greatest in countries where dog rabies is highly endemic. Areas of high risk include parts of Colombia, Ecuador, El Salvador, Guatemala, India, Mexico, Nepal, the Philippines, Sri Lanka, Thailand, and Vietnam.

Preventive Measures

Avoid animals that behave abnormally. They may act either "mad", viciously biting and agitated, or lethargic and paralyzed, refusing to eat or drink. Excessive salivation (foaming at the mouth) may indicate rabies. Other indications may be daytime activity on the part of normally nocturnal animals like foxes, bats, skunks, or raccoons, and an absence of their usual fear of humans.

It's best to leave all stray animals strictly alone, no matter how cute, forlorn, or winsome. If camping outdoors, carefully mind clothing and other gear. One rabies victim was bitten by a rabid skunk that had crawled inside his sleeping bag.

Another important preventive measure is pre-exposure immunization against rabies. It should be considered by travelers who will be at high risk of exposure. (See Appendix A, pp. 305–306.)

Rabies Symptoms

The incubation period of rabies in humans is 10 days to 2 years, averaging 3–7 weeks. It's shorter when bites occur on the face, head, or upper body.

Tingling and pain near the bite is an early symptom. Malaise and fever follow, accompanied by restlessness which increases to uncontrollable agitation. A rabies victim develops excessive salivation and intense thirst. Excruciatingly painful spasms of the throat are triggered by the slightest stimulus, even swallowing: thus the term, "hydrophobia." Death follows from asphyxia, exhaustion, or general paralysis.

This is definitely a disease to avoid.

Treatment of Animal Bites

Any wound from an animal bite, or exposure to saliva, should be cleaned to excess. **Repeatedly flush the wound with soap and water. Don't** attempt to close the wound. Medical help may be necessary to adequately flush a deep puncture wound. **Good cleansing may be the most important factor in preventing rabies.**

Rabies Antiserum and Vaccine

In the United States, rabies antiserum and vaccine are normally given only under the following conditions:

1. If the animal is obviously rabid or develops rabies during a ten day confinement period following capture;

2. When the animal can't be observed or examined and if the bite was unprovoked or the animal was behaving unusually, and rabies is known to be present in the area.

As a traveler in a foreign environment, however, assume that **any animal bite carries the risk of rabies.** Never rely on assurances to the contrary, no matter how official. The only exceptions are in the handful of countries considered rabies-free, listed at the end of this section.

After thoroughly cleaning a bite, scratch, or abrasion exposed to saliva, get immediate medical attention where rabies vaccine is available. The sooner treatment is started, the greater the chance of preventing rabies. Even when the animal can be confined and observed for ten days, treatment should be initiated immediately. It can be discontinued if the animal proves healthy. **You require treatment even if you have had pre-exposure Rabies vaccine.**

The new human diploid cell rabies vaccine (HDCV) is a vast improvement over its predecessor. Discomfort and side effects aren't a concern. The full series of HDCV consists of only 5 shots, given over 4 weeks. In addition to the vaccine, rabies immune globulin must be taken to provide immediate protection *if* no pre-exposure rabies vaccine was obtained.

Many developing countries use vaccines other than HDCV. They may have inactivated nerve tissue vaccine (NTV) or inactivated suckling mouse brain vaccine (SMBV). Both carry an increased risk of potentially harmful reactions. If given a choice, use HDCV. Otherwise, use whatever is available. It's better than getting rabies. None of these vaccines are contraindicated during pregnancy.

If human rabies immune globulin is not available, it should be possible to obtain antiserum derived from horses. A skin test is required before taking the antiserum to prevent a possible allergic reaction.

Rabies treatment schedule:
following possible exposure with no pre-exposure vaccination:

1. 5 intra-muscular (IM) injections of HDCV, 1 cc. each. The first dose

is given as soon as possible after exposure. Subsequent shots are given on days 3, 7, 14, and 28 following the initial dose. All injections should be given into the upper arm (deltoid muscle).

2. In addition, 20 IU/kg. of body weight of HRIG (human rabies immune globulin) should be given within 8 days of exposure. Half the dose is infiltrated into the wound area, the other half given IM into the buttock.

following pre-exposure vaccination:

1. 2 IM doses of HDCV are needed, 1 cc. each. The first is given as soon as possible, the second 3 days later. No HRIG is necessary.

Side effects — HDCV may cause pain, redness, swelling and itching at the injection site. Less commonly there's headache, nausea, abdominal pain, muscle aches, or dizziness. For headache or localized symptoms, take 2 aspirin or Tylenol every 4–6 hours as needed. Cold packs to the injection site are also helpful. The same measures are useful for any local pain or low-grade fever that develops from HRIG.

Countries Reported Free of Rabies
(does not include rabies transmitted by bats)

Americas — Bermuda, Saint Pierre, Miguelon
Caribbean: Anguilla, Antigua, Barbuda, Bahamas, Barbados, Cayman Islands, Dominica, Guadeloupe, Jamaica, Martinique, Montserrat, Saint Christopher (St. Kitts) and Nevis, Saint Lucia, Saint Martin, Saint Vincent, Turks and Caicos Islands, Redonda, Virgin Islands (U.K. and U.S.) Netherlands Antilles (Aruba, Bonaire, Curacao, Saba, St. Maarten, and St. Eustatius)
Europe — Cyprus, Faroe Islands, Finland, Gibraltar Iceland, Ireland, Malta, Norway, Sweden, United Kingdom, Bulgaria*, Portugal*
Asia — Bahrain, Brunei, Darrussalam, Japan, Kuwait, Malaysia (Malaysia Sabah*), Maldives*, Oman* Singapore, Taiwan
Oceania — American Samoa, Australia, Belau (Palau), Cook Islands, Federated States of Micronesia (Kosrae, Ponape, Truk, and Yap), Fiji, French Polynesia (Tahiti), Guam, New Zealand, Pacific Islands, Trust Territory of the USA, Papua New Guinea
Kiribati, New Caladonia, Niue, Northern Mariana Islands, Samoa, Solomon Islands, Tonga, Vanuatu
Africa — Mauritius*

*Denotes countries that have only recently reported an absence of rabies. This should be considered a provisional status.

Typhoid Fever

The culprit in typhoid is the bacteria *Salmonella typhi*. Infection is spread primarily through contaminated food, water, or milk. Outbreaks can often follow earthquakes, floods, hurricanes, drought, and other disasters. **Take special precautions to purify water following any disruption of normal water supplies.**

Vaccination is not as good a preventive measure as water purification and good handwashing by infected individuals. Vaccination is 70–90% effective and is important for travel in areas with a known risk of typhoid. India, Mexico, and Peru are very high risk areas.

Signs and Symptoms

Untreated, typhoid fever sometimes shows three characteristic stages. The first is marked by flu-like symptoms. These include increasing fatigue, headache, cough, general body aches, sore throat, and often nose bleeds. There may be abdominal pains, constipation, diarrhea, or vomiting. There is a classic "stepladder" fever, with the maximum temperature increasing daily for seven to ten days. It's generally highest in the evenings.

In the second stage the fever stabilizes. There is either "pea soup" diarrhea or constipation, possibly with abdominal distention. Severe weakness with delirium or coma may result. There may also be a characteristic rash, with rose-colored spots that turn white (blanch) with pressure. Fever is accompanied by a pulse which is markedly slow. If there are no complications, symptoms slowly subside over another 7–10 days. The fever decreases, again in step-ladder fashion.

Sometimes these classic stages are not present. There may only be milder symptoms with recurrent fevers. **All recurrent fevers require medical evaluation.**

Treatment

If typhoid is suspected, get medical treatment as soon as possible. Blood cultures, stool tests, and/or urine tests are required to identify typhoid.

Adults are usually treated with ciprofloxacin or chloramphenicol. The latter can be given either intramuscularly (IM) or intravenously (IV). **By any route chloramphenicol should never be taken except under medical supervision.** Its side effects are dangerous and can be life-threatening.

Bedrest and adequate hydration are important. High calorie, low residue foods are likely to be the best tolerated. Reduce fever by applying cool compresses as needed.

Preventing the Spread of Illness

To prevent infecting other individuals observe good handwashing, especially after using the bathroom. Avoid preparing foods for others, as well as handling plates or utensils. Avoid intimate or sexual contact until treatment is complete. Keep food screened from flies, which may also spread the disease.

Mononucleosis

Mononucleosis is a viral infection. It's transmitted directly through kissing, and indirectly through coughing, sneezing, and sharing food, utensils, or cigarettes.

The incubation period is 5–15 days. Signs of infection include fever, sore throat, fatigue, and increased sleepiness. Lymph nodes may be enlarged and slightly tender, especially in back of the head and neck. There may be muscle aches and decreased appetite. At times there's a red, flat or slightly raised, generalized body rash. If a lab is available, diagnosis can be confirmed with a mono spot or heterophil blood test.

Treatment

The main requirement is rest and increased fluid intake. For pain or fever, take one aspirin orally four times a day. For a sore throat, use warm saline gargles three times a day. If unable to maintain a nutritional diet, vitamin supplements may be useful. Avoid contact sports until recovery is complete. There's an increased possibility of injury to the spleen during illness. Complete recovery may require up to 4–6 weeks.

Brucellosis (Malta or Undulent Fever)

Brucellosis is a bacterial infection that occurs worldwide. It's contracted from ingesting contaminated, unpasteurized milk or dairy products from cows and goats. It's also an occupational hazard for people who work with these animals, or with pigs, dogs, cats, or wild animals. The bacteria can enter the body and cause infection through broken skin.

Symptoms

Onset is slow with increasing tiredness, weakness, loss of appetite, headache, stomach ache, swollen lymph nodes, and possibly joint pain or constipation. Fever may be absent or severe. When present, it usually starts in late afternoon accompanied by chills. It rises in the evening with profuse sweats and falls again in the early morning.

Acute cases without complications may resolve completely in 2–3 weeks. Often the fever recurs after short periods of absence. **Any recurrent fever requires prompt medical evaluation.**

Treatment

Obtain medical help to distinguish brucellosis from other causes of fever. **This is especially important during pregnancy.** Spontaneous abortion is a frequent complication of brucellosis. Brucellosis is usually treated with either:

1. tetracycline, 500 mg. orally every six hours for 3–5 weeks, **or**

2. Bactrim, 2 tablets orally twice a day for 3–5 weeks.

Both medications are contraindicated during pregnancy. This illness is preventable. **Avoid unpasteurized dairy products.**

Plague, Typhus, and Leprosy

These diseases are virtually nonexistent among travelers. Plague in recent years has been a public health problem primarily in Vietnam. The last reported case of typhus in a U.S. traveler was more than 30 years ago.

Leprosy, too, has vanished as a concern among travelers . . . almost. If you travel in northern Mexico or the southwestern U.S. (Texas, New Mexico, and Arizona), you will have to refrain from eating the armadillo tacos. Believe it or not, several recent cases of leprosy were traced to this source, and the organism which causes leprosy has been isolated from the paw pads of local armadillos.

Tropical Diseases

8

With few exceptions, travelers in urban areas infrequently encounter the diseases we discuss here. Many tropical diseases are really hazards of rural areas, poverty, and native lifestyles. Schistosomiasis, for example, mostly affects rural agricultural workers exposed to canal and irrigation water. It's also prevalent in villages near rivers and lakes where sanitation facilities and potable water systems don't exist. By the same token, travelers to these areas — dependent on the same water supply — are definitely at risk for schistosomiasis. Anyone who travels in a predominately rural area must be aware of local health hazards and precautions. This is especially true for missionaries, field researchers, service volunteers including Peace Corps members, agricultural workers, or others living in a rural setting.

It's also important to document or make a written note of travel in endemic areas where exposure to infection may have occurred. Delayed symptoms are sometimes possible months or even years after leaving the area. **Any recurrent fever or ulcerated lesion or sore which doesn't heal requires medical evaluation as soon as possible.**

Protozoan Infections

Leishmaniasis

Leishmaniasis is a protozoan infection transmitted by certain biting sandflies. Different forms of the disease appear in different parts of the world. When the infection is generalized (spread throughout the body), it's called visceral or systemic leishmaniasis. When localized (limited) to the skin or mucous membrane, it's called cutaneous or mucocutaneous leishmaniasis.

Systemic Leishmaniasis

The systemic form, known as Kala-azar or dum-dum fever, occurs in several South and Central American countries. It's also found in Africa, India, southern Russia, the Near and Middle East, and along the Mediterranean coast.

The incubation period varies widely, averaging 3–8 months. Symptoms have a gradual onset. There may be vague abdominal pain, fever, weakness, decreased appetite, coughing, weight loss, muscle aches, and constipation or diarrhea. The skin may be pale, dry, and scaly. It sometimes acquires a gray tone, particularly on the hands and feet ("Kala-azar" means literally "black disease"). Fever may be recurrent, or high and spiking, with chills, sweats, and even nose bleeds. The liver and spleen are enlarged. A primary skin lesion at the site of the sandfly bite is rare.

Because most of the symptoms are nonspecific, identification of the disease requires laboratory testing. Antimony compounds and other medications are available to treat the disease. **Any recurrent fever requires medical evaluation.**

Cutaneous and Mucocutaneous Leishmaniasis

Cutaneous leishmaniasis, affecting only the skin, is known outside the Americas as oriental sore, tropical sore, Bangladesh or Delhi boil. It occurs in China, India, Africa, the Mediterranean, and the Near and Middle East. In these areas it's predominantly an urban disease. It's common in the larger cities of the Middle East such as Teheran, Baghdad, Aleppo, and Damascus. It's also found in northwest India and Pakistan and around the Mediterranean, including Italy and North Africa. In urban areas, the lesions are dry and usually occur singly. They grow slowly and may persist a year or more unless treated.

In the Americas, leishmaniasis of the skin is a predominantly rural infection. It's common among people living or working near the edge of jungles and forests. Several forms occur from Mexico and Central America south to northern Argentina. The disease is prevalent in Chile and Uruguay. The authors have seen several cases in Guatemala, where tourists camping at the popular Mayan ruins of Tikal were affected. In the Americas, lesions are moist rather than dry and multiple lesions occur more often.

Lesions may take weeks to months or even years to develop. They can occur anywhere on the body, including the mouth, nose, and face. They may vary in appearance, even on the same person.

The lesion begins as a small, sometimes itchy nodule. It grows, becomes encrusted, and ulcerates. The ulcer is usually shallow and circular, with a well-defined hard, raised, red border. There may be a discharge, either clear or with pus. The ulcer may grow to an inch (2–3 cm) or more across. Sometimes new smaller lesions spring up around it.

The lesions are painless and are neither tender nor itchy unless secondary infection occurs. Lesions around the nose may produce nose bleeds or nasal obstruction.

Treatment

All forms of leishmaniasis require medical attention. Skin lesions usually spread and may be disfiguring. Although lesions may eventually heal after many months, they almost inevitably become infected if not treated.

Leishmaniasis is often more quickly identified in the regions where it's known and can be diagnosed virtually on sight. Back home it may be quite mysterious, requiring weeks and repeated biopsies to identify. **Any persistent lesion that does not heal requires medical evaluation.** Formerly, lesions were treated with a locally injected antimony compound. They're now usually treated with stibogluconate sodium (Pentostam).

Trypanosomiasis (sleeping sickness & Chagas disease)

Sleeping Sickness

Sleeping sickness, transmitted by the tsetse fly, occurs in West, Central, and East Africa. It ranges between 20°N. and 20°S. latitudes, where the tsetse fly lives only in scattered localities near certain lakes and rivers with damp, shady vegetation.

There are two forms of sleeping sickness, both bad. The nasty Gambian form is found in West Africa, Zaire, Uganda and the southern Sudan, with strongholds along the main branches of the Congo and Niger rivers. It's also found in Gambia, Guinea, Ghana, and Sierra Leone.

The even nastier Rhodesian form is largely limited to East Africa, including Kenya, Uganda, Tanzania, Zambia, Malawi, Mozambique, and Zimbabwe National Park in Rhodesia. It is responsible for several deaths among travelers on safari in East Africa.

Although the risk of infection is small, travelers entering endemic areas should know both preventive measures *and* early signs of disease.

The latter is necessary so that effective treatment can be obtained. **Early treatment is essential.** The longer treatment is delayed, the less likely it is to be effective.

Typically, tsetse fly bites are painful. After a bite from an infected fly, local redness and swelling may appear within minutes, subsiding in a few hours. This is followed in several days by a characteristic reddened, firm, raised nodule or tumor. It's usually about one inch (2–3 cm.) across. It may be accompanied by swelling, or surrounded by a diffuse, reddened, plaque-like area. This is the so-called "trypanosomal chancre."

The chancre usually occurs on exposed parts of the body — often the legs, but also the hands or head. It's sometimes said to resemble a boil. Although itchy and tender to mildly painful, the chancre is never as painful as a boil. The nodule subsides spontaneously in 1–2 weeks, with no apparent scarring.

The chancre is an identifying sign of infection that almost always occurs in travelers. (It does not necessarily occur in local inhabitants, who have some immunity.) It's especially severe with the Rhodesian form of sleeping sickness.

Once alerted by development of the chancre, quick medical attention will prevent the infection from spreading. If neglected, the second phase of the disease occurs with dissemination of the parasites throughout the blood stream.

Symptoms of generalized infection usually develop within 10-21 days of the bite. The protozoa cause recurrent fever, tiredness, insomnia, and headache. The fever is irregular, accompanied by a fast pulse which may persist after the fever subsides. Lymph nodes are often enlarged, soft, rubbery, and painless. They can frequently be felt high in the back of the neck. The face, feet, and legs may appear swollen. Six to eight weeks after the onset of illness, a patchy red rash may develop on the chest, back, or elsewhere. Untreated, progressive damage occurs to the heart, nervous system, and other organs.

Prevention

Some protection from tsetse flies can be provided by protective clothing and repellents. There's also a chemical prophylaxis for individual travelers, given in the form of intramuscular injections. However, it's not recommended. This is because the length of effective protection against the Rhodesian form of sleeping sickness is uncertain. The procedure also masks the trypanosomal chancre, which otherwise provides a reliable early warning of infection. Without this sign, diagnosis is vastly more complicated if an illness accompanied by fever does occur. Normally diagnosis and treatment of early sleeping sickness is easy, rapid, and effective.

American Trypanosomiasis (Chagas' Disease)

Chagas' disease exists throughout rural areas of southern Mexico, and in Central and South America. The "kissing bug" or "assassin bug" that spreads the infection is large and nocturnal. It usually inhabits only the poorer adobe and thatch-roof huts in tropical areas.

Victims of the "kissing bug", usually asleep, are often bitten about the face. When the bite occurs near the eye, there may be a characteristic one-sided conjunctivitis ("pink-eye") and swelling of the eyelid. This is called "Romana's sign." Otherwise the bite causes local redness and swelling.

Symptoms of infection which may occur 2–3 weeks following the bite include daily fever, and a rash on the chest and abdomen. The rash consists of pinhead small red spots; there is no pain or itching.

Symptoms diminish over several months. There may or may not be further symptoms or damage to internal organs, including the heart.

Prevention and treatment

Mosquito netting is an effective barrier against kissing bugs at night. The bugs can also be controlled with insecticides. Although contact is unlikely, travelers should choose their sleeping quarters carefully with an eye for prevention. This disease has long been considered incurable, although new drugs appear promising. Treatment requires medical supervision.

Blood Flukes and Other Parasitic Worm Infections

There are a variety of parasitic worms that infect the blood and lymphatic system, or organs such as the liver, lungs, bladder, and intestines. These are not your run-of-the-mill intestinal parasites discussed in Chapter 6, "Stomach and Intestinal Disorders." Rather, they have complex life cycles involving intermediate hosts. They are commonly transmitted by insects or contact with fresh water, not by ingestion of contaminated food.

Repeated exposure and reinfection is generally necessary to produce symptoms of disease from these parasites. Anyone living or traveling where these diseases are widespread should take precautions against them. This is especially true for extended visits. On rare occasions even minimal exposure to some diseases, such as schistosomiasis, can have devastating consequences.

Filariasis

Filariasis is an infection of the lymphatic system with tiny threadlike nematode worms. Several species of mosquitoes transmit these. The disease occurs in scattered urban and rural areas of the tropics and subtropics worldwide. The disease is slow to develop, usually no earlier than 8–12 months after infection. Signs and symptoms, caused by inflammation and obstruction of lymph channels, include swelling of lymph vessels and glands. There may also be swelling of the scrotum, arms, or legs.

Swelling may be preceded or accompanied by fever, sweating, malaise, loss of appetite, nausea, and vomiting. After leaving an endemic area, early symptoms which may have arisen during an extended stay gradually disappear. Occasionally, though, the initial symptom is a recurrent fever that develops within a few months of leaving an endemic area.

Elephantiasis, the gross enlargement of a leg, arm, scrotum, or other part, is still frequently seen among natives where infection is widespread. This rarely occurs without a decade or more of chronic disease.

Prevention and Treatment

Mosquito precautions (see pp. 38–40) will help reduce exposure. People who face years of continuous mosquito exposure, such as missionaries, Peace Corps volunteers, or field researchers, might want to consider a prescription drug regime (diethyl-carbamazone) to prevent infection.

The vague symptoms, especially in travelers who spend a short time in an endemic area, make an early diagnosis difficult. Anyone with recurrent fever should seek medical help for diagnosis and treatment. The drug of choice, diethyl-carbamazone, should only be taken under medical supervision. Full control of infection may require repeated treatments over a period as long as one year.

Schistosomiasis (Bilharziasis)

This is a potentially dangerous infection from trematode worms known as blood flukes. It's a rural disease, transmitted through an intermediate host, the fresh water snail. These snails generally require standing or slow-moving water, usually dirty or muddy, with aquatic vegetation and exposure to sunlight. They are found commonly in streams, ponds, small dams, shores of lakes, lazy rivers, and canal or irrigation water.

The snails become infected from eggs passed in human urine and feces. In time, they release free-swimming larva. These are capable of penetrating the skin within 15 minutes of contact. In such areas, it's hazardous to drink, wade, or bathe in untreated water.

Contact frequently causes a mild form of "swimmer's itch." This is an itching, prickling sensation with local redness or swelling that lasts up to three days. Usually within 2–8 weeks a general allergic reaction begins with fever, malaise, muscle pains, and often hives (urticaria).

The severity of all schistosome infections in most cases depends on the degree of exposure to larvae. Although frequent re-exposure is usually necessary for symptoms to develop, this is not always true. Adult worms live up to 20 years in the body. Because tissue damage occurs from the myriad eggs produced over this time, long term consequences can easily accrue. In addition, some individuals with minimal exposure have developed paralyzing spinal cord disease.

Additional symptoms vary according to the type of schistosomiasis responsible. There are three forms.

Urinary Schistosomiasis

This variant is found throughout Africa and adjacent islands. It's heavily present in Egypt, particularly along the Nile. In the Mediterranean and Middle East it occurs only in a few scattered areas. It occurs nowhere else with the exception of Bombay province in India.

This form may cause only a mild allergic reaction. Three to six months after infection, but sometimes up to 2 years or more, there may be local symptoms of urinary frequency and urgency. Characteristically there is blood in the urine, often at the end of urination. Rectal symptoms, with blood or pus in the stools, are possible. Progressive and irreversible damage to genital, urinary, and other organs can occur if the infection is not treated.

Intestinal Schistosomiasis

This one is found predominantly along the Nile valley, in Africa from the southern Sahara to about 15°S. latitude, and in Madagascar. In the Middle East it rarely occurs outside Yemen, except for a few places in Saudi Arabia. It's also common in a wide coastal band of South America, extending from near Barranquilla in northern Columbia through Venezuela and Brazil to about 20°S. latitude, or just north of Rio de Janiero. In Brazil this region extends west across the highlands and far into the Amazon basin. The infection also exists in the Caribbean, mainly in Puerto Rico and Santa Lucia.

The general allergic reaction is often severe. Headache, nausea, vomiting, abdominal pain, and severe diarrhea with bloody stools may accompany it. Six to eight weeks after infection (but sometimes up to two years or more) dysentery develops. Symptoms include severe colicy pains, diarrhea, passage of blood and mucus in the stools, fever, weakness, and weight loss. Untreated, symptoms endure for 6–12 months with increased severity at intervals of 2–3 weeks. Damage to abdominal organs is cumulative and irreversible.

Asiatic Schistosomiasis

This is the most dangerous form. It's found only in southeastern China, the Philippine Islands (including Leyte, Mindanao, and southern Luzon), Sulawesi (Celebos), and a few areas of Laos and Kampuchea. It may have been eliminated in Japan.

The initial reaction is usually severe, with vomiting, diarrhea, abdominal pain and cramps. There may be a dry cough. After several weeks, blood and mucus often appear in the stools as diarrhea becomes increasingly severe. Untreated, damage is progressive not only to abdominal organs but throughout the body.

Prevention: schistosomiasis precautions

Observe the following precautions to reduce or eliminate potential schistosomiasis exposure in endemic areas:

1. Don't swim in fresh water lakes or ponds that might be contaminated by nearby inhabitants.

2. Don't swim, bathe, or drink from slow-moving fresh water rivers and streams.

3. Avoid contact with irrigation or canal water.

4. Be wary of oceans, beaches, or bays near river or sewage outlets.

5. If wading is necessary to cross potentially contaminated water, use hightop rubber boots. If the skin becomes wet, dry off quickly (within 5-10 minutes) to prevent skin penetration by larvae.

6. Never drink untreated water from potentially contaminated lakes or streams. Larvae are destroyed by the water purification measures recommended in Chapter 4 — boiling, iodine, filters, or chlorine (see pp. 80–83.

7. Water can be made safe for bathing by the above measures or by allowing it to stand in a container for at least 3 days.

Although fast moving clear streams and rivers may be safe, there is no practical way for the traveler to distinguish infested from uninfested water. Swimming pools, if chlorinated, are considered safe.

Treatment

Medical evaluation is mandatory to diagnose schistosomiasis. Laboratory exams, usually of stool or urine for ova and parasites, and occasionally a rectal biopsy, may be needed to identify the parasite. The earlier that diagnosis and treatment is made, the sooner potential damage can be limited.

Praziquantel is effective against all forms of schistosomiasis. The usual dose is 20 mg./kg of body weight taken orally 3 times a day for one day.

Other Parasitic Infections

Stool exams may reveal other parasites, including flukes, as well as tapeworms. Treatment of all these parasites requires medical attention. For reference, a chart of lab results and the indicated treatment is included at the end of this chapter.

Guinea Worm Infection (Drancunculosis, Dragon Worm, Fiery Serpent)

These worms are encountered in West, Central, and East Africa. They can also be found in Afghanistan, Sudan, Egypt, Pakistan, Iran, Turkey, southern Russia, western and southern India, Burma, New Guinea, South America, and some of the Caribbean islands.

Guinea worm may be one of the oldest known parasites. Moses in the Bible (Numbers, 21) refers to fiery serpents which plagued the Israelites on their travels along the Red Sea.

Human infection is the result of ingesting contaminated water containing a microscopic intermediate host, the cyclops. Freed from the cyclops by digestive juices, larvae burrow out of the stomach or upper intestines and migrate into body tissues. After 10–14 months, the female worm is mature enough to produce young. It then burrows outward toward the skin, most commonly in the legs and feet.

Many people complain of a deep, stinging pain at the site where the worm nears the surface. When the worm reaches the surface, a raised lesion (or group of lesions that grow together into one) develops. It enlarges for 1–2 days, forming a reddish blistering area one to three inches in diameter. The blister then ruptures, leaving an ulcerated lesion with the head of the worm often visible within the ulcer.

Until the female worm reaches maturity, there are no symptoms in a majority of cases. When symptoms do precede blistering, they may include generalized itching, a hive-like rash, nausea, vomiting, watery diarrhea, fever, wheezing, and possibly shortness of breath.

These symptoms usually disappear completely with the development of the lesion, or at the latest by the time it has ruptured. The growth of the blister may be accompanied by itching and intense pain that is relieved by immersion in cold water. A frequent complication is secondary bacterial infection. Tetanus is also a concern.

Prevention

Infection is easily prevented by any of the water purification methods discussed in Chapter 4 — boiling, iodine, filters, or chlorine (see pp. 80-83).

Treatment

Pain, tenderness, and swelling are quickly relieved with treatment. The worms will emerge or are easily removed. Any one of the following medications can be used:

1. Flagyl, 250 mg. orally 3 times a day for 10 days; **or**

2. thiabendazole, 25 mg./kg. of body weight twice a day for 3 days; **or**

3. niridazole (Ambilhar) 25 mg./kg. of body weight per day, divided in 2 doses and taken morning and evening for 10 days (in other words, each dose is 12.5 mg/kg of body weight). Maximum: 1.5 grams per day.

When drugs aren't available, slow extraction taking many days is necessary. Extraction should start after 2–3 days of wet compresses to the lesion. This allows the worm to discharge its eggs, after which it's easier to remove.

One end of a thread is attached to the worm's head, the other to a stick about which the worm is gently wound, a little each day. This may take a while as the worms can be two feet long. Patience is required to avoid breaking the worm. Keep the ulcerated area clean, dry, and covered to prevent secondary infection. If this occurs, use one of the following:

1. dicloxacillin 500 mg. orally, 4 times a day for 10 days; **or**

2. erythromycin 250 mg. orally, 4 times a day for 10 days; **or**

3. Keflex or Velosef 500 mg. orally, 4 times a day for 10 days. Obtain a tetanus booster if needed.

Parrot Fever (Psittacosis)

Many travelers are attracted to the wonderfully colorful tropical birds of the world — handling them in the markets or keeping them as pets while living or working abroad. Caution is required, as many of the birds carry *Chlamydia*, a bacteria that can cause lung infections in humans.

Fever develops 1 to 3 weeks after exposure. Onset may be slow or abrupt. It's accompanied by chills, headache, backache, fatigue, muscle aches, and sometimes a bloody nose. There is a cough, dry initially, which becomes productive as pneumonia progresses.

Treatment

Parrot fever is treated with tetracycline 500 mg. orally, 4 times a day for 2–3 weeks. Rest, fluids, and aspirin, 2 tablets up to 4 times a day for fever, headache, and muscle aches, are also appropriate. If allergic to tetracycline, an alternative medication is erythromycin 500 mg. orally, 4 times a day for 2–3 weeks.

Prevention

A course of antibiotics will rid parrots of any Chlamydia bacteria they might harbor. European formulations of injectable Vibramycin, if available, can be given to the parrot intramuscularly. These are required only once every 6 days. Unfortunately American preparations of Vibramycin for injection are considered too irritating by some veterinarians.

The full course of oral antibiotics for parrots lasts 45 days and must be adhered to rigorously. The dose for parrots is Vibramycin (doxycycline) 8–12 mg. per lb. twice a day for 45 days. Syrup formulations are the easiest to measure and handle. An alternative is chlortetracycline (syrup form), 20 mg. per lb. 3 times a day for 45 days.

Leeches

To travelers in the tropical rain forests of New Guinea, India, Indochina, and elsewhere, it may seem like bloodthirsty little gremlins are hiding under every leaf and rock. Slithering stealthily, they attach themselves to the skin like murderous hickeys, producing a trickle of blood at the site.

There are 2 types of leeches — land and aquatic. Neither appears to cause any disease. Their bite is painless, and the main problem with leeches, after their removal, is itching and secondary infection.

Land Leeches

A photographer and an anthropologist we know trekked for 10 days in the New Guinea jungles. They pulled an average 100 leeches off each person daily. In one 3-hour stretch, they pulled 292 leeches from 1 person alone. As a result of their experiences, they provide the following information and advice:

1. Don't pull off an attached leech, or a sore will develop a few days later. Remove the leech with insect repellent, lemon juice, salt, vinegar, or tobacco juice. Or, if you are feeling generous, let it fall off when it's finished with you.

2. DEET insect repellent is particularly effective. Put a drop on the leech and not only will it fall off, it will curl up, shrivel, and die.

3. Heat from a lighted match, applied to the body of the leech, may also be effective, but isn't recommended due to the possibility of burn injury.

4. Leeches are sticky. In removing them, they will stick to the hand. Immediately roll them between forefinger and thumb (decreasing the stickiness) — then throw them away.

5. Leeches are diurinal creatures. Don't worry about sleeping on the ground at night, even in heavily infested areas.

6. You can remove a leech from the eye by shining a flashlight close to it. The leech will move toward the light and off of the eye.

Treatment

To reduce itching, take Benadryl 25-50 mg. or Atarax 25 mg. orally 3–4 times a day. This will also help reduce secondary infection from scratching. Drowsiness is a frequent side effect of these medications.

Prevention

Insect repellents such as dibutyl or dimethyl phthalate, DEET, Indalon, or Rutgers 6–12 will help ward off leeches. The repellent should be applied to clothing as well as skin, although dimethyl phthalate should not be used on rayon. Repellent is usually effective for 3–5 hours if you are not sweating or exposed to water.

In leech-infested territory, wear knee-high boots (preferably waterproof), and closely woven pants tucked into the boots. An Australian friend who has lived in Africa suggests rubbing Vaseline petroleum jelly over exposed skin. This prevents leeches from attaching and resists being washed off.

Aquatic or Water Leeches

Aquatic leeches are found only in fresh water, primarily in North Africa, western Asia, Indonesia, and southern Europe. They are less common than the terrestrial variety, but more dangerous.

Water leeches are acquired by drinking or bathing in infested water. They can attach themselves to the mouth, throat, nose, lungs, vulva, vagina, male urethra, and other internal sites.

In the nose they may cause bleeding, obstruction, and persistent headaches. Lodged in the throat, they may cause continuous coughing with a bloody discharge, difficulty swallowing, hoarseness, and possibly even suffocation. In the lungs they may produce chest pain and shortness of breath. Elsewhere they cause other localized symptoms.

Treatment

Internal leeches should be removed by medical personnel. In the mouth or nose, a strong saline solution swished, gargled, or lavaged may remove leeches.

Prevention

Don't drink or bathe in infested waters. Water for all purposes should be filtered, then boiled. If you can't do both, one or the other will at least be effective in removing leeches.

See the table for stool exams on the next page.

Quick Reference:

Stool Exams for Fluke and Tapeworm Ova and Parasites

When lab reports indicate the presence of tapeworms or flukes, medical attention must be obtained immediately. The following information is provided for reference only.

Exams show presence of: Treatment:

Tapeworms (cestodes)

Taenia saginata Taenia solium Diphyllobothrium latum Diphyllobothrium pacificum Diphyllobothrium mansonii	For the treatment of all tapeworm infections, take either niclosamide, four 500 mg. tablets (2 grams) chewed thoroughly, or praziquantel, 10–20 mg. per kg. of body weight, as a single oral dose (except Hymenolepsis nana).
Hymenolepsis nana	The drug of choice for Hymenolepsis is praxi-quantel, 25 mg. per kg. of weight in a single oral dose. The alternative is niclosamide, four 500 mg. tablets (2 grams) chewed thoroughly as an initial does, then two 500 mg. tablets daily for 6 successive days.

Blood Flukes

Schistosoma mekongi Schistosoma japonicum Schistosoma haematobium Schistosoma mansoni	The drug of choice is praziquantel, 20 mg. per kg. of body weight 3 times a day for 1 day.

Intestinal Flukes (trematodes)

Heterophyes heterophyes Metagonimus yukogawai Fasciolopsis buski	The drug of choice for intestinal flukes is praziquantel, 25 mg. per kg. of body weight, 3 times a day for 1 day. An alternative for Fasciolopsis is niclosamide, four 500 mg. tablets chewed thoroughly, as a single oral dose.

Liver Flukes

Clonorchis sinensis Opisthorchis viverrini	The drug of choice is praziquantel 25 mg. per kg. of body weight, taken 3 times a day for 2 days to treat Chlonorchis or 1 day to treat Opisthorchis.
Fasciola hepatica	The drug of choice is Bithromol, 30–50 mg. per kg. of body weight every other day for 10–15 doses.

Avoiding and
Treating Ear Disorders

9

Any ear infection is potentially dangerous and should receive treatment. When problems do occur, they can affect any part of the ear — external, middle, or inner ear structures. The risk of injury or infection is greatly increased by two activities: sticking foreign objects in the ear, or swimming in contaminated water.

The Outer Ear

Wax Obstruction

Blockage of the external ear canal with wax is a frequent problem in childhood. Adults are also susceptible. Dust is sometimes a contributing factor, and you might need protective ear covering (such as ear plugs or a bandana) in some environments. When necessary, wax should be removed regularly by washing with warm water. This is best done while showering, or with the aid of a wash cloth or bulb syringe.

Don't attempt to remove ear wax with Q-tips or other objects. A Q-tip acts as a trash compactor, often tamping the wax into an immobile brick. This may block the ear canal so that normal hearing is impossible. Other objects can scratch the canal, leading to infection. You can even puncture the ear drum (tympanic membrane).

Wax contains enzymes and other necessary substances to protect the ears, much as tears protect the eyes. Remove it only if there is:

1. a sense of fullness or feeling that the ear is plugged up;
2. a sense of hearing through water (water trapped in the ear after swimming or showering);
3. diminished hearing due to wax buildup.

There might be ringing in the ear and on rare occasions an earache, but wax alone should not cause any other symptoms.

Removal of a wax plug is often best done professionally. If no medical help is available, wash the ear out with warm water. Fill an ear or bulb syringe, if available, with equal amounts of hydrogen peroxide and warm water. Some clinics use a dental water-pik filled with warm water on the softest possible setting. If necessary, first soften the ear wax with Debrox. Place 5–10 drops into the ear twice daily for up to 4 days.

In Isolated Areas

If you're unsuccessful in removing wax, medical help is unavailable, and you have no Debrox, use 2–4 drops of Cortisporin Otic solution in the affected ear 3–4 times a day for 5–7 days. This should soften and loosen the wax so it can be washed out as described above. If there is no improvement, obtain medical help.

Infection of the Outer Ear (Otitis Externa, "Swimmer's Ear")

Infection occurs frequently after swimming in contaminated water. Q-tips or other foreign objects can also cause infection in the ear canal. They scratch the skin, creating a place for bacteria to breed.

Symptoms

Itching and pain within the ear canal are the primary symptoms. There may be decreased hearing, or a sense of fullness or obstruction in the canal. A colored, pus-filled discharge may also be present.

To distinguish between a middle and outer ear infection, pull upward and outward or down and outward on the external parts of the ear on either side of the canal (the auricle and tragus, see diagram). Pain or discomfort that is increased by this action indicates an outer ear infection. Then tap over the mastoid bone just behind the ear (see diagram). **If pain is present, this is an emergency. Get medical help immediately.**

Treatment

Treat outer ear infections with Cortisporin Otic Solution (ear drops), a mixture of polymixin B sulfate, neomycin sulfate, and hydrocortisone which may be available under other brand names. Apply 4 drops in each affected ear 4 times a day for 1 week. Keep the head tilted for 3–5 minutes after applying drops to allow the medication to reach the entire area.

If medicine isn't available, you can make your own ear drops. Mix together equal volumes of vinegar, 70% isopropyl alcohol, and water. Purify the water by boiling for 5 minutes, if needed, to make sure it isn't contaminated. Use as above: 4 drops four times a day for 7 days.

The ear must be kept dry for at least 1 week — no swimming, and no water in the ear when bathing. For discomfort or pain take 1 or 2 aspirin or Tylenol up to 4 times a day.

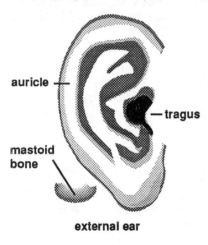

external ear

Indications for medical attention

Get medical attention promptly if there is:

1. no improvement after 3-4 days, or infection occurs after a week of treatment. A laboratory culture may be needed to make sure the cause isn't a fungus;

2. swelling so severe that ear drops cannot be administered;

3. pain or tenderness of the mastoid bone (see drawing);

4. an allergic reaction to the medication;

5. concurrent diabetes.

Never stick anything in your ear smaller than your elbow.

Surfer's ear

Recurrent exposure of the ear canal to cold water may lead to progressive bone growth within the canal. Eventually this causes severe hearing loss. It also increases the risk of infection in the outer ear. The condition is preventable. Always wear good form-fitting ear plugs when swimming or surfing in cold water.

Treatment

Surgical removal of the excessive growth is the only treatment. There is no regression of the bone growth once it has taken place.

The Middle Ear

Middle ear infections may result in permanent hearing loss and other severe damage if not treated promptly. For this reason, **medical evaluation is required for any infection of the middle ear.**

Bacterial Infection (Acute Bacterial Otitis Media)

A bacterial middle ear infection is occasionally associated with bacterial infection of the nose and throat. Bacteria can travel through the eustachian tubes to the middle ear. When this occurs, sputum or nasal discharge, usually tinged gray, green, or yellow, may accompany the infection.

Symptoms

Symptoms include earache or pain, possibly with a sense of fullness, decreased hearing, and elevated temperature. Occasionally there is headache, nausea, or vomiting. As mentioned, there may be a recent or con–current upper respiratory infection. For treatment, obtain medical evaluation.

Treatment in Isolated Areas

In areas where medical help isn't immediately available, start one of the following medications:

1. ampicillin, 500 mg. orally 4 times a day for 10 days or amoxicillin 500 mg. 3 times a day for 10 days; **or**

2. erythromycin 250 mg. orally 4 times a day for 10 days; **or**

3. Bactrim DS or Septra DS 1 tablet orally, twice a day for 10 days; **or**

4. Keflex or Velosef 500 mg. orally, 4 times a day for 10 days.

Seek medical attention as quickly as possible. If pain is still present after 48 hours and you haven't yet obtained medical care, switch to one of the other antibiotics and continue seeking medical help.

Along with antibiotics, oral decongestants or antihistamine decongestants are usually required for 7-10 days. Any of the following can be used:

1. Entex L.A. one orally twice a day; **or**

2. Sudafed 60 mg. orally three times a day; **or**

3. Dimetapp one tablet orally twice a day; **or**

4. Actifed one tablet orally three times a day; **or**

5. Drixoral one tablet orally twice a day.

If any of the following conditions develop either before or after you start treatment, **medical help is urgently required:**

1. recurring or continued elevation of temperature, or lack of improvement after 2-3 days of antibiotic therapy;
2. development of a headache, stiff neck, lethargy, nausea, or vomiting;
3. development of pain over the mastoid bone (see illustration, p. 190);
4. increasing pain, possibly with a sudden decrease in pain which may be accompanied by a flood of drainage from ear canal (ruptured ear drum).

Fluid in the Middle Ear (Serous Otitis Media or Eustachian Tube Dysfunction)

A noninfectious condition of fluid accumulation sometimes occurs. This happens because of a blocked eustachian tube, often from an allergic condition (hay fever or runny nose) or an upper respiratory infection.

Symptoms

There's a sense of fullness in the ear with some hearing loss. There may be a snapping or crackling sensation when swallowing, yawning, or blowing the nose.

Treatment

Treat with an oral decongestant or antihistamine decongestant as described above for otitis media. If the condition is accompanied by a stuffy nose unrelieved by an oral decongestant, use a nasal spray such as Afrin or Neosynephrine (oxymetazoline hydrochloride) in addition to the decongestant. Wait a few minutes, squeeze your nose, hold your mouth shut, and blow. This should pop open the eustachian tube.

Nasal spray must be used sparingly: one whiff twice a day for no more than 3 consecutive days. It shouldn't be used for a chronic, ongoing condition. Obtain medical help if there is no improvement in 3–5 days.

The Inner Ear

Dizziness or a spinning sensation, ringing in the ears, and varying degrees of hearing loss usually indicate inner ear problems. In severe cases there may also be nausea or vomiting. **These symptoms should receive prompt medical evaluation.**

Some medications, especially some antibiotics, may cause hearing loss or ringing in the ears. These include aspirin, streptomycin, neomycin, kanamycin, vancomycin, and gentamycin. If hearing problems occur while taking any of these, stop immediately and consult a doctor.

Treatment in isolated areas

For treatment of dizziness or a spinning sensation when medical care isn't readily available, try meclazine 25 mg. orally, 3 times a day until you can obtain medical help.

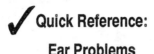

Quick Reference:

Ear Problems

Problem/Symptom	Possible Cause
earache	
with runny nose, sore throat, possibly fever	middle ear infection (otitis media) *or* blocked eustachian tubes
with pain when the earlobe is pulled, and/or discharge from the ear; possibly decreased hearing	external ear infection (otitis externa)
with tooth or jaw pain	possible cavity, dental abscess, or sinusitis
decreased hearing, with sense of fullness or of water in ear after swimming or bathing	wax obstruction
hearing loss, with or without ringing	requires medical evaluation
ringing in the ears while taking aspirin or antibiotics	possible aspirin or drug toxicity

Ear Conditions Requiring Medical Treatment

1. hearing loss;

2. a ruptured or punctured ear drum;

3. bleeding from the ear;

4. earache or pain not due to outer ear infection;

5. any unexplained or persistent ringing in the ears, dizziness, spinning sensation, or difficulty with balance;

6. mastoid bone tenderness or pain;

7. an ear infection under treatment that fails to improve within 48 hours;

8. any ear infection accompanied by headache, fever, neck stiffness, nausea, vomiting, or lethargy.

Treating
Eye Disorders

10

Eye medications are extremely potent. Always observe the following precautions when using eye medications:

1. Eye drops are labeled "sterile ophthalmic solution." Be careful not to confuse them with "otic" ear medications.

2. Eye medications must be sterile. Avoid touching the container to the eye or any other surface.

3. To instill eye drops: blink after each drop, but don't close eyes tightly. Ointments: warm tube slightly in your hands, squeeze ointment onto the lower lid, then close the eyes but don't squeeze them tightly shut.

Use of Dangerous Medications

In many Third World countries, antibiotic eye medications may be encountered which contain chloramphenicol (Chloromycetin or other brands). This drug can cause a severe disease of the blood.

Don't take any eye medications which contain chloramphenicol unless under the care of an eye specialist.

Conjunctivitis or "Pink Eye"

Conjunctivitis is an inflammation of the white part of the eye, the conjunctiva. Your eye gets pink or "bloodshot." It's the most common eye disease. Usually the cause is viral or bacterial. Occasionally, chemical irritation, parasites, a fungal infection, or allergies cause conjunctivitis.. On rare occasions, most often in young men, burning on urination and joint pain (see "Reiter's syndrome," p. 197) may accompany it.

Allergic Conjunctivitis

"Hay fever" and other allergic reactions can affect the eyes. Symptoms include itching, redness, and watering. This invariably affects both eyes, and is never accompanied by pus or other discharge. It's usually a recurrent problem and may be accompanied by sneezing and itching of the nose, ears, and roof of the mouth. Travelers with a history of hay fever should add appropriate medications to their first aid kit prior to travel.

Treatment

Oral antihistamines (see pp. 284–285) are usually sufficient for the treatment of symptoms. For more severe symptoms try Naphcon-A Ophthalmic Solution, 1 drop in each eye every 3–4 hours as needed. **Don't** use these medications if a rash is present around the eyes.

Bacterial Conjunctivitis

When the cause is bacterial, a discharge containing pus accompanies the inflammation — most noticeably in the morning. Waking up, your eyelids may be stuck together with encrusted, dried yellow matter. For treatment, obtain medical evaluation.

Treatment in Isolated Areas

Apply sulfacetamide sodium 10% (10% Sodium Sulamyd Ophthalmic or Bleph-10 Liquifilm Ophthalmic), 1 or 2 drops to the affected eye 4 times a day for 5–7 days. **Don't** use this medication if you're allergic to sulfa drugs.

An alternative treatment is gentamicin sulfate (Garamycin Ophthalmic) ointment or solution. Use the ointment or apply 1 or 2 drops of the solution to the affected eye 3 times a day for 5–7 days.

Before using either medication, clean off any encrusted matter from the eyelids. To do this effectively, first apply cool moist compresses to the eyes for several minutes. After starting treatment, make your eyes feel better with warm compresses 3 times a day.

Conjunctival infections can be very contagious. Wash your hands thoroughly before and after touching the eyes. Be careful not to pass infection from one eye to the other. **Don't** share towels, washcloths, or pillows with anyone else.

Stop treatment and get medical help immediately if there is:

1. worsening of the condition or development of vision problems after starting treatment;

2. no improvement in 2–3 days;

3. development of an allergy or sensitivity reaction to the medication. This is usually indicated by itching or a constant burning sensation;

4. sharp stabbing eye pain.

Other Eye Infections

Possible Exposure to Gonorrhea or Chlamydia

When an eye infection occurs following a casual sexual encounter or after known exposure to gonorrhea or chlamydia through sexual contact, **get medical help immediately.** Medical evaluation is always required if an eye infection is accompanied by an abnormal discharge from the penis or vagina. Gonorrheal infections usually affect only one eye, not both.

Orbital Cellulitis

Redness and swelling of the eyelid, accompanied by pain and fever, is a medical emergency. The cause is bacterial and potential complications include abscess into the brain. **Medical attention must be obtained immediately.**

In isolated areas. If medical care is not immediately available, start one of the antibioitics listed below **while seeking medical attention as quickly as possible.**

1. dicloxacillin 500 mg. orally, 4 times a day for 10 days; **or**

2. erythromycin 500 mg. orally, 4 times a day for 10 days; **or**

3. Keflex or Velosef 500 mg. orally, 4 times a day for 10 days.

Sties

A sty is an inflammation of one of the oil glands located on the eyelid. This results in a tender red lump or swelling on the lid margin which eventually becomes capped by pus. Pain or sensitivity to touch is proportionate to the swelling.

Treatment

Apply warm compresses to the area for 10 minutes, 3–5 times a day. Use antibiotic ointment or eye drops for 2–5 days as suggested for conjunctivitis. The sty should come to a head, open, and drain the pus with relief of symptoms. Obtain medical help if:

1. sties are a recurring problem;
2. infection spreads;
3. the sty does not resolve within 3–5 days.

Reiter's Syndrome

Conjunctivitis accompanied by painful joints (arthritis) and burning on urination (nonspecific urethritis) is usually Reiter's syndrome. It's most common in young men. The joints most frequently affected are the ankle and the knee, usually on one side only. There is often a discharge from the penis and there may also be a rash or fever. This syndrome is a reaction following venereal exposure to the bacteria chlamydia, or diarrhea caused by either shigella or yersina bacteria.

Treatment

Seek medical attention for treatment. If medical care isn't readily available, the anti-inflammatory drug Indocin helps relieve joint pain. Take 25–50 mg. orally 3 times a day. Obtain medical evaluation after starting treatment.

Physical Injury to the Eye

Foreign Bodies

Wash or flush out with water a small foreign object, such as an eyelash or grain of sand, for 5–10 minutes as needed. An alternative is to gently flick it out with the twisted fibers on the end of a Q-tip or cotton swab. This requires the help of a mirror or another person. If a foreign object is suspected, **never rub the eyes**. This may cause further injury. If a foreign object has punctured or protrudes from the eye, **don't** attempt to remove it. Protect it from being touched or bumped if possible and get medical help immediately.

After removing any small foreign object which hasn't punctured the eye, obtain medical help if:

1. sensation of scratchiness, abrasion, or presence of a foreign body persists;
2. there is swelling, pain, or discoloration of the eye;
3. there is bleeding from the eye.

Chemical Contact

Eye injury including blindness can occur rapidly from chemical contact. Acids or bleach are common causes of eye injury; alkaline chemicals are particularly dangerous. Chemicals must be removed **immediately and thoroughly** to stop eye damage.

Immediate Treatment

Flush the eye immediately with large amounts of cool water for 20–30 minutes, or longer if burning continues. Use a gentle but sufficient stream from a hose or faucet, or water from any other available source — bucket, pan, drinking fountain, stream, or lake. Rinse the eye from the inner to the outer corner, away from the nose and the unaffected eye. Keep the eyelid open and wash under it thoroughly. **Don't** use any eye medications. Get medical attention as quickly as possible, preferrably from a hospital emergency room or an eye specialist (ophthamologist).

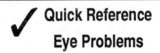

✔ Quick Reference
Eye Problems

Problem/Symptom	Possible Cause
eye red, with discharge; eyelids encrusted, stuck together in a.m.; usually one eye, may spread to the other	conjunctivitis ("pink eye")
both eyes red, watery, itching	allergic conjunctivitis
scratchy or abrasive sensation and watering in one eye	foreign body
red, swollen lesion on either eyelid, often with small amount of pus	sty
tenderness around cheekbones or the eyes, or pressure behind the eyes; no redness of the white part of the eyes (conjunctiva); with headache, nasal discharge, occasionally fever	sinusitis
light hurting the eyes, with severe, throbbing headache	migraine
light hurting the eyes, with severe headache, fever, neck stiffness	meningitis*
eye(s) red with a discharge, possibly stuck together in a.m.; joint pain, burning on urination with discharge from penis (usually affects young men); symptoms following sexual intercourse or episode of diarrhea	Reiter's syndrome
blurred vision in one eye becoming progressively worse ("A curtain came down over my eye")	retinal detachment*

*requires immediate medical evaluation

Quick Reference:

Eye Conditions Requiring
Immediate Medical Attention

1. Exposure to chemicals of any kind.

2. Visual disturbances: any blind spot that develops in the field of vision; blurred vision, especially in one eye, becoming progressively worse; double vision; dimness or decreased vision. Spots (floaters) may require medical evaluation if they persist or recur.

3. Eye pain, either sudden or slowly developing, if not due to sinus problems.

4. Light hurting the eyes (photophobia) if not related to known migraine headaches, or if accompanied by stiff neck and severe headache.

5. Redness or discoloration just around the iris (colored circle) of either eye; or an irregular (not round) pupil (small black circle).

6. Uncontrolled infection, inflammation, itching, or persistent burning.

7. Presence of a rash around the eye (may indicate a herpes infection).

8. Infection following known or possible exposure to venereal disease (gonorrhea or chlamydia) through sexual contact.

9. Conjunctivitis with concurrent joint pain and burning with urination (Reiter's syndrome).

10. Development of allergy or sensitivity to any eye medication.

Treating Nasal Problems

Hay Fever (Allergic Rhinitis)

Hay fever is an allergic response to airborne irritants in the environment. These include pollen, dust, sudden temperature changes, and animal dander (bits of skin, hair, or feathers). Unfortunately, travelers usually don't have control over these environmental factors. Preventive measures that may work at home aren't always effective when traveling in new environments.

Symptoms

Symptoms of hay fever include sneezing and often itching of the ears, eyes, nose, and throat. The eyes may be red, watery, and itchy. There may be a dry (non-productive) cough. There is usually a clear watery nasal discharge or a stuffy nose. Attempts to relieve nasal itching and congestion often result in the "allergic salute" — rubbing the nose upward and outward with the edge of the forefinger.

Treatment

Consult a doctor if the condition becomes chronic, interferes with daily activities, or is accompanied by wheezing. Otherwise there are generally no serious complications.

You can treat most conditions with an antihistamine. Frequently used are Actifed, one tablet orally 3 times a day, or Drixoral, Dimetapp, or Seldane, one tablet orally twice a day. Drowsiness is a common side effect. If wheezing occurs, seek medical attention as quickly as possible.

Treatment in Isolated Areas

In isolated areas, treat wheezing with an Alupent (metaproterenol sulfate) or Albuterol (Salbutanol, "Proventil") inhaler, or, if these aren't available, an epinephrine inhaler 3–4 times a day until you can find medical attention (see "How to Use an Oral Inhaler," p. 290).

Sinus Problems

Sinus problems may arise from either bacterial or nonbacterial causes. Drainage passages become blocked, and pressure differences can then result in varying degrees of pain.

Symptoms

There may be a frontal headache, over or behind one or both eyes. Pain is usually greatest in the morning and lessens during the day. It's increased by bending the head down and forward. There may be tenderness when tapping or pressing just above and below the eyebrows or below the cheekbones (see diagram below). Sometimes the pain is in one or both cheeks. It may feel like a toothache in the upper jaw, but there's no facial swelling and no tenderness of any tooth if pressure is applied. Fever and chills, nasal discharge and, frequently, a foul-tasting postnasal drip, cough, and headache may all be associated with sinusitis.

Nonbacterial Sinusitis

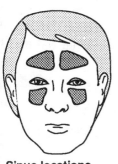
Sinus locations

Nonbacterial sinusitis may have an allergic or viral cause. It can accompany or follow an attack of hay fever or a common head cold. Antibiotics are of no value. Sinusitis from these causes is characterized primarily by a nasal discharge that is clear or watery — never thick, opaque, or green colored.

If the cause is viral it may be associated with muscle aches, a low fever (under 101°F (38.3°C).), and a dry cough. Sneezing often accompanies it if the cause is allergic. There may also be burning, itching, and watering of the eyes and/or mouth.

Treatment

Nonbacterial sinusitis is treated with decongestants and antihistamines. Use **one** of the following:

1. Entex L.A., 1 orally twice a day; **or**
2. Sudafed, 60 mg. orally 3 times a day; **or**
3. Actifed, 1 tablet orally 3 times a day; **or**
4. Dimetapp, 1 orally twice a day; **or**
5. Drixoral, 1 orally twice a day.

In addition, steam inhalation (from a bowl of hot water or shower) will help loosen and clear blocked passages. Get plenty of rest and drink lots of fluids.

Bacterial Sinusitis

Sinusitis of bacterial origin may be severe. It's characterized by a thick nasal discharge which is usually colored green or yellow, has a foul taste, and which lasts for more than 7 days. It's **never** clear. There may be a cough, usually producing green or yellow sputum. Weakness, fever, nausea, vomiting, and sinus pain or "headaches" over the face, or with facial tenderness (see diagram p. 201), are all possible. These symptoms vary individually with the degree of infection.

Treatment

In addition to the measures described above for nonbacterial sinusitis, you need antibiotics to curb the infection. The medications, listed in order of preference, are:

1. Bactrim DS (same as Septra DS) 1 tablet orally, twice a day for 10 days (**don't** take if allergic to sulfa drugs); **or**
2. ampicillin 500 mg. orally 4 times a day, or amoxicillin 500 mg. 3 times a day, for 10 days (do NOT take either medication if allergic to penicillin); **or**
3. tetracycline 500 mg. orally, 4 times a day for 10 days; **or**
4. erythromycin 250 mg. orally, 4 times a day for 10 days; **or**
5. Keflex or Velosef 500 mg. orally, 4 times a day for 10 days.

Rest and drink plenty of liquids. For fever or pain, take 2 aspirin or Tylenol up to 4 times a day as needed.

Indications for medical treatment

Get medical attention for any sinus condition if:

1. there's no improvement within 3–4 days of treatment;
2. there's redness or swelling around the eye.

If a sinus problem fails to improve with treatment and is accompanied by jaw pain, this may indicate a possible tooth disorder — get medical or dental help for evaluation and treatment.

Nosebleed

A nosebleed is usually due to the rupture of a small blood vessel in the sensitive inner lining of the nose. These vessels are fragile, exposed, and easily damaged. A nosebleed can occur from colds or other infections, hay fever, exposure to dry air, irritation from nose picking, vigorous blowing, or trauma. Medical evaluation is usually necessary only when:

1. the bleeding is very great or cannot be stopped within 20 minutes;
2. the nose is or may be broken;
3. there's an increased tendency to bruise or bleed elsewhere on the body;
4. the nosebleeds recur frequently.

Treatment

Sit up in a chair, lean forward, and breathe through the mouth. Apply pressure to the bleeding site by pressing the nostril closed with the thumb, or by pinching both nostrils shut. If necessary, gently pack a small amount of tissue (not cotton balls) one-half inch inside the affected nostril, enough to make it bulge slightly. Then apply pressure to the outside of the nose. Maintain pressure for 5–10 minutes. Avoid blowing the nose for several hours to keep from dislodging the clot.

Prevention

When nosebleeds are due to excessively dry air, you can usually prevent them with some lubricating ointment. Place a small pea-sized amount on a fingertip or Q-tip and rub it up inside each nostril several times a day and at bedtime, as needed. Use any commercial ointment, such as Vaseline, Vicks VapoRub, or A and D Ointment. If not available, a topical antibiotic ointment can be used.

Quick Reference:

Causes of a Runny Nose

Problem or Symptom	Possible Cause
Thick, greenish yellow nasal discharge with frontal headache or pain behind the eyes or face which is increased by bending forward	bacterial sinusitis
Clear watery or white nasal discharge with frontal headache or pain behind the eyes or face which is increased by bending forward	nonbacterial sinusitis
Clear watery or white nasal discharge with itchy eyes, nose, and mouth; sneezing	allergy (allergic rhinitis)
Clear watery or white nasal discharge with mild fever	cold
Clear watery or white nasal discharge with muscle aches, fever, chills	flu

Dental Problems: Gum and Tooth Disease   12

Satisfactory dental care is sometimes more difficult to find than medical care in developing nations. Even in countries with superb dental schools, care may be scarce outside the urban centers. In rural areas the most sophisticated dental tool is often a pair of pliers; "anesthetic" may be the brand name of a locally distilled beverage. It's a good idea when traveling to have any required dental work performed in a large major city, after obtaining a reliable referral.

Cavities

The bacteria in plaque convert sugar to acid. As this eats through tooth enamel, cavities form. They commonly occur between the teeth, along the gumline, on molar surfaces, and behind the last molars. These are the areas that require special attention when cleaning.

Discolorations of the tooth that are soft when probed indicate cavities. If you're in an isolated rural area for an extended time, a cavity can sometimes be found early with the help of a small dental mirror, a dental pick, and a friend.

Once located, clean and fill a cavity to prevent further damage. A dentist is needed because of the technical skills, specialized tools, and anesthetic that you may require. If a dentist isn't immediately available, you'll need to provide interim care for a simple toothache and possibly emergency care for advanced disease. For new cavities, or old ones exposed when fillings are lost, use the following temporary measures.

Temporary Cavity Care

If there is no pain, scrape out all debris from the cavity. Rinse thoroughly: swish and spit, using a mixture of equal parts hydrogen peroxide and water. When pain is present, relieve it first by applying a few drops of clove oil to the affected area with a cotton swab or small cloth. Then rinse the area as previously described. "Oil of cloves" is a numbing sedative that also promotes some dental healing. Make it part of your first aid kit for travel in rural areas.

If necessary for pain, take Vicodin 1 tablet 3–4 times a day, or 1 or 2 aspirin or Tylenol with 30 mg. of codeine every 6 hours. **Never** put aspirin directly on the painful tooth or gum. This is one home remedy that causes damaging and painful tissue burns.

After cleaning, find a dentist — within 24 hours when toothache pain is continuous or severe. If this is impossible, temporarily fill the cleaned cavity. This should be done only when:

1. pain is absent, slight, or intermittent; and

2. heat relieves, not intensifies pain.

Use one of the filling materials listed below. The first 2 are commercial preparations. Both are inexpensive and available without prescription from dental supply stores in the U.S. If not obtained before leaving, equivalent preparations may be available in major cities.

1. "Cavit" is a handy temporary filling that lasts 1–2 weeks — time enough to find a dentist. It's the easiest of the 3 preparations to use, and comes in a small tube.

   Instructions. Before applying, add a drop of clove oil. The cavity shouldn't be dried. Contents of the tube are squeezed onto the cavity area, then patted down with a piece of moistened cotton. It can also be pressed into the cavity with a finger. In contact with saliva, Cavit begins to harden in an hour or two and sets completely in 1 day. Avoid any pressure on the new filling for 30 minutes, and avoid eating or chewing for a couple of hours.

2. "I.R.M." (Intermediate Restorative Material) is a more durable filling. It's less convenient than Cavit, as it requires mixing from 2 containers. The liquid clove oil base is added to a powdered mixture of zinc oxide and eugenol cement, forming a putty. After drying a few minutes, this

is pressed into the thoroughly cleaned cavity to harden. The cavity must be completely dry or bonding will not occur. Don't swallow this preparation.

3. Warm soft candle wax can also be used as a temporary filling material. It will not survive exposure to temperature extremes. Apply a few drops of clove oil before inserting the wax. Mix the warmed wax with wisps of cotton fiber from a cotton ball before using to create a slightly stronger material.

Lost Fillings

The above materials can be used for temporary cavity care if fillings become loosened or dislodged. Clean and keep the filling. A dentist will be able to evaluate its potential reuse.

Toothaches and Other Tooth Pains

Simple Toothache (Partial Simple Pulpitis)

Without regular dental exams, a toothache is often the first sign of a cavity. When a cavity reaches or is near the inner tooth (the pulp), injury may occur from either bacterial infection or temperature extremes. At first the pain is intermittent and slight. It's intensified by cold and relieved by heat. Dental care needs to be obtained at this stage so that the tooth and pulp can be saved without extensive procedures. Take 1 or 2 Tylenol or aspirin orally every 6 hours for pain, with codeine if necessary for extreme discomfort, or Vicodin, one tablet orally 3–4 times a day.

Advanced Tooth Disease

Untreated, simple toothache pain becomes increasingly severe until it's intense and continuous. **It should never be permitted to reach this stage.** You'll require dental care for pain control and extraction or other procedures.

Tooth abscess (periapical abscess)

Sometimes pressure builds within a tooth as a result of injury or infection. Pain is either intermittent, sharp, and throbbing, or continuous and intense, even excruciating. In contrast to simple toothache pain, it's intensified by heat and relieved by cold. Tapping on or near the tooth increases the pain.

The pressure often causes infection and inflammation in the tissues underlying the tooth. Indications are facial swelling, fever, local pus formation, and often a persistent bad taste in the mouth. **When these symptoms occur, antibiotics must be started immediately.** If uncontrolled, the infection may spread throughout the blood or to bones of the face and jaw.

Treatment in Isolated Areas

If dental or medical care isn't immediately available, start **one** of the following antibiotics, listed in order of preference. Continue taking the medication for the full 10 days, or until treatment can be found.

1. penicillin VK 500 mg. orally, 4 times a day for 10 days; **or**
2. tetracycline 500 mg. orally, 4 times a day for 10 days; **or**
3. erythromycin 250 mg. orally, 4 times a day for 10 days; **or**
4. Keflex or Velosef 500 mg. orally, 4 times a day for 10 days.

To relieve pain, take 1–2 aspirin or acetaminophen (Tylenol), with codeine if needed, 3–4 times a day or Vicodin, 1 tablet 3–4 times per day. This may be necessary for a day or two until the swelling subsides. By this time you should have obtained medical or dental care, but it's urgently required if the pain and infection fail to improve, become worse, or recur after starting antibiotics. Once the infection has been successfully treated, dental care is still required to remedy the underlying cause.

Tooth Injury or Trauma

Chipped or Broken Teeth

The teeth of adults are more likely to shatter from a blow than are childrens' teeth. A tooth that is knocked out, chipped, or broken can often be saved if it can be professionally splinted and stabilized within an hour. When help is more than an hour or so away, success rates are unfortunately too low to warrant this effort.

It's sometimes possible to press the tooth back into place, using clove oil to reduce pain if necessary. First lick the tooth clean (saliva is preferable but water can be used when the tooth is very dirty). If it will not stay in place, keep it in your mouth while en route to a dentist or emergency room. The tooth can also be kept in cold milk, or as a last resort wrapped in a damp cloth. Use a cold compress on the face to reduce swelling of the injured area. Take 1 or 2 Tylenol, with codeine if necessary, every 4–6 hours or Vicodin, 1 tablet 3–4 times per day as needed for pain.

Control of Bleeding

Following injury to the teeth and gums, excessive bleeding can be controlled by applying direct pressure with a gauze bandage or clean cloth. If bleeding doesn't stop, rinse the mouth with warm salt water and place a used tea bag (cooled after steeping in hot water for 5–10 minutes) over the area. Hold with firm pressure for 20–30 minutes. The tannic acid in the tea bag helps to stop the bleeding.

Gum Disease

Inflammation of the Gums (Gingivitis)

Inflammation or infection of the gums can sometimes be a sign of vitamin deficiency, allergic reaction, or the onset of diabetes or other disease. Usually, however, the cause is plaque. This gradually builds up beneath the gum margin. Plaque, calculus, and bacterial products all irritate the gums, causing inflammation.

The earliest and sometimes only sign of gingivitis is bleeding. In contrast to healthy gums, inflamed gums bleed readily when touched, brushed, or flossed. After a prolonged time they may become swollen, and bluish or red in color. If the condition isn't corrected, the gums become progressively detached from the teeth. The gums recede, and the underlying bone ultimately erodes away.

Treatment

A dentist must remove calcified plaque. Good diet and daily oral hygiene is required to prevent recurrence. Under normal circumstances, antibiotics and mouthwashes are of no value.

Trenchmouth

Also called Vincent's infection, trenchmouth is a noncontagious infection of the gums. Small ulcers form along the gum margin or between the teeth, covered with a grayish membrane. These bleed readily. Unlike gingivitis, the lesions are painful. Swallowing and talking may be difficult. Usually there's swelling of lymph nodes in the neck, but no fever.

Treatment

Have your teeth cleaned professionally to prevent infection from recurring. Plaque and calculus are the root of the problem.

Control symptoms by rinsing the mouth several times daily for a few days with a mixture of equal parts hydrogen peroxide solution (3%) and warm salt water (1 teaspoon in 1 pint of water). This preparation is available over the counter in the U.S. as "Amosan" (add one package to a glass of water, rinse or gargle). Similar preparations are available in most countries.

Conscientious oral hygiene is essential. Rest and a good diet with vitamin supplements of B complex (1 daily) and C (500-1000 mg. daily) are also helpful.

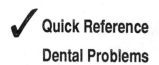

Quick Reference

Dental Problems

Problem/symptom	Possible cause
tooth pain	
intermittent; intensified by cold, relieved byheat	early cavity
continuous; intensified by heat, relieved by cold; possibly with fever or facial swelling	abscess
pain only when biting down on tooth	possible cracked tooth, filling, or early abscess
bleeding from the gums, without pain or fever	gingivitis
gums red, painful; bleed easily	Trenchmouth
sores around lips; blistering, painful	probable cold sore (herpes simplex)

Any sore or ulcer in the mouth which does not heal within 10 days requires medical evaluation. If the sore follows oral sex with a new or casual partner, medical evaluation including a test for syphilis is required.

Respiratory Problems 13

The lungs are a branching system of air passages that become progressively smaller. This system, the "respiratory tree," ends in tiny air sacs (alveoli) where inhaled air interacts with the blood.

The throat (pharynx), vocal cords (larynx), and the air passages that connect the nose, sinuses, and middle ears make up the upper respiratory system. The trachea, bronchi, and alveoli — the lungs — make up the lower respiratory system.

Upper Respiratory Disease

Viral Infections

Viruses are a frequent cause of upper respiratory infections. In order to treat these infections properly, it's important to understand the difference between viral and bacterial infections. Antibiotics work well against bacterial infections because both bacteria and antibiotics work *outside of the body's own cells*. Viruses, on the other hand, pass *inside* the cells where antibiotics cannot reach them. Therefore antibiotics have *no* effect on viruses, and will *not* help cure viral infections.

The Common Cold

Cold symptoms vary, depending partly on which of over 200 different viruses is the cause. Symptoms may include sneezing, a runny or stuffy nose, watery eyes, a mild, dry sore throat, headache, and tiredness. There may be muscle aches, nausea, or plugged-up ears. Nasal discharge is watery and either whitish or clear. There may be a mild cough with a small amount of whitish or clear sputum. A low grade fever (less than 101°F (38.3°C)) is also common.

These symptoms usually disappear in 3–14 days. Since the cause is viral, antibiotics don't help. Symptoms can sometimes be confused with influenza, nonbacterial sinusitis, or hay fever.

Treatment

The traditional prescription is to rest and drink plenty of fluids — still good advice. Nutrition is important, and can include your favorite recipe for chicken soup.

Treat mild fever and aches with 1 or 2 tablets of aspirin or Tylenol up to 4 times a day if needed. Do warm salt water gargles (1 teaspoon salt in 1 pint of water) several times a day for a sore throat. Avoid smoking to prevent complications.

Oral decongestants may be useful. Try Sudafed (pseudoephedrine HCl.) 60 mg. up to 3 times a day or Entex LA (phenylpropanolamine HCl. and guaifenesin) twice a day to lessen secretions and to decrease any sensation of "popping" or fullness in the ears. If nasal discharge is clear and accompanied by itchy, burning, watery eyes, the cause may be allergic rather than viral (see "Hay fever," pp. 200–201).

Decongestant nasal sprays, such as Afrin or Neosynephrine, should be used only if other decongestants aren't available. Strictly follow directions on the package — usually 1 whiff in each nostril no more than twice a day. **Don't use nasal sprays for more than 3 days at a time.** Otherwise, these products may cause a "rebound" effect which makes symptoms even worse once they are discontinued.

Flu, or "Viral Upper Respiratory Syndrome"

Cold symptoms accompanied by a high temperature (101°–103°F (38.3°–39.4°C)), chills, and general body or muscle aches, usually indicate a flu virus. Fatigue can be severe. Related symptoms may include decreased appetite, nausea, vomiting, diarrhea, sore throat, and headache.

Fever can last 3–5 days, while other symptoms, including fatigue, often last 3–14 days. Recovery should be complete in 7–21 days. If symptoms persist beyond this time, or recur, obtain medical evaluation.

Treatment

The cause is viral and antibiotics are of no benefit. Treatment is the same as for the common cold, with bedrest recommended until the fever subsides. Resume activities slowly.

Symptoms Requiring Medical Attention

Most often a cold, flu, or other viral upper respiratory infection runs its course uneventfully. **The following conditions require immediate medical attention:**

1. wheezing;
2. shortness of breath with chest pain or a dry, painful cough, with or without a fever;
3. severe pounding headache, high fever, and neck pain or stiffness increased by bending the head forward or bringing the knees to the chest;
4. coughing up blood;
5. an earache that doesn't clear with decongestants.

Other Upper Respiratory Infections

Sore Throat

The majority of sore throats are viral in origin, especially when accompanied by other head cold symptoms. These include a dry cough, stuffy nose, and whitish-clear sputum or nasal discharge. Sore throats with a viral cause don't respond to antibiotics, and these shouldn't be used.

To relieve throat discomfort, gargle with warm salt water (1 teaspoon salt in a pint of purified or boiled water (see pp. 80–83) 3–4 times a day. A soft or liquid diet and throat lozenges may also be helpful. One to two aspirin 3–4 times per day will also help decrease discomfort.

"Strep" Throat

A "strep" throat is an infection due to a form of streptococcus bacteria. You must treat it with antibiotics to prevent potentially dangerous complications.

A throat culture is the only way to accurately identify a strep throat. There are no reliable physical signs or symptoms. The so-called "classic" features of strep throat occur in only a small percentage of cases. These features are:

1. fever;
2. tonsils that are swollen, red, and covered with white spots;
3. a beefy red sore throat;

4. tender enlarged lymph nodes in the front of the neck.

Even when all of the above are present, odds are only about 60% that the cause is streptococcus, although these odds are a little higher for persons under the age of 25.

Throat cultures can usually be done at a doctor's office, clinic, or medical laboratory. Results are frequently ready in 24 hours, or in 15 minutes if monoclonal antibody tests are available. It's cheaper and quicker to go directly to a medical laboratory for the throat culture. Then take the lab report to a doctor. *This is necessary only if the report shows the presence of Group A beta-hemolytic streptococcus.* Other forms of streptococcus are often present normally and don't need treatment. If in doubt, ask a doctor.

Treatment

Obtain treatment when the lab report is positive for "Group A beta-hemolytic streptococcus." A doctor will usually prescribe either penicillin VK, erythromycin, or ampicillin. These are given 250–500 mg. (depending on the severity of the signs and symptoms) orally 4 times a day for 10 days. Symptoms disappear after a few days, but it's important to complete the entire 10 day course of antibiotics. Medical follow-up is necessary if an allergy to the medication develops or if there is no improvement in 2–3 days.

Other causes of a sore throat

If the lab report does not show strep, and the sore throat is associated with fatigue, low grade fevers, increased sleepiness, and decreased appetite, mononucleosis is a possible cause (see pp. 172–173).

Persistent sore throat following sexual contact

If a sore throat persists following oral sex (with someone other than an established, exclusive partner), gonorrhea, chlamydia, or syphilis are possible causes. Obtain medical attention for evaluation. A blood test for syphilis and a throat culture for gonorrhea and chlamydia should be done. If any are positive, further evaluation and/or treatment are required.

Chronic sore throat

If tests for strep throat and mononucleosis are both negative and a sore throat persists for more than 3 weeks, the cause may be allergic or bacterial.

Treatment in isolated areas — A trial of antibiotics may be started. Take *one* of the following:

1. erythromycin, 250 mg. orally, 4 times a day for 10 days, **or**

2. doxycycline, 100 mg. orally twice a day for 10 days, **or**

3. tetracycline, 250–500 mg. orally, 4 times a day for 10 days.

If the sore throat continues after taking antibiotics, try an antihistamine for 7 days. If there is still no improvement, obtain medical evaluation.

Sinusitis. See pp. 201–203.

Allergic rhinitis. See pp. 200–201.

Ear pain. See Chapter 9.

Lower Respiratory Disease

Acute Bronchitis

Bronchitis (inflammation of the bronchi) is usually caused by a viral or bacterial infection. It's often accompanied by cold symptoms. It's characterized by a cough, usually dry at first but with increasing sputum production.

There may be pain centered in the upper chest with coughing, or coughing may be accompanied by a sensation of tightness in the chest. Temperature is often mildly elevated, 101°F (38.3°C) or less. When there are no complications, *the key to treatment of bronchitis is the character of the sputum.*

Viral bronchitis

A cough which produces clear to whitish sputum indicates the cause is probably viral. Antibiotics are of no benefit. Symptoms should diminish within 5–7 days, although coughing may persist a week or two. Follow the general guidelines below. If the sputum changes from clear to yellowish-green, see "Bacterial bronchitis" for additional treatment measures.

Treatment guidelines for bronchitis

The secretions that lungs produce must be kept thin and loose so they can be coughed up. Otherwise, a secondary bacterial infection is likely. Adequate fluid intake is very important. Drink at least 2–3 liters (quarts) per day. You may also need other measures, such as vaporizers and cough expectorants. See "Care of a cough" at the end of this chapter for a summary of recommendations.

In addition to drinking plenty of fluids, adequate rest is important. Take 1 or 2 aspirin or Tylenol as needed up to 4 times a day for fever or pain. Smokers who continue to smoke will prolong their illness and risk potential complications.

Bacterial Bronchitis

If coughing produces a large amount of colored sputum (more than two tablespoons a day), the cause is probably bacterial. Sputum often appears yellowish at first, changing to dark yellow or yellow-green. In this case antibiotics are needed in addition to the treatment measures described above.

Treatment

Obtain medical help to make sure there is no pneumonia, and to start the appropriate antibiotics.

Treatment in isolated areas — When medical care is not available, consider a course of oral antibiotics. The drugs of choice, listed in order of preference, are:

1. erythromycin 250 mg. orally, 4 times a day for 10 days; **or**

2. ampicillin 500 mg. orally 4 times a day for 10 days (don't take if allergic to penicillin); **or**

3. tetracycline 500 mg. orally 4 times a day for 10 days (only if allergic to penicillin and erythromycin is not available); **or**

4. Bactrim DS (Septra DS) one tablet orally, twice a day for 10 days (**don't** use if allergic to sulfa drugs); **or**

5. Keflex or Velosef 500 mg. orally, 4 times a day for 10 days.

Symptoms Requiring Immediate Medical Attention

Obtain medical care immediately if bronchitis is accompanied by any of the following:

1. shaking chills and fever above 101°F (38.3°C);

2. fever lasting more than 3 days;

3. chest pain, not related directly to coughing.

    Any of the above symptoms may indicate pneumonia.

4. Wheezing, or difficulty inhaling or exhaling (these may indicate airway obstruction — a potential emergency. See "Asthma," p. 218).

Pneumonia

Pneumonia is an inflammation of the lungs. Infectious causes are usually viral or bacterial, but may sometimes be fungal. Travelers should be aware of other potential causes as well, such as inhaled smoke or chemicals, tuberculosis, and roundworm or other parasitic infections.

Symptoms

Pneumonia can occur without chest pain. More often, though, chest pain is present and may be described as "stabbing." Coughing frequently increases this pain, though it may or may not initially produce phlegm or sputum. Breathing is usually rapid. There is an elevated temperature that either becomes increasingly worse, or lasts more than 72 hours. **These symptoms require immediate medical attention.**

Other symptoms which may be present include headache and shaking chills. Phlegm is usually produced soon after the onset of coughing and the resultant sputum may be yellow, green, gray, or brown.

Sputum that is rust-colored, thick, and sticky is often characteristic of pneumococcal pneumonia. The onset of symptoms is extremely rapid, with increased breathing and pulse rates.

Treatment

Regardless of cause, pneumonia always requires medical evaluation as quickly as possible. Chest x-rays, blood tests, and sputum gram stains are standard. Severe cases may require further measures, including hospitalization. **Never** start antibiotics unless medical help is unavailable.

Initially, complete bed rest is essential. Drink plenty of fluids. For fever or pain, take 1 or 2 aspirin or Tylenol tablets as needed up to 4 times a day. **Don't take any other pain killers, cough suppressants, or other medications unless prescribed by a doctor.**

Treatment in isolated areas

In addition to the above measures, if medical help is more than 36–48 hours away, start antibiotics if signs of pneumonia are accompanied by any of the following:

1. severe shortness of breath;
2. a temperature above 103°F (39.4°C);
3. rapid progression of symptoms, with sputum that is rust-colored, thick, and sticky (suspected pneumococcal pneumonia).

The recommended antibiotics, in order of preference, are:

1. erythromycin 250 mg. orally, 4 times a day for 10 days; **or**
2. tetracycline 500 mg. orally, 4 times a day for 10 days; **or**

3. Bactrim DS (Septra DS) orally, 1 tablet twice a day for 10 days; (**don't** use if allergic to sulfa drugs); **or**

4. Keflex or Velosef 500 mg. orally, 4 times a day for 10 days.

Medical care must still be obtained as quickly as possible. Some strains of pneumococcal bacteria, especially in South Africa and New Guinea, are resistant to many antibiotics. It's always best to get medical care before starting any antibiotics.

Asthma

An attack of asthma can be triggered by pollen, dust, animal dander, or other airborne particles. It can also result from viral or bacterial respiratory infections, inhaled irritants (physical or chemical), psychological stress, or vigorous exercise.

Symptoms

Asthma is characterized by shortness of breath, wheezing (a high pitched noise from the airway during inhalation and/or exhalation), and a sensation of tightness in the chest. A cough is usually present. Coughing may bring up thick secretions of mucus.

Asthma is usually, but not always, an ongoing condition. *Travelers with a history of asthma should carry their usual medications and know how and when to use them.* They should also consult with their doctor prior to travel regarding any special medications to take along. Medical care is necessary if asthma is not relieved with the usual medications, or if an underlying bacterial infection is the suspected cause.

Travelers with no history of asthma or chronic lung disease should get medical attention at the onset of wheezing. Wheezing should be considered the first sign of a possible life-threatening emergency.

You don't need to be an asthmatic to have an asthma attack. On a camping trip, one of the authors experienced severe respiratory difficulty accompanied by wheezing — suddenly and for no apparent reason. Sitting around the campfire, a fellow camper had thrown sulfur-bearing rocks onto the fire to spark some color. Downwind, invisibly, the sulfurous fumes provoked a nearly lethal reaction.

Treatment

During a first attack of asthma, it's important to stay calm. Reduce the work of breathing: sit up, lean forward, support the upper body with arms folded across a table or desk if available. Drink lots of fluids to keep secretions thin and loose. **Don't** smoke. Get medical help as soon as possible, including a follow-up evaluation once the initial attack subsides.

Treatment in isolated areas

Asthma symptoms may sometimes accompany bronchitis, either viral or bacterial. If symptoms of bacterial bronchitis are present and no medical help is available, then, in addition to the above measures we suggest starting one of the following oral antibiotics (listed in order of preference):

1. erythromycin 250 mg. orally, 4 times a day for 10 days; **or**

2. ampicillin 500 mg. orally, 4 times a day for 10 days (**don't** take if allergic to penicillin); **or**

3. tetracycline 500 mg. orally, 4 times a day for 10 days (only if allergic to penicillin and erythromycin is not available); **or**

4. Bactrim DS (Septra DS) 1 tablet orally, twice a day for 10 days (**don't** use if allergic to sulfa drugs); **or**

5. Keflex or Velosef 500 mg. orally, 4 times a day for 10 days.

Get medical help as quickly as possible.

For wheezing, you may use an Alupent (metaproterenol sulfate) or Albuterol ("Proventil") inhaler. If these aren't available, you can use an epinephrine inhaler, but it has the potential for more side effects. For further information on these drugs and how to use an inhaler, see p. 290. Drink plenty of fluids, and **don't** smoke.

If none of the inhalers are available, one option is to take Alupent 20 mg. orally 3–4 times a day, or an equivalent medication such as Brethine 2.5 mg. 3 times a day. Severe wheezing with shortness of breath that doesn't respond to any of these measures is a medical emergency requiring immediate attention.

Care of a Cough

Secretions produced by the lungs must be coughed up to prevent a bacterial infection either from starting or from becoming worse. **Productive coughing (coughing which produces phlegm) should always be encouraged rather than suppressed.** The following measures will help keep secretions loose and thin so that coughing can be effective:

1. Drink plenty of fluids — 2 or 3 quarts (liters) a day.

2. Keep the room comfortably warm and humidified if possible.

3. Use a vaporizer if available, or try steam inhalations several times a

day. Take hot steamy showers, or heat water over a stove and transfer it to a basin. Cover your head and the basin with a towel to enclose the steam. Be careful to avoid burns. Eucalyptus leaves added to the water will help open air passageways.

4. Cough medicines should contain an expectorant such as guaifenesin. Avoid cough suppressants as much as possible. If necessary for sleep, use a cough suppressant such as codeine or terpine hydrate.

5. Smokers must not smoke. Cigarette smoke paralyzes the structures (cilia) that sweep pulmonary secretions out of the lungs so they can be picked up and properly disposed of by a good cough.

Symptomatic Treatment of Fever and Indications for Medical Evaluation

Mild fevers (less than 102°F (38.9°C) can be treated with aspirin, Tylenol, or ibuprofen and increased fluid intake. In addition, fevers above 102°F (38.9°C) may require tepid water sponge baths.

Obtain medical evaluation for:

1. any recurrent fever;
2. any fever over 104°F (40°C);
3. any fever accompanied by chest pain and/or shortness of breath, with or without a productive cough;
4. any fever accompanied by yellowing of the skin or eyes (jaundice);
5. fever accompanied by severe headache, nausea, vomiting, and neck stiffness.

See our Quick Reference guides on the following pages.

Quick Reference

Common Causes of a Cough

Symptoms	Possible Cause
Nonproductive, or dry cough	cold, flu, allergy, smoking, viral bronchitis, post-nasal drip, pneumonia or asthma
with:	
clear nasal discharge, fever, sore throat, muscle aches	flu, cold with post-nasal drip
watery, itchy eyes, nose, mouth	hay fever (allergic rhinitis)
wheezing*	asthma, bronchitis
mild fever	bronchitis
chest pain, fever, possibly shortness of breath*, chills	pneumonia
Productive cough with white or clear sputum:	viral bronchitis, flu, cold, asthma, pneumonia (occasionally)
with:	
slight fever	cold, viral bronchitis
fever, muscle aches, fatigue	flu
wheezing*	asthma, viral bronchitis
Productive cough with green, dark yellow, gray, or brownish sputum:	bacterial bronchitis (most common cause), pneumonia, asthma with bacterial upper respiratory infection
with:	
slight fever	bacterial bronchitis
chest pain when not coughing, fever, chills*	pneumonia
wheezing*	bacterial bronchitis, asthma
Productive cough with green or yellow sputum and nasal discharge, pain behind the eyes which is increased when bending over	bacterial sinusitis
Productive cough with bloody or blood-tinged sputum*	pneumonia (usually blood streaked with yellow-green sputum), tuberculosis, severe parasitic infection, tumor
Cough with wheezing	bronchitis, asthma
Cough with shortness of breath, difficulty breathing*	asthma, pneumonia
Chronic or persistent cough*	smoking, tuberculosis, asthma, chronic bronchitis, parasitic infection

*Requires immediate medical attention

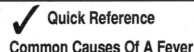

Quick Reference

Common Causes Of A Fever

Symptom	Possible Cause
Accompanied by a cough, with:	
chest pain, shortness of breath, cough usually productive with colored sputum, occasionally non-productive	pneumonia
productive green or yellow sputum, sometimes with wheezing	bacterial bronchitis, asthma with or without underlying bacterial infection
muscle aches, fatigue, headache, chills, nausea	flu, "viral upper respiratory syndrome"
nasal discharge, headache, pain behind eyes or face increased by bending over; cough dry or productive	sinusitis
fatigue, headache, sore throat, "stepladder" fever; cough non-productive	typhoid fever
Without a cough, but with:	
chills, fatigue, sore throat, with or without cold symptoms	flu, "viral upper respiratory syndrome", strep throat, viral sore throat, tonsillitis, mononucleosis
nausea, and/or vomiting, diarrhea; muscle pain, abdominal pain, possibly headache or chills	gastroenteritis
burning on urination, urinary frequency, small amounts **and**:	
no back pain	urinary tract infection (bladder infection)
back pain, nausea and/or vomiting	kidney infection
fatigue, shaking chills that come and go periodically; occasionally with diarrhea	malaria
severe lower abdominal pain	appendicitis, pelvic inflammatory disease
bloody diarrhea	schistosomiasis, intestinal bacterial infections/dysentery
chills, severe headache, nausea, vomiting neck stiffness	meningitis*
skin locally red, swollen, tender; progressively larger area	cellulitis

*If meningitis is suspected, don't take antibiotics. Get immediate medical evaluation.

Sexually Transmitted Diseases, Gynecology

14

Problems Common to Men and Women

Genital Ulcers

There are many possible causes of genital ulcers or lesions in men and women following sexual contact. Some of these occur more frequently in the tropics. Although the lesions sometimes have identifying characteristics, in practice they are hard to distinguish without laboratory tests. **All genital-rectal ulcers or sores require medical evaluation. Aways have a syphilis blood test done.**

Syphilis

Syphilis is extremely dangerous if *untreated* or *under* treated. The organism (Treponema pallidum) is capable of damaging any organ of the body.

Acute primary syphilis

The first sign of infection occurs 10–90 days after exposure, averaging 3 weeks. A painless ulcer may appear on the penis, or on the labia, clitoris, inner vaginal wall, or cervix. It may also occur in the mouth, on the lips or tongue, or in the rectum.

The classic lesion begins as a dull red flat spot. It develops into a raised lesion which then ulcerates. It has a hard, clearly defined border. The base of the ulcer is smooth and shiny and becomes covered with a gray film. It is always *painless*, unless complicated by a secondary infection.

The classic lesion occurs about 50% of the time. The lesion otherwise varies considerably in appearance. In women, it may go unnoticed. Lymph nodes are usually enlarged, painless, and nontender.

If syphilis is suspected, do not fail to get medical attention. Insist on a syphilis blood test (RPR) or a darkfield microscopic exam from a qualified lab. If any of these are positive, repeat VDRL blood tests in 1 month, and again 3, 6, and 12 months after treatment. This may seem like a lot of testing, but it's the only insurance against possible undertreatment and a potentially devastating infection.

Treatment — The usual treatment is a single intramuscular injection of 2.4 million units of Bicillin, a form of penicillin. Treatment should be obtained only in a medically supervised setting as the medication may cause a dangerous allergic reaction. **Don't** obtain treatment through a pharmacy or other nonmedical setting, even when such treatment is offered.

If you're allergic to penicillin, or if Bicillin is not available, the alternative treatment is either:

1. tetracycline 500 mg. orally, 4 times a day for 2 weeks; **or**

2. doxycycline 100 mg. orally, twice a day for 2 weeks.

Avoid sexual contact throughout treatment and for 1 week afterwards. Notify partners that may have been exposed. Don't forget the repeat blood tests. If any of these are positive, get medical attention immediately.

Chancroid

Chancroid is a genital lesion that is relatively rare outside the tropics. In tropical regions it's often spread by prostitutes. It is caused by an organism called *Hemophilus ducreyi*.

Symptoms

Four to seven days following exposure, 1 or more raised, red lesions develop in the genital area. Within 24–48 hours the lesion becomes pustular and ulcerates. It has a soft, ragged, undefined border. A pus-like gray or yellow discharge covers the base of the ulcer. It bleeds easily when scraped.

When more than one is present, the ulcers may converge, becoming larger than 1 inch (about 2 cm) across. The ulcer is painful. These features help distinguish it from the hard, clear, painless ulcer produced by syphilis. Lymph nodes in the groin may be enlarged and tender. Women frequently have no symptoms, while men always have very painful ulcers.

Treatment

As with any genital ulcer, you must obtain medical evaluation. Treatment varies in different geographical areas depending on the drug-resistant properties of local strains of bacteria. Usually, chancroid is treated with one of the following:

1. erythromycin 500 mg. orally, 4 times a day for 7 days; **or**

2. Ceftriaxone, one 250 mg. intramuscular injection; **or**

3. Bactrim DS, 1 tablet twice a day for 7 days.

If you're allergic to penicillin, don't take Ceftriaxone except under medical supervision. If allergic to sulfa drugs, don't take Bactrim.

LGV and Granuloma Inguinale

Lymphogranuloma venereum (LGV), granuloma inguinale (Donovanosis), and other diseases have a higher incidence in the tropics. They are difficult to identify without experience and laboratory tests. **Obtain medical attention for any unidentified lesion, rash, discharge, or other genital problem.** There may be a danger of transmission and possibly serious damage to affected tissue. Blood tests should be done to rule out the possibility of syphilis for **any** undiagnosed genital lesion.

Genital Herpes. (See pp. 121–122).

 Quick Reference:

Typical Signs of Ulcerative Genital Lesions

	Syphilis	Chancroid	Herpes	LGV	Granuloma inguinale
Primary lesion	raised, smooth lesion may be pustular	red, raised lesion, blister (vesicle)	raised, pimple-like (vesicular) or pustular lesion	raised, smooth blister-like	raised, smooth lesion
Border	well defined	red, ragged	red	variable	rolled, elevated
Base	red, smooth with gray film	pus yellow to gray, bleeds easily	red, smooth	variable	red, rough
Pain	rare	present	present	variable	rare
Lymph nodes	firm, non-tender	tender, rubbery	tender, firm	tender	pseudo

Sexually Transmitted Diseases — Men

Whether or not you acquire an infection from sexual contact, there's usually no lack of opportunity to do so. This is often truest for those traveling alone. With few exceptions, all sexual encounters carry a risk of developing disease — some, of course, more than others.

Gonorrhea

Gonorrhea is one of the most common sexually transmitted diseases. It has been increasingly resistant to standard doses of antibiotics in many areas of the world. Among these are the Philippines, Thailand, Singapore, South Korea, and West Africa, especially in Ghana, Cote d'Ivoire (formerly the Ivory Coast), Nigeria, and Kenya.

Symptoms

Initially there's burning on urination accompanied by a clear or milky discharge. This occurs approximately 2–10 days after contact. Within a day or two the discomfort increases and the discharge turns yellow, yellow-green, or cream-colored. Urination is frequent with a sense of urgency and burning. The tip of the penis is often tender, red, and swollen.

Diagnosis

If there's any doubt about the cause, a medical laboratory or doctor can Gram-stain and/or culture the discharge. These will show the presence of the causative bacteria, Neisseria gonorrhea.

Nongonoccocal Urethritis (NGU)

This infection is even more common than gonorrhea. Symptoms are virtually the same as for gonorrhea and can easily be mistaken for it. The discharge usually remains clear or milky. Diagnosis is based on the absence of gonorrhea bacteria in a Gram-stain of the discharge.

Treatment of Gonorrhea and Nongonoccocal Urethritis (NGU)

Obtain medical care for evaluation and treatment. As indicated, it's usually impossible to tell the difference between gonorrhea and NGU infections without laboratory tests. In addition, about a third of men with a urethral discharge have a combination of both gonorrhea *and* NGU. The following lab tests should be obtained prior to treatment:

1. gonorrhea culture
2. syphilis blood test
3. Gram-stain of the discharge

Treatment in isolated areas

If medical care isn't available, all penile discharges should be treated with 2 drugs (ceftriaxone or spectinomycin injection, followed by either doxycycline or tetracycline) to cover the possibility of infection by both gonorrhea and NGU. Note that the recommended treatment is different for heterosexual and homosexual men, and in geographical areas where drug-resistant strains of gonorrhea are present.

During treatment for either infection, it's important to increase fluid intake. Avoid both alcohol and coffee, which are irritating to the urethra. There should also be no sexual contact until at least 3–4 days after completing treatment. If sexual contact does occur, use a condom. **Condoms are recommended for any casual sexual contact to help prevent disease.**

Treatment schedules (for reference)

The following is the current treatment schedule for both gonorrhea and nongonococcal urethritis. If allergic to penicillin, don't take Ceftriaxone except under medical supervision.

A. All NGU infections in men should be treated with either:

    1. doxycycline 100 mg. orally, twice a day for 7 days; **or**

    2. tetracycline 500 mg. orally, 4 times a day for 7 days.

B. For gonorrhea in heterosexual men, or homosexual men with only urethral contact:

    1. Ceftriaxone (Rocephin) 250 mg. IM (intramuscular injection) **and** either doxycycline or tetracycline as for NGU; **or**

C. For gonorrhea in homosexual males with oral and/or rectal contact:

    1. Ceftriaxone 250 mg. IM injection;

D. Treatment of gonorrhea if allergic to penicillin and unable to take Ceftriaxone:

For heterosexual males, either;

    1. doxycycline or tetracycline as for NGU; **or**

    2. spectinomycin 2 grams IM injection.

For homosexual males:

    1. rectal contact: spectinomycin 2 grams IM;

    2. oral contact: ciprofloxacin 500 mg. orally taken as a single dose.

Treatment of Gonorrhea in Drug-resistant Areas

In any country where antibiotic resistant strains of gonorrhea are known to exist, check with local medical practitioners or the public health department for the recommended treatment. If this isn't possible, current recommended treatments are as follows:

1. For all sites of contact, Ceftriaxone 250 mg. IM injection; **or**
2. For urethral or rectal infections, spectinomycin 2 grams IM injection; **or**
3. For oral sites, ciprofloxacin 500 mg. orally taken once as a single dose.

If symptoms persist during treatment, or recur following treatment, medical evaluation is required.

Partner Contact

Make sure sexual partners are also treated so that infection isn't transferred back and forth, ping-pong style.

Gynecology and Sexually Transmitted Diseases — Women

In medical practice it's not surprising to find that areas relating directly to women have changed significantly. The women's movement has transformed traditional practice to meet newly expressed and developing needs. It has brought a style of medicine with greater sensitivity and understanding of women's bodies and problems specific to women.

These changes include an increased awareness and understanding of gynecological problems, including vaginal and urinary tract infections, birth control, and sexually transmitted disease. These are particularly appropriate concerns for women who travel, who may need to make decisions without access to their usual medical resources.

We reiterate the importance of adequate preparation before traveling. Consider carefully your contraceptive choices, obtain a Pap smear as part of a pretravel physical if necessary, and make breast self-examination a personal skill, especially for extended travel. These topics are detailed in Part I.

Chlamydia

Chlamydia is an organism spread through sexual contact that may not produce symptoms initially. Like gonorrhea, it can spread to the upper genital tract (the uterus and fallopian tubes) and cause infection (PID). In males the organism causes nongonococcal urethritis (NGU), with symptoms of burning on urination and a penile discharge. As with gonorrhea, symptoms in your male partner may be the first indication of infection.

Gonorrhea

Gonorrhea is one of the most common sexually transmitted diseases. It's increasingly resistant to standard doses of antibiotics in many areas of the world. Among these are the Philippines, Thailand, Singapore, South Korea, and West Africa, especially in Ghana, Cote d'Ivoire (formly the Ivory Coast), and Nigeria.

Gonorrhea may produce a pus-like, yellowish discharge from the vagina. It's sometimes accompanied by urinary burning and frequency. When present, these symptoms usually occur from 1-3 weeks after exposure to infection.

There may, however, be no symptoms or such minimal ones that they are easy to overlook. The first indication of infection is often from a male sexual partner who develops burning with urination and a discharge from the penis. If not discovered early, gonorrhea may go undetected until it produces more generalized symptoms, usually of PID (Pelvic Inflammatory Disease — see below).

Pelvic Inflammatory Disease (PID)

PID refers primarily to infections of the uterus and fallopian tubes. Infection is usually caused by either gonorrhea or chlamydia bacteria. The consequences of infection can be quite serious. They include:

1. complete scarring of the tubes leading to sterility;
2. partial scarring of the tubes, greatly increasing the risk of ectopic (abnormal) pregnancy, itself an emergency;
3. severe infection with abscess formation, requiring hospitalization and possibly surgery.

The symptoms are varied, but usually include **mild to severe lower abdominal pain**. It's usually felt on both sides but may not be equally painful on both sides. It may be accompanied by one or more of the following:

1. nausea and/or vomiting;
2. fever and chills;
3. vaginal discharge or bleeding;
4. pain with intercourse.

> **If either PID or gonorrhea infection is suspected, get medical attention immediately.**

Treatment of Suspected PID in Isolated Areas

If medical help is more than 24 hours away, consider starting antibiotics. The following is also the appropriate treatment schedule following diagnosis of gonorrhea or chlamydia, or when a male partner is diagnosed with gonorrhea or chlamydia or develops a urethral discharge with or without burning on urination:

1. ceftriaxone 250 mg. intramuscularly (IM),

   and, in addition, take one of the following oral medications concurrently:

2. doxycycline 100 mg. orally, twice a day for 10 days; **or**

   tetracycline 500 mg. orally, 4 times a day for 10 days.

   Don't use either of the above medications during pregnancy. Instead, take one of the following:

   erythromycin, 500 mg. orally 4 times a day for 10 days **or** 250 mg. orally 4 times a day for 20 days.

> **After starting any of the above antibiotics, medical assistance must still be obtained as quickly as possible.**

Urinary Tract Infections (UTIs)

Urinary tract infections are very common. All things considered, it's remarkable they don't recur constantly. The short length of the urethra, its proximity to bacteria of the vagina and rectum, and the abundance of ways that bacteria can be spread in the area, including intercourse, all predispose to such infections.

You can encounter other contributing circumstances during travel. These might include an absence of hygenic facilities, long rides with an unemptied bladder, and inadequate fluid intake. Other factors which may play a role include tight pants and jeans, or undergarments made of non-breathing synthetic fabrics. New sexual partners are often implicated as a cause, as intercourse may be especially intense.

Preventive Measures

Drink plenty of fluids. See Nutshell™ Guide (pp. 97–98) for a list of beverages which are safe to drink. If urinary tract infections are a recurrent problem, avoid citrus drinks, coffee, and alcohol. All of these are urinary tract irritants.

Use underwear made with a cotton crotch. It will absorb excessive moisture which otherwise promotes bacterial growth. Avoid irritants such as vaginal sprays or deodorants as well as excessively tight clothing.

On long bus or train rides, it's a good idea to empty the bladder frequently if possible. It is also a basic principle to avoid any practice, sexual or otherwise, that transfers germs from the rectal area to the vagina.

Symptoms of Bladder Infection

The indications of a bladder infection (cystitis) are straightforward and easily recognizable, if not maddeningly familiar. Most common are sensations of urgency and burning with urination There is an increased frequency of urination, with disappointingly small results. Even without other symptoms, these symptoms by themselves usually indicate a bladder infection.

When they occur, treat symptoms promptly. Otherwise infection may travel up the urinary tract from the bladder to the kidneys.

Treatment

Simple urinary tract infections, with no abnormal vaginal rash or discharge, no back pain or fever, and no nausea or vomiting, are easily treated. Oral antibiotics are prescribed for 3–7 days. Drink plenty of water or other fluids throughout the course of antibiotic therapy. Vitamin C supplements can also be taken to acidify the urine.

Treatment of urinary tract infections in isolated areas

When medical help isn't available, use any one of the following treatments, listed in order of preference:

1. Bactrim DS (Septra DS), one tablet orally twice a day for 3 days.

   Don't take Bactrim or Septra if you are allergic to sulfa drugs.

2. amoxicillin 500 mg. orally 3 times a day for 3 days or ampicillin 500 mg. orally 4 times a day for 3 days. These are equivalent treatments.

   Don't take amoxicillin or ampicillin if you are allergic to penicillin.

3. If allergic to penicillin: tetracycline 500 mg. orally, 4 times a day for 3 days.

   If you're pregnant, use ampicillin. If allergic to penicillin, the alternative during pregnancy is Nitrofurantoin, 100 mg. orally 4 times a day for 10 days.

After treatment, signs of a bladder infection may occasionally reappear after 2 or 3 days. If this occurs, obtain medical attention. The bacteria and the most effective antibiotic for treating it will need to be identified through a urine culture and sensitivity. Then, one of the above drugs will usually be prescribed for 7 days.

Vaginal yeast infections are a frequent side effect of antibiotic therapy. Vaginal yeast medications can help prevent infection if used while taking antibiotics (see p. 234).

The burning sensations that accompany a bladder infection are often extremely uncomfortable. They can be relieved with Pyridium (phenazopyridine HCl) 200 mg. orally, 3 times a day for no more than 2 or 3 days. This medication can be taken along with the antibiotics. It turns the urine bright orange, so don't panic.

Indications for medical assistance

When accompanied by an unusual vaginal discharge, symptoms of a urinary tract infection require medical evaluation. The symptoms may be due to a vaginal infection, not to a bladder infection.

Get medical help immediately if symptoms of a urinary tract infection are accompanied by any of the following:

1. chills or fever (102°–105°F (38.9–40.6°C));
2. back or flank pain (a dull ache in the back along the rib margin);
3. nausea and vomiting.

These may all be signs of a kidney infection.

Emergency treatment in isolated areas

If any of the above signs of kidney infection develop and you are close to medical care, get immediate help. Don't take **any** medications. If unable to access medical care immediately, start **one** of the following medications, listed in order of preference:

1. Bactrim DS (Septra DS) one tablet orally, twice a day for 14 days;
   Don't take Bactrim or Septra if you are allergic to sulfa drugs.
2. amoxicillin 500 mg. orally, 3 times a day for 14 days or ampicillin 500 mg. orally, 4 times a day for 14 days (these are equivalent treatments);
   Don't take amoxicillin or ampicillin if allergic to penicillin.
3. Norfloxacin 400 mg. orally, twice a day for 14 days.

Head **immediately** for the nearest physician or medical care facility whether antibiotics are started or not.

Vaginal Infections (Vaginitis)

Infections of the vagina are common, especially under travel conditions. Physical stress and environmental or dietary changes may be contributing factors. In addition, vaginal yeast infections may occur as a side effect of antibiotic therapy. There are many different organisms that can cause vaginal infections. It's difficult to diagnose and effectively treat infections without laboratory facilities. If there are signs of a vaginal infection, obtain medical evaluation. This is essential after any sexual contact that carries the risk of gonorrhea, syphilis, or other venereal disease.

If medical care isn't readily available, an accurate diagnosis can sometimes be made from the clinical signs (the physical observations that can be made without laboratory help). This is often true for recurrent infections, after becoming familiar with their identifying characteristics.

Yeast Infections

These are common occurrences. Conditions which may contribute to infection include pregnancy, diabetes, and stress, including long hard days of travel in tropical climates. Other contributing factors include douching and the use of oral contraceptives, antibiotics, and synthetic garments which trap heat and moisture.

Yeast infections are characterized by thick, white secretions that resemble cottage cheese. Swelling and itching around the vulva and labia can be mild to severe.

Treatment

Most yeast infections can be cured with one of the 1- or 3-day treatments listed below. For severe or persistent infections, use a 1-week or longer treatment method. Insert the medication — suppository, cream, or tablet — into the vagina each night at bedtime. The medication should be put in following intercourse, not before. Otherwise it will get squashed out and not do any good.

Butoconazole (Femstat) — 2% cream. Apply 5 gms. (one full applicator) at bedtime for 3 days, or 6 days if pregnant.

Clotrimazole (Gynelotrimin, Mycelex)

— 10% cream. Apply 5 gms. (one full applicator) as a single application.

— 100 mg. vaginal tablet. Use one tablet vaginally at bedtime for 7 days, or two tablets at bedtime for 3 days.

— 500 mg. vaginal tablet. Use one tablet vaginally once.

— 1% cream. Apply 5 gms. (one full applicator) at bedtime for 7–14 days.

Miconazole (Monistat)

— 2% cream. Apply 5 gms. (one full applicator) at bedtime for 7 days.

— 100 mg. vaginal suppository. Use one suppository vaginally at bedtime for 7 days.

— 200 mg. vaginal suppository. Use one suppository vaginally at bedtime for 3 days.

— 1200 mg. vaginal suppository. Use one suppository vaginally once.

Teraconazole (Terazol)

— .4% cream. Apply 5 gms. (one full applicator) at bedtime for 3 days.

— 80 mg. vaginal suppository. Use one suppository vaginally once.

Ticonazole (Vagistat)

— 6.5% ointment. Apply 4.6 gms. at bedtime once.

Some women find that a yeast infection inevitably follows use of ampicillin or other antibiotics. Use an antifungal vaginal medicine as a preventive measure along with antibiotic therapy.

Symptomatic relief of vaginal infections

If vaginal medications aren't available and you have symptoms of itching, redness, swelling, or irritation of the labia, wash the area free of any discharge. Apply a thin coating of sterile lubricant such as K-Y jelly or diaphragm jelly to protect the skin. If these aren't available, use a 1% topical hydrocortisone cream to the area to reduce symptoms. **Don't** apply hydrocortisone cream if herpes lesions are present.

A doctor friend of ours suggests trying aspirin or antihistamines orally for symptomatic relief, especially if no other treatments are available.

Trichomonas ("Trich")

When seen under the microscope, *Trichomonas* organisms appear to be cute little creatures with wiggly tails. Infections are less pleasing, characterized by a profuse yellow-green, foamy, bubbly discharge, usually with a very foul odor. There is mild itching of the vulva.

Treatment

1. Flagyl 2 grams (8 tablets) orally, taken as a single dose.
2. If infection isn't cured with the above dose, try Flagyl 500 mg. orally, twice a day for 7 days.

   Don't use Flagyl during pregnancy. An alternative is:
3. Clotrimazole (Mycelex vaginal tablets or 1% cream), inserted vaginally each night before sleep for 7 days.

   Male sexual partners should be treated at the same time with the single,

2 gram dose of Flagyl, provided there are no contraindications. After exposure, males may harbor infection in their urethra, usually without any symptoms. Left untreated, they may well reintroduce infection. Partners undergoing treatment should refrain from intercourse until both have completed treatment. If intercourse does take place, use condoms.

For symptomatic relief of itching and irritation, see p. 215, "Yeast Infections."

Bacterial Vaginosis (Formerly Called Nonspecific Vaginitis, Hemophilus, Gardnerella, or Corynebacterium).

This is an inflammation caused by overgrowth of bacteria in the vagina. A thin discharge is produced, usually whitish with a fishy or foul odor. Mild itching may be present.

Treatment

Flagyl is usually effective. If infection recurs, male partners should be treated simultaneously. The dose is:

1. Flagyl 500 mg. orally, twice a day for 7 days.

   Don't use Flagyl during pregnancy. The following medication can be used during pregnancy, or if treatment with Flagyl is ineffective:

2. Clindamycin 300 mg. orally, twice a day for 7 days.

   For symptomatic relief of itching and irritation, see p. 234.

Use of Acid-base Balance
To Help Identify Vaginal Infections

The acid-alkaline balance of the vagina changes when different infections are present. In isolated areas when medical care isn't available, use litmus paper to test the pH of any vaginal discharge. The normal pH is 4.5. Yeast infections cause the pH to drop below 4.5 (they are more acidic). In trichomonas infections the pH is usually 5 or higher. In bacterial vaginosis, the pH is usually 4.5 or higher. These readings provide some confirmation when accompanied by the symptoms of infection previously described.

Use of Douches

Don't douch on a regular basis. It washes out normal vaginal bacteria and can lead to vaginal infection. Douching may also push bacteria into the uterus. This may result in pelvic inflammatory disease (PID). Statistically, women who douche have a 4 times greater incidence of PID.

Quick Reference:
Common Vaginal Infections

	Yeast	Trichomonas	Bacterial vaginosis
Discharge	white, scant to moderate, clumped or cottage cheese-like	profuse, yellow or green, often frothy	mild to moderate, thin, white or gray
pH	less than 4.5	equal to or greater than 5	equal to or greater than 4.5
Odor	none	fishy	fishy
Irritation	redness of labia & opening to vagina	redness of opening to vagina	none
Typical symptoms	vulvar itching &/or irritation with increased discharge	profuse discharge, mild irritation	slightly increased discharge with bad odor
Treatment required for sexual partner	no	yes	yes, if infection recurs following treatment

Special Concerns of Women

Pregnancy Testing and Possible Pregnancy

Missed period with the possibility of pregnancy. When cause for concern, this situation requires different responses depending on circumstances. We suggest the following:

1. If using birth control pills:

   • regularly with no missed pills: no pregnancy test should be needed unless 2 consecutive periods are missed.

   • with 1 or more missed pills: a pregnancy test is advised.

2. If using an IUD:

   • obtain a pregnancy test immediately. If the results are positive, indicating pregnancy, obtain medical care as soon as possible.

3. If using any other form of birth control (or no birth control): a pregnancy test is advised.

 **Quick Reference:**

Gynecologic Symptoms That Require
Immediate Medical Evaluation

See a physician immediately for any of the following signs and symptoms, whether already receiving treatment or not:

1. Lower abdominal pain (not associated with normal menstrual pain or diarrhea), accompanied by any of the following:
   - chills or fever;
   - pain with intercourse;
   - spotting after intercourse;
   - loss of appetite, nausea, or vomiting;
   - abnormal vaginal discharge.

   These are usually indications of PID (Pelvic Inflammatory Disease). Symptoms are often, but not always, accompanied by a foul vaginal odor or discharge which may be more intense during or following menstruation.

2. Urinary urgency, frequency, and burning, accompanied by any of the following:
   - chills or fever – 101°F (38.3°C) or greater;
   - pain in the back or side;
   - nausea or vomiting.

   These symptoms usually indicate kidney infection.

3. abnormal vaginal bleeding;

4. problems with contraception (birth control pills, IUD's, diaphragms, etc.);

5. vaginal infections.

Pregnancy Tests

A standard urine pregnancy test (UCG) does not provide a valid test result until 6 weeks after the last menstrual period. Other urine pregnancy tests on the market, based on monoclonal antibodies, are as accurate as blood tests. They detect pregnancy as soon as 10 days following conception. Blood tests (BHCG) are more expensive, but are considered slightly more reliable than standard UCG's and are valid 7 days following conception. The blood test is the test most widely available in many Third World countries.

In most developing nations you can save money by going directly to a laboratory for a blood or urine pregnancy test. To be accurate, urine samples for a UCG should not be dilute. Obtain a sample from the first voiding in the morning. Don't drink a lot of liquids prior to the test.

If the pregnancy test is negative and contraceptive techniques have been faultless (no missed pills, IUD string in place, use of condom, diaphragm and foam, etc.), repeat the test in 7-10 days. During this time abstain from intercourse. If the second test is also negative, pregnancy is extremely doubtful. Missed menstrual cycles could be due to stress from travel or other sources.

Missed menstrual cycles accompanied by a breast discharge and/or headache with visual disturbances require medical evaluation. Otherwise obtain medical evaluation if normal menstruation does not resume within 6 months. Even when periods are irregular and abnormally spaced, pregnancy is still possible. Don't dismiss the need for contraceptive measures.

If tests indicate pregnancy, consider your diet, medications, lifestyle, and travel plans to avoid harming the fetus. If considering an abortion, bear in mind that this is safest when done within the first 12-15 weeks of pregnancy.

Menstrual Cramping (Dysmenorrhea)

Cramping is common just before and during menstruation. In the past it was considered normal and inevitable, regardless of degree. This is no longer the case.

Treatment

A number of medications have proven effective in reducing discomfort. These include ibuprofen 400 mg. (Motrin, Nuprin, etc.), indomethecin 25 mg. (Indocin), and Naprosyn (Naproxen) 250 mg. The directions for administration are identical, regardless of which is used. Take 2 tablets orally when cramps first begin, then 1 every 4–6 hours until cramps are gone.

Injuries to Bone and Muscle

15

Strains, Sprains, Fractures, and Dislocations

With the exception of simple sprains and strains, most acute injuries to muscles, joints, ligaments, tendons, and bones require medical evaluation. Unfortunately, many bone fractures are difficult for even the most experienced practitioner to identify. An x-ray is usually required if there is any doubt about a bone being broken.

First, some definitions:

Sprains occur when the ligaments that support the joints are torn or stretched, usually by overextending or twisting a joint beyond its normal range. This kind of injury is seen frequently in ankles, knees, and wrists.

Strains are injuries of the muscles, from overextension or overexertion. These cause swelling and moderate to intense pain with movement. Strains are common in muscles of the back and arms from lifting.

Fractures are broken bones. They are called *open* fractures if bone protrudes from the skin. *Closed* fractures do not protrude and are often difficult to detect without x-rays.

A **dislocation** is the displacement of any bone from its normal position in a joint. This occurs most often to shoulders and fingers.

Treatment of Sprains and Strains

Minor sprains and strains are treated identically. During the first 24–48 hours, a cold pack or compress, such as ice, wrapped in a towel, is applied to the area for 15–20 minutes 4 times a day. Keep cloth or other material between the ice and the skin. Elevate the injured area at least 12 inches above the level of the heart to further reduce swelling and pain. After 24–48 hours, apply heat to the area for 15–20 minutes, 3–4 times a day to further reduce swelling.

For pain and swelling, take either aspirin, 1 or 2 tablets orally every 4–6 hours, *or* one of the following nonsteroid anti-inflammatory medications:

1. ibuprofen (Motrin or Advil) 400–600 mg. orally, 4 times a day; **or**

2. naproxen (Naprosyn or Anaprox) 250–500 mg. orally twice a day; **or**

3. indomethacin (Indocin) 25 mg. orally 2–3 times a day; **or**

4. piroxicam (Feldene), 1 capsule orally once a day; **or**

5. diflunisal (Dolobid) 1 tablet twice a day.

See contraindications for nonsteroid anti-inflammatories in Part III before taking any of these medications.

For severe pain not relieved by the above measures, obtain medical evaluation.

In Isolated Areas

When medical help isn't available, for severe pain take aspirin or Tylenol with 15–30 mg. of codeine, 1 or 2 orally every 4-6 hours or vicodin, 1 tablet 3 or 4 times per day. For severe muscle spasm, a muscle relaxant may also be necessary. Use one of the following or an equivalent muscle relaxant. Avoid use of Valium as it may be habit-forming.

1. Parafon Forte DSC 1 or 2 tablets orally every 4–6 hours; **or**

2. Robaxin 500 mg., 2 tablets 4 times a day; **or**

3. Flexeril 10 mg., 1 tablet 3 times a day.

Use of an "Ace wrap" or supportive bandage.

An "Ace wrap" or elastic bandage is sometimes used to support an injured joint, most commonly the ankle, knee, or wrist. When using an elastic bandage, or a substitute such as a long strip of cloth, be sure it isn't too tight. Remove and rebind the joint less tightly whenever a wrap causes discomfort, skin discoloration, numbness, or pain in or beyond the joint.

Treatment of Other Muscle, Bone, or Joint Injuries

Any injury more severe than a minor strain or sprain **requires medical evaluation and treatment.** Immobilize suspected fractures or injured joints with a Sam Splint, a multipurpose splint that can be molded into many shapes (see p. 43), or any other splint material, while seeking medical attention.

 Quick Reference:

Injuries Requiring Medical Evaluation and Treatment

Medical evaluation and/or x-rays are required as soon as possible for the following injuries:

1. all open fractures;
2. any dislocation (any injury causing joint deformity);
3. inability to walk or bear weight after an ankle or knee injury;
4. a "snap, crackle, or pop" (the Rice-Krispie syndrome) heard at the time of an injury;
5. any injured area, especially a joint, that becomes hot, tender, swollen, or painful;
6. any joint injury with moderate to severe swelling;
7. any injury where there is tenderness or pain over the bone;
8. whenever there is doubt about a bone being broken;
9. any joint that becomes painful or disabling without an identifiable cause (for example, waking up in the morning with a tender, un-movable wrist or knee).
10. any injury that isn't improved after 2 weeks of treatment.

Women fewer than 20 weeks pregnant should not have x-rays unless medically required and authorized. If x-rays are deemed necessary, have a lead apron placed over the abdomen — provided one is available and the abdomen or back are not needed in the x-ray.

Burn Injuries

16

Burns caused by heat are classified by the degree (depth) of injury to the skin. Treatment varies depending on the degree, extent, and location of injury. Although some aspects differ, the evaluation and treatment of external burns from electricity or acidic and alkaline chemicals is the same as for thermal injuries.

First Degree Burns

First degree burns affect only the outermost layer of skin. They cause redness but not blistering. They may be painful, but swelling is absent or minimal. A nonblistering sunburn is a common example.

Treatment

Following brief contact with a hot object, immerse the burned area immediately in cold water or apply a cold wet cloth until the pain subsides. **Never** apply butter, grease, or other home remedies to any burn.

Cool water or damp cool cloths are soothing and effective for local pain. Take one or two aspirin orally as needed every 4–6 hours to reduce swelling and pain. Infection is unlikely.

Second Degree Burns

Second degree burns cause incomplete injury to the skin below its surface layer. Blistering is a characteristic sign. The skin may appear moist or oozing. Redness, pain, and swelling are usually present for several days. Injuries from spilled hot liquids and severe sunburn are examples.

Treatment

Apply cold water or a cold wet cloth to the burn area until the pain subsides. **Don't** break blisters. Intact skin is the best defense against infection. Some second degree burns require immediate medical care; indications are summarized at the end of this chapter.

The main goal of care in minor second degree burns is to prevent infection. Bathe the injured area for 20–30 minutes, using lukewarm water. If the water isn't reliably treated and clean, boil it first for 5 minutes, then allow it to cool.

After bathing, pat the surrounding skin dry, but allow the burn to air dry. Don't blow on it. Dress the burn by putting on a thin layer of Silvadene Cream, if available, then cover it with sterile gauze or gauze pads.

Repeat this procedure every 12 hours, or more often if needed to keep the gauze bandages clean. Before changing, soak off dressings that are dry and stick to the wound. For blistering burns from a deep sunburn, apply topical Neosporin or other antibacterial ointment to help prevent infection.

Relieve pain with 1 or 2 aspirin or Tylenol as needed every 4–6 hours. For extensive burns, **don't** use aspirin. For moderate to severe pain, take 1 or 2 Tylenol with 15–30 mg. of codeine every 4–6 hours, or Vicodin, 1 tablet up to 4 times a day, as needed.

Tetanus

Get a tetanus booster if you haven't had one within the previous 5 years.

Infected second degree burns require immediate medical attention. Infection delays healing and increases tissue damage. Infected burn wounds need to be cultured before the appropriate antibiotics can be prescribed. Signs of infection are:

1. yellow or greenish pus draining from the burn or present on the dressing;
2. a foul odor coming from the burn or dressing;
3. fever greater than 101°F (38.3°C).

Treatment of Infected Burns in Isolated Areas

If you're more than 2 days from medical care and develop signs of infection, start antibiotics and head for the nearest medical care facility as quickly as possible. Continue bathing and dressing the burned areas, with care not to spread the infection. Use one of the following antibiotics:

1. dicloxacillin 500 mg. orally, 4 times a day for 10 days; **or**
2. erythromycin 250 mg. orally, 4 times a day for 10 days; **or**
3. Keflex or Velosef, 500 mg. orally, 4 times a day for 10 days.

Third Degree Burns

Third degree burns destroy all layers of the skin. Fire, prolonged contact with hot substances, and electricity are frequent causes of third degree burns. The burned area may be charred, or turn as hard and white as the edge of a fried egg. There is little or no pain because nerve endings in the skin are destroyed.

Treatment

All third degree burns, even small ones, require immediate medical evaluation — preferably at a hospital or burn center. In contrast with milder burns, **don't** apply ice or cold water compresses to third degree injuries. Don't attempt to remove stuck or charred clothing or apply any ointments or medications.

While awaiting or during transportation to medical care:

1. Cover burned areas loosely with a sterile dressing if available. Otherwise, use a clean sheet or cloth, preferably ironed or dried in the sun.
2. Elevate burned extremities.
3. Keep the injured person calm and lying down, or supported with pillows if there are burns on the face or neck.

Burns Requiring Special Treatment

Second Degree Burns Involving Adjacent Skin Surfaces

Burns to areas of the body where skin comes in contact with skin, such as the fingers, toes, armpit, or groin, require special care. Sterile vaseline gauze dressings should be placed between the adjacent skin surfaces. Obtain medical care immediately for these injuries.

Electrical Burns

Electrical burns must also receive immediate medical evaluation and treatment. Damage is often internal and may not be readily apparent.

 **Quick Reference:**

Burns Requiring Immediate Medical Attention

1. Any third degree burn.
2. Any electrical burn.
3. The following second degree burns:
   - of the face (including eyes, nose, and ears);
   - of adjacent skin surfaces, such as the fingers, toes, armpit, or groin;
   - covering more than 10% of the body surface. This can be quickly estimated, counting the injured person's hand (from base of palm to fingertip) as 1% of the body surface. More than 10 handspans requires immediate care;
   - in adults over age 50, diabetics, or anyone with circulatory or immune system impairment, including those taking steroid medications.
4. Signs of secondary infection in any burn:
   - green or yellow drainage (pus) on the burn or dressing;
   - a foul smelling wound or dressing;
   - an elevated temperature greater than 101°F (38.3°C).
5. Whenever smoke, gas, or chemical inhalation has or may have occurred. The following are indications for immediate medical help even if there are no other injuries:
   - exposure to fire in an enclosed space such as a house, hotel room, subway, theater, etc.;
   - singed nasal hairs;
   - soot in the nose, mouth, throat, or sputum;
   - burns of the face, nose, or mouth;
   - hoarseness, coughing, wheezing, or difficulty breathing;
   - presence of a headache after possible exposure to fire or smoke.

Exposure to Heat and Cold

17

Heat Exposure

Problems from heat exposure — cramps, exhaustion, or "heatstroke" — are normally preventable. They're due to excessive loss of water and salt.

These conditions are unlikely except on very hot days, especially when the humidity is high. The cause is profuse sweating over an extended time (as from working or hiking), *accompanied by inadequate replacement of water and salt.* Other sources of water loss — diarrhea, vomiting, or consumption of alcoholic beverages — may intensify symptoms. Cold beer may sound great, but it will increase rather than replace body water losses.

For normal to moderate levels of activity, salt replacement shouldn't be necessary. Don't use salt tablets except when you can't avoid extended daily physical labor under hot, humid conditions.

At the first sign of any heat-related symptoms, stop all activity and take preventive measures. Otherwise, symptoms may progress to heat stroke, which is often fatal.

Prevention of Heat-Related Problems

When traveling, allow yourself time to adjust to warmer climates. Go slowly and don't try to do too much too soon. Avoid serious activity for a few days after arrival in a warm, humid environment. It may take as long as 8–10 days for your body to adapt to the heat, especially if you've just flown south to escape a long, cold winter.

Drink plenty of fluids — even if you're not thirsty, but avoid alcohol and caffeine. Get enough rest and sleep. Maintain a good diet. Wear loose-fitting clothing, preferably of cotton rather than stuffy synthetic materials. Above all, don't push it — but drink lots of fluids if you do.

Heat Cramps

Heat cramps are painful muscle spasms, usually of the arms, legs, or abdomen. They occur when large amounts of fluid lost from sweating are replaced only by water. Heat cramps were formerly common in steelworkers, for example, who did not replace lost salts during exposure to high heat for 8–12 hour stretches.

When profuse sweating occurs over a prolonged period, fruit juices and beverages such as Gatorade are preferable to water for fluid replacement. If these are unavailable, water with added salt or salt tablets may be necessary.

Treatment

Stop all activity. Replace lost fluids by drinking a minimum of 1 glass (8 ounces) of juice or water every 15 minutes for an hour. Add 1 teaspoon of salt per glass. Gently massage and stretch the painful areas. Rest for 1–3 days.

Heat Exhaustion

Symptoms of heat exhaustion include weakness, headache, dizziness, nausea, and possibly fainting ("heat collapse.") The skin is cool, pale, and clammy. The pulse rate is usually under 100. There may be vomiting, diarrhea, or muscle cramps. Body temperature remains normal or is only slightly elevated (less than 100°F (37.8°C)).

Treatment

Stop all activity. Get out of direct sunlight if possible and lie down in the coolest available place. Elevate and support the feet about 8–12 inches above the head. Unless there is vomiting or unconsciousness, replace fluids orally with juices or cool water: a minimum of one glass every 15 minutes for an hour. Add one teaspoon of salt per glass.

Cool down by any available means, such as wetting the skin with cool or tepid water and vigorous fanning. If ice is available, place an ice pack or cold compress in the armpits, behind the neck, and in the groin. **Don't** leave an ice pack on for more than 15–20 minutes at one time to avoid frostbite. You can reapply it after 15–20 minutes. **Don't** take aspirin or alcoholic beverages.

Indications for medical assistance
Obtain medical help immediately for any of the following:

1. vomiting or unconsciousness. Don't give oral fluids if either is present;

2. symptoms that worsen or persist beyond one hour;

3. cessation of sweating, accompanied by a sudden, rapid rise in temperature. **This is heatstroke — an emergency.**

Heatstroke (Sunstroke)

Heatstroke is a life-threatening emergency. It may occur suddenly, or follow heat exhaustion — when the latter condition is not promptly corrected.

Sweating Fails

This is sometimes an early warning that may precede other symptoms by an hour or more. The skin is red, hot, and dry. The pulse rate is rapid — well over 100. The person affected becomes listless, confused, or unconscious as the body temperature rises rapidly to 105°F (40.6°C) or higher.

Treatment

Cool the victim **immediately** using any means available. If possible, place the person undressed in a tub of cold water. Otherwise, bring the body temperature down with rubbing alcohol, cold packs, cool water and fanning, etc. Check the body temperature and stop treatment when it reaches 100–101°F (37.8–38.3°C). Recheck the temperature every 30 minutes for 3–4 hours as there will often be a rebound temperature rise. **Get medical help as quickly as possible.**

Exposure to Cold

Frostbite

Exposure to freezing temperatures may cause frostbite. Factors that predispose a person to frostbite include old age and diseases of the blood vessels, cigarette smoking, consumption of alcohol, and use of constrictive clothing or poorly fitting shoes.

Ice crystals form in affected tissues, most often the nose, ears, fingers, and toes. The skin is initially red, with a prickling or itchy sensation. Joints become stiff, their movement progressively slowed. With continuous exposure the skin turns white or yellow with a firm, waxy feel. There may be paralysis, with numbness or pain.

Injury from frostbite is much like a burn and is graded accordingly:

First degree frostbite: freezing of the topmost layer of skin without blistering or peeling. Numbness, redness, and swelling are usually present. Pain is minimal or absent once the area has been rewarmed.

Second degree frostbite: freezing with blistering or peeling, usually with a risk of infection from broken skin. It's often accompanied by pain after rewarming.

Third degree frostbite: freezing that causes complete skin death, with possible injury to deeper tissues. As with burns, there is no pain once the area is rewarmed. There is also no return of color or other sensation.

All second and third degree frostbite requires immediate medical attention.

Prevention of Frostbite

Observe the following precautions:

1. keep clothing dry;

2. don't drink alcohol;

3. wear warm, well-fitted clothing; cover your hands and face, including nose and ears;

4. use a windbreaker;

5. move around to keep circulation going and body heat up — don't stay in one position for a long time;

6. to prevent windburn, use sunscreens with a cream or grease base on any exposed skin

Treatment of Frostbite

When outdoors, cover frostbitten areas with warm, dry clothing. Warm fingers and hands under the armpits. When the toes or heel are affected, it's necessary to remove footwear, dry and rewarm the feet, and re-cover with dry socks. This requires some form of shelter, which should be sought as soon as possible once any frostbite occurs.

Rewarm frostbitten areas quickly to minimize injury. This should

never be done by rubbing them (especially with snow!) or with dry heat, as from a campfire. Because of decreased sensation, either method can unwittingly cause further damage.

Procedure for rewarming frostbitten tissue

Place the affected area in water heated to 100–104°F (37.8–40°C). This should feel hot, but not so hot that prolonged immersion causes pain or burning. Test the water first with an elbow or other area with normal sensation. If water is not available, wrap the affected areas in warm blankets or additional clothing.

Stop rewarming when the skin becomes pink or feeling returns. Exercise fingers and toes to increase circulation. Hot coffee, chocolate, tea, soup, or other nonalcoholic beverages will help increase body temperature. After rewarming, elevate an affected extremity to reduce swelling.

Rewarming shouldn't be done while there is a risk of re-exposure to frostbite. Wait instead until a shelter is found where warmth and proper care can be maintained.

Other guidelines:

1. avoid alcoholic beverages (they increase heat loss);

2. leave blisters unbroken to protect against infection;

3. use sterile gauze or vaseline gauze between toes and fingers to keep them separated if needed;

4. protect against infection in the same manner as for equivalent burn injuries. If the skin is broken, apply antibiotic ointment and cover with a sterile, non-stick dressing such as vaseline gauze.

After rewarming, get medical attention immediately for any second or third degree injury. Signs include:

1. blistering or broken skin;

2. moist, oozing skin with pain or swelling;

3. areas which remain white, gray, numb or cool.

Following injury from frostbite, watch for secondary bacterial infection (see pp. 104–105).

Hypothermia

Hypothermia — when body temperature falls below normal — occurs due to overexposure to the cold. Alcohol consumption is frequently a contributing cause. Victims of accidents, and especially near drownings, often suffer from hypothermia, but excessive heat loss can happen to anyone who is poorly clothed, tired, and hungry on cold, wet, windy days. Diabetics, the elderly, and people with cardiovascular disease are particularly vulnerable to the cold.

The earliest sign of hypothermia is shivering. It may become uncontrollable and then, after several hours, stop completely as the stores of fuel for the muscles (glycogen) are used up. Progressive symptoms of hypothermia are slurred speech, mental confusion, and inappropriate behavior, followed by fatigue, sleepiness, unconsciousness, and death.

Prevention

Be prepared for cold, wet, or windy weather. "Keep warm, keep moving, and keep dry." Wear proper clothing, in layers, which allow you to add or remove garments as needed to keep warm or to avoid unnecessary sweating. Wool clothing retains heat even when wet, and a wind breaker may be crucial to minimize wind chill. Protect your hands, feet, and especially your head from the cold. Wet clothing should be replaced as soon as possible with dry garments. Eat well, carry snacks, and get plenty of rest, as hunger and fatigue increase your vulnerability to cold weather.

Treatment

Always treat the hypothermic person gently. Never rewarm a person too quickly as this can cause heart problems which may be fatal. First obtain shelter. Replace wet clothing with dry. Use a blanket or sleeping bag to warm the person up. Apply insulated hot water bottles, if available, to the neck, groin, and chest. Be careful not to burn the skin. As an alternative use your own body heat by snuggling close to the person if required. Obtain medical help as quickly as possible.

Surviving Animal Hazards

18

Marine Animal Hazards — Stings

Stingrays and Other Fish _Scorpion Fish._

Stings from fish with venomous spines are fairly common. They can occur from a variety of species with local or widespread geographic distribution. All have one or more bony spines covered with an envenoming sheath.

Stingrays cause most incidents as they often nestle in shallow, sandy bays or near beaches when warm waters are likely to be shared by bathers. When disturbed, the serrated spine at the base of their lashing tail may cause either a ragged cut or a small puncture wound. Frequently part of the sheath, or on rare occasions even a broken spine, remains embedded in the tissues. All of this material must be removed.

Other species with venomous spines include dogfish, catfish, weeverfish (in the Atlantic and Mediterranean), scorpionfish (widely found in tropical and temperate seas, especially around coral reefs), and stonefish. The latter is a coral reef dweller of the tropical Indian and Pacific oceans.

Symptoms

From any of these fish, tissue damage may occur locally at the site of the sting. The main effect though is immediate and severe pain. Without treatment it may increase in intensity for up to an hour or more, then subside over several hours or even days. Deaths from stonefish have occured.

Treatment

The toxins of all these species are heat sensitive. The most effective treatment for stings is immersion of the affected part in hot water. The water should be as hot as can be tolerated without causing a burn. Relief from pain is usually instantaneous.

Soaking should continue for 60–90 minutes or until most of the pain is gone. To maintain an effective but tolerable water temperature, it's best to let the injured person regulate the addition of hot water to the soaks. This reduces the possibility of a burn injury.

Take 1 or 2 aspirin or Tylenol up to 4 times a day for pain. Obtain a tetanus booster if needed, and watch for secondary infection. If parts of the sheath or spine remain, obtain medical help for their removal. Ragged cuts may require suturing, which should be done within 6–8 hours of the injury.

Prevention

If caught when fishing, cut scorpionfish off the line and never handle them. Avoid stingrays by shuffling your feet noisily through flat, sandy bottoms. Don't step, run, or jump in suspect areas.

One of the authors, crossing a shallow channel in Baja California waters known to be infested with stingrays, nonetheless suffered a sting and laceration in spite of faithfully doing the "stingray shuffle." Further protective measures were then copied from a local group of research scientists. They employed a long stick, waving it through the water and sand to clear a path ahead of them in the shallow channels.

Jellyfish   CORAL ~~RASH~~ CUTS,

Jellyfish have tentacles covered with nematocysts – microscopic envenomating stingers. A single tentacle may fire hundreds of these on contact. Only a few actually penetrate the skin, creating a red raised welt or lesion, usually in one or more discontinuous lines surrounded by inflamed tissue.

Symptoms

Pain may be severe and itching is common. Occasionally there may be headache, nausea, weakness, sweating, and watering of the eyes and nose.

Prevention

You can often avoid incidents by knowledge of the seasonal occurrence of jellyfish in local areas, and by noting the presence of jellyfish washed ashore. These shouldn't be handled. Nematocysts are capable of discharging their poison for up to several hours out of the water.

Treatment

Pour ocean water over the injured area. Don't rinse with fresh water or let remaining bits of tentacle dry out, as this causes more nematocysts to discharge into the skin. If present, remove the tentacles with gloved hands or an instrument such as a knife blade or piece of wood. Saturate the area with either a mixture of baking soda and water for 10 minutes, or vinegar or Domeboro's solution for 30 minutes. Then sprinkle baking soda, flour, or dry sand on the injured area. Scrape, don't rub, this off with a knife blade or other instrument. Wash the area again with salt water. Apply Itch Balm Plus to reduce itching, swelling, and pain. In Australia, antivenom is available for treatment of stings from certain species of jellyfish.

Stinging Corals and Sea Anemones

If you touch stinging corals and sea anemones, they can produce a localized red rash. If necessary, treat as indicated for jellyfish stings.

Cone Shells

Cone shells found in tropical and subtropical regions can inject poison through a single, dart-like tooth. Shell collectors are the most frequent victims. Injuries can occur through clothing, such as a shirt, blouse, or pants pocket.

Symptoms may include localized pain, redness, and numbness at the site of injection. Giddiness, double-vision, difficulty in swallowing or speaking, and difficulty in breathing can occur in severe reactions. Recovery is usual, although fatal respiratory failure has occurred.

Treatment

First aid measures are of little value. In areas where highly toxic reactions have been noted, primarily in the Indian ocean and South Pacific, obtain medical attention.

Other Marine Hazards

Sea Urchins

Sea urchins are found worldwide. Their spines can break off in the skin, causing intense local pain and inflammation.

Treatment

Remove spines immediately or they may cause infection or destructive tissue changes. Deeply imbedded spines may require surgical removal under local anesthesia.

If superficial spines can't be pulled or worked out, they can sometimes be dissolved by vinegar soaks, 3–4 times a day for 10–20 minutes. Apply wet vinegar compresses between soaks. After spines are removed, clean the wound thoroughly and watch for secondary infection.

Ciguatera Fish Poisoning

Poisoning can occur from eating certain tropical reef fish, usually between 35° north and south latitude. The fish most often involved are red snapper, grouper, barracuda, amberjack, surgeonfish, sea bass, and moray eel. Toxin is especially concentrated in the eggs (roe).

Ciguatera poisoning occurs sporadically in all subtropical and tropical areas of the Pacific and Indian oceans, and in the West Indies. Outbreaks are episodic, often thought to occur after storms, changes in currents, or other natural or even man-made disturbances of the coral reef systems.

Prevention

Unfortunately there's no way to identify affected fish, and the toxin itself is not destroyed by heat. The only preventive measure is to avoid eating large reef fish or those fish in the area known to be toxic.

Symptoms

Ciguatera poisoning involves some very distinctive symptoms, usually occuring 2–6 hours after ingestion of the toxic fish. These include:

- tingling or numbness of the mouth;
- dizziness, blurred vision, or temporary blindness;
- reversal of hot and cold sensations.

When present, these neurological symptoms can be disabling for weeks, months, or even years. Other common symptoms are:

- diarrhea, vomiting, and abdominal cramps;
- sweating, chills, muscle and joint pain.

In very severe cases, death may occur from respiratory paralysis.

Treatment

Treatment measures are primarily supportive. Obtain medical care if symptoms suggest ciguatera poisoning after eating reef fish.

Spiders and Scorpions

Spider Bites

Spiders are almost universally venomous, but only a few have fangs long or strong enough to penetrate human skin. Among these, the two most often responsible for injury are the black widow spider and the brown recluse or violin spider. Black widows are large, shiny black spiders with a red hourglass marking on their abdomens. Brown or violin spiders are light brown in color, marked with a violin shape on their backs. They are usually less than 1/2 inch long. Fortunately, bites can often be prevented by observing a few precautions.

Prevention

Use gloves to protect the hands when working in areas commonly inhabited by spiders. These include woodpiles, garages, sheds, barns, and other rustic structures. If living or camping in rural areas, check clothing and shoes before putting them on. Netting used at night to prevent mosquito bites will also protect against other insects, including spiders.

In some rural areas, black widow bites occur more frequently in men than women. The spiders often establish webs in the darkness under outhouse seat covers, and they are sufficiently territorial to attack any anatomy which invades their space. Use a stick or broomhandle to periodically dismantle these webs. The silk is very strong, tacky, and adherent, and can be easily rolled up onto the stick and discarded. Otherwise, exercise appropriate caution. This is a rude way to start the day after leisurely morning coffee.

Treatment

Many bites attributed to spiders are actually caused by mosquitos, fleas, bedbugs, ticks, or other insects. If a spider bite is witnessed, capture the spider in a jar or other container if possible. Obtain medical evaluation, taking the spider with you for identification. Ice placed on the bite often helps to reduce pain.

Any bite which becomes ulcerated (crater-like) requires medical treatment. This may indicate a bite from the brown or violin spider. Whether or not from a spider bite **any ulcerated skin lesion requires medical evaluation.**

Scorpions

Most scorpions are small, nocturnal, and not particularly shy about

haring human space or accessories. This includes shoes, pants, sleeping
ags, and bed linen. As with spider bites, many scorpion stings can be
revented by observing a few precautions.

revention

Encounters with scorpions are more likely at night, particularly after
ain or periods of high humidity. Always check bedding at night before re-
iring. Anything crawling on you in the dark should be quickly flicked or
rushed off rather than swatted or smashed. Mosquito netting might even
e necessary at night when camping in some remote areas. In the morning,
nspect and shake out shoes, socks, pants, and other apparel before use.

Most stings occur to the hands or feet. Wear gloves and boots when
andling or moving rocks, logs, firewood, or lumber, or working around
heds or barns.

reatment

The majority of stings, especially in adults, cause only a local reaction
vith redness, swelling, or pain. Apply ice to the sting to reduce pain, and
eep the area below the level of the heart. **If more severe symptoms de-
elop, get medical attention as soon as possible.** Antivenom is availa-
le locally in parts of the world where it's sometimes needed, primarily
1exico, North Africa, India, and the Middle East. Be especially cautious
n these areas.

Stings from Flying Insects

Bees, wasps, hornets, yellow jackets, and ants of the order *hymenop-
era* are a major threat to hypersensitive individuals because of anapha-
axis, a fatal allergic reaction. In the nonallergic, stings may be painful
ut are not life-threatening. The pain is immediate, quickly followed by
welling and redness which may last 2–3 days. Symptoms subside
radually.

Removal of a Stinger

Any stinger left in the skin should be carefully teased, scraped, or
licked out with a pin, pointed knife, or fingernail. **Don't** use tweezers or
ingers. This is likely to squeeze out more venom from the poison sac at-
ached to the stinger.

reatment

Use the "Extractor" in your first aid kit to suction out as much venom as possible. Then apply an ice pack to the site to relieve pain and slow absorption of the toxin, and elevate an affected extremity to reduce swelling. An antihistamine may help reduce swelling and pain. Take Benadryl 25–50 mg. or Atarax 25 mg. orally, every 6 hours as needed.

Soothing lotions such as calamine, Domeboro's solution, or a paste of baking soda and water applied to the sting often help to relieve discomfort. Applying raw onion to the site is reputed to be effective — worth a try in a pinch.

For severe swelling, obtain medical evaluation and treatment.

Hypersensitivity Reactions

Increasingly severe responses to subsequent stings indicate hypersensitivity reactions. Each sting further sensitizes the individual. A local reaction greater than 6 inches (15 cm) across, and redness, swelling, or itching in areas other than the sting site, are early signs of allergic reaction. Headache, nausea, abdominal pain or cramps, and weak rapid pulse, wheezing, or labored breath are signs of advancing severity.

Even with no prior history of allergy, **it's best to get medical attention immediately for any generalized reaction**, including skin reactions away from the sting area. There's a possibility of a life-threatening progression of symptoms.

Treatment of Hypersensitivity Reactions

In addition to the measures previously described, apply a loosely constricting band 3–4 inches above a sting on an extremity. Make sure 1 or 2 fingers can easily be slipped underneath and a pulse can be felt in the hand or foot beyond. Loosen this for 1 minute out of every 10, and move it 2–4 inches above any swelling that occurs. **Obtain transportation to medical care immediately.** Obtain an allergy kit for future use.

**Emergency treatment for stings in
known hypersensitive individuals**
If you're stung, use your allergy kit as directed, or follow these steps:

1. Immediately give the injectable epinephrine.

2. Take the oral antihistamine (usually 50 mg. of Benadryl).

3. Apply the loosely constricting band 3–4 inches above a sting on an extremity as previously described.

4. Remove the stinger if present by flicking, not squeezing. Then use the "Extractor" to remove the venom.

5. Apply ice or a cold compress.

6. Get medical attention promptly, keeping the affected area *below the level of the heart*.

Use of epinephrine

Don't use inhalants. Absorption is too low to counteract a serious allergic reaction. Epinephrine **must** be injected. If unsure about or reluctant to use the epinephrine injection, **use it anyway**. The oral antihistamine alone will not save your life in a severe reaction, but epinephrine will. In severe reactions, wheezing or respiratory difficulty is an ominous sign and can develop within 5 minutes of the sting. Oral medications will not begin to work before 15–45 minutes. Effective first aid requires both medications if you have a history of allergic reaction. After using the epinephrine, immediate medical attention is still needed for further evaluation and treatment. If you have angina, **don't** use the epinephrine without the prior consent of your physician.

Centipedes and Millipedes

Centipedes

Some of the larger centipedes can bite, causing a sudden, painful local reaction with redness and swelling. This usually subsides within 48 hours, and rarely is there tissue damage or infection.

Treatment

Use ice or a cold compress on the site to reduce pain. Apply a topical steroid cream (1% hydrocortisone cream) or Itch Balm Plus if needed to reduce swelling and inflammation. Take Benadryl, 25–50 mg. orally twice a day for 1–2 days, and one or two aspirin up to 4 times a day as needed for discomfort.

Millipedes

Millipedes don't bite, but if you handle them, they may secrete a toxin that causes burning and itching. Some species can spray a highly irritating toxin that may cause acute inflammation of the eyes.

Treatment

Use soap and water to thoroughly clean the affected skin. Don't use rubbing alcohol. Apply a topical steroid ointment (1% hydrocortisone) or Itch Balm Plus to the skin if there is redness, swelling, or irritation. Benadryl and aspirin can be taken as indicated above if necessary to reduce inflammation and discomfort.

If toxin is sprayed or rubbed into the eyes, immediately irrigate the eyes with large amounts of water. Obtain medical attention.

Allergic Reactions

If an allergic reaction occurs, follow the procedure for using a bee sting allergy kit if one is available. Then get medical help.

Snakebite

Like some of the tropical diseases, snakebite is primarily an occupational hazard. In industrialized countries most bites occur to snake handlers. Elsewhere, particularly in the tropics, farmers or others who work the land in rural areas are the likely victims of venomous land snakes. Net fishermen are the most frequent victims of sea snakes.

The possibility of snakebite should not be of great concern unless you plan to spend extended time traveling or working in rural areas where snakes are a known hazard. Even then, by following suitable precautions and knowing emergency medical procedures, you should be reasonably safe from this hazard.

Prevention

1. Avoid the unnecessary capture, killing, or harassment of snakes.
2. Always wear closed shoes and protective clothing outdoors in rural areas.
3. Take clear paths and avoid tall grass, bushes, or heavy groundcover and walk slowly.
4. Keep hands and feet out of places that can't be seen, as when climbing ledges or stepping over logs.
5. Inspect clothes, shoes, and bedding before use when camping.
6. When walking at night, wear shoes and use a flashlight.
7. Know the first aid measures for snakebites.
8. **Know the location of the nearest clinic or source of anti-venom.**
9. When fishing, always cut sea snakes from a fishing line, **never** handle them.

Snakebite — an Unpredictable Event

The degree of poisoning from the bite of a venomous snake isn't predictable. The amount of venom injected and the individual's response to it vary greatly. About 30% of bites from venomous snakes are "dry bites" — no venom is injected at all.

For purposes of treating snakebite assume that all bites are venomous until proven otherwise. Medical attention should be obtained as quickly as possible. Antivenom is always the treatment of choice when poisoning from snakebite has occurred. The quicker you obtain it, the better the chance of minimizing tissue damage or preventing death.

Types of Poisonous Snakes

There are three broad classes of poisonous snakes: vipers, cobras, and sea snakes. Vipers are represented in North America by rattlesnakes; in Central and South America by the tropical rattlesnake, fer de lance, and bushmaster; and in Central and South Africa by the common puff adder. Cobras, such as the yellow cobra, spitting cobra, Egyptian cobra, and black mamba, are present in Central and South Africa. Cobras are also found in the Far East, including India and Southeast Asia. Sea snakes are found in the Pacific Ocean, but not in the Atlantic.

Viper Poisoning

Bites that result in immediate local swelling and edema (accumulation of fluid) are usually unmistakable signs of viper poisoning. These signs appear within 3–5 minutes, often after only a minute or two. Pain, redness, and bleeding at the site of the fang marks are common. Other signs of envenomation include a metallic taste in the mouth, and tingling in the back, ears, or around the mouth. If no symptoms develop within 30 minutes following a viper bite, *it's unlikely that envenomation has occurred.*

When viper poisoning does occur, untreated cases may lead to progressive swelling and destruction of local tissue. In severe cases, there may be generalized symptoms such as vomiting, abnormal bleeding, difficulty breathing, circulatory collapse, and death.

Cobra and Sea Snake Poisoning

Unlike vipers, the bites of sea snakes and most cobras produce little or no local swelling. When these symptoms do occur, it's usually not for 1–2 hours or more following the bite.

Severe sea snake poisoning may produce generalized muscle aches within 1-1/2 – 3 hours. This can progress to muscle paralysis and death.

Cobra venom may cause numbness or tingling and weakness of the bitten extremity. Drooping eyelids are often the first sign of general poisoning, with slurred speech, increasing muscle weakness, lethargy, and paralysis. This may progress to respiratory failure. Signs of cobra poisoning can occur within 15 minutes, or be delayed up to 10 hours.

First Aid for Snakebite

First aid recommendations have changed over the years. The use of ice or cold water on a bitten extremity is no longer advised, since it may increase rather than decrease local tissue damage. In addition, a snakebite victim should **never** drink alcoholic beverages. It will only speed absorption of venom into the general circulation.

Tourniquets vs. Loosely Constrictive Bands

The majority of snakebites occur on the extremities. Use of a tourniquet — a band so tight that it interferes with the arterial blood flow — isn't recommended. It may cause the needless loss of an entire limb.

However, a loosely constricting band applied 2–4 inches above the bite may be helpful. It's purpose is to restrict the flow of blood and lymph back to the heart. This may delay symptoms of general poisoning until antivenom can be obtained.

Loosen the constricting band enough that a finger can easily be slipped underneath. You should be able to feel a pulse in the foot, ankle, or wrist below the band. If used, the constricting band should be loosened for 1 minute out of every 10 and reapplied 2–4 inches above any swelling that occurs.

Removal of Venom Through Suctioning

The best tool for removing snake venom is "The Extractor." It creates more powerful suction than either traditional suction cups or oral suctioning. Application requires use of only one hand; no cutting or incisions are required. The only thing better than 1 of these devices for snakebites is possibly 2 of them. This might be required for bites from large snakes, where the fang marks are widely separated.

If an "Extractor" isn't available use any snakebite suction device. Or use your mouth, provided there are no open sores or gum disease — this could poison you too. Suctioning is a useful first aid measure only in the initial 20–30 minutes following the bite. After this time there is no evidence that suctioning provides any benefit.

Incision of a Snakebite

Incision of a snakebite prior to suctioning is still a matter of controversy. Its use, in conjunction with a loosely constrictive band above the bite, is governed by the following considerations:

. It's useful only for poisoning from vipers, not from cobras, coral, or sea snakes.

. It's used only on bites of the extremities, never on the face or trunk.

. It should not be used if the victim can be transported within 30 minutes to a facility where antivenom is available. In this case, it only delays effective treatment.

Procedure

If incision and suction are indicated, wipe the area clean. Use an alcohol pad if available. Make a single shallow cut over each fang mark **just deep enough to cut through the skin**. The cut shouldn't be more than 1/16th inch (2–3 millimeters) deep or 1/8th inch (1/4 to 1/2 centimeters) long. **Don't make an 'X'. Don't make more than 1 or 2 incisions.**

This cut should be parallel to the long axis of the extremity — that is, parallel to the tendons, arteries, nerves, veins, long bones, and muscles. **Never cut into or across these structures.**

Suction for 20–30 minutes only. After you complete the incision and suction, treat as for any skin wound. Wash thoroughly, and apply hydrogen peroxide and antibacterial ointment. Cover with a clean or sterile dressing.

Other First Aid Measures

In most cases of snakebite the victim will need reassurance and calming. After moving at least 30 feet away from where the bite occurred, have the person lie down and rest. After other first aid measures, immobilize the bitten extremity with a sling or splint and carry the victim, if possible, to the nearest source of antivenom.

Always keep the bitten area *below* the level of the heart.

Even if poisoning does not occur and antivenom is unnecessary, treat bites like any other puncture wound. Obtain a tetanus shot if necessary and watch for secondary infection.

 **Quick Reference:**

Emergency First Aid Treatment
of Venomous Snakebite

1. Assume that every bite is a serious medical emergency and immediately begin first aid measures.

2. Move away from the snake, then sit or lie down, remain calm, avoid unnecessary movement, and keep the bitten area below the level of the heart.

3. Apply a constricting band about 2 inches above the bite. Move it progressively above any swelling that occurs.

4. Use the Sawyer Extractor or other available snakebite suction device, or use oral suctioning, for 30 minutes. If a known source of antivenom is less than 30 minutes away, don't waste time with oral suctioning. Proceed immediately to medical care.

5. Remove all rings, jewelry, or other constrictive items from the affected extremity.

6. Head directly for medical help. Immobilize the bitten area **below** heart level. Carry or assist the victim to help, by stretcher if possible. If alone, walk slowly towards help, resting periodically.

7. Drink plenty of fluids to avoid dehydration.

8. **Never** use ice on a snakebite.

Dealing with Insomnia   <u>19</u>

At one time or another almost everyone experiences difficulty falling or staying asleep. Causes can be emotional (anxiety, grief, or depression), physiological (stimulants such as the caffeine in coffee, colas, or tea), or environmental (noisy neighbors and barking dogs).

In Third World countries you may encounter unaccustomed barriers to a good night's sleep: strange hotels, dripping faucets, lumpy matresses with sinkhole springs, hot sticky tropical nights, buzzing mosquitos, itchy bites or rashes, crowing roosters, and even intestinal parasites. Just thinking about it is enough to keep you awake at night.

Treatment

It's important to remember that a night without sleep will not cause any harm. Worrying about lost sleep can easily entertain you past daybreak.

The easiest bad habit to acquire following recurrent insomnia is the use of alcohol as a sedative at night. This produces a poor quality, unrestful sleep. The accumulating anxiety about restless sleep can continue the pattern of alcohol use in a vicious circle. Use of alcohol frequently wakes people up in the middle of the night with dehydration, thirst, and the need to urinate. Returning to sleep is often a struggle without additional quantities of alcohol. It's easy to see that this is a self-defeating and unhealthy endeavor.

Don't

1. Drink alcohol regularly as a sedative before bedtime.
2. Drink stimulants with caffeine (coffee, colas, many teas) in the evening.
3. Take an afternoon nap.
4. Use prescription or over-the-counter sleeping pills on a regular basis, as they may be habit forming.
5. Combine alcohol with sleeping pills or other sedatives — ever.

Do:

1. Establish a regular time to retire for the night and a relaxing nighttime ritual. This may be showering or bathing, reading a book or magazine, or other quiet activity.
2. Get out of bed if you're not sleepy. Do something productive but not overly stimulating — listen to the radio, or do some light reading by low, soft light.

As a last resort, an antihistamine that produces drowsiness as a side effect may help. Try 25–50 mg. of Benadryl an hour or so before bedtime. This may cause a "hangover" feeling the next morning. Another medication used occasionally for insomnia is a sleeping pill, Halcion (triazolam). Avoid regular use as it may be habit-forming.

Indications for Medical Evaluation

When nothing works and insomnia continues, sleeplessness may be due to intestinal parasites. This can occur with or without other symptoms. Stool exams should be obtained (see Chapter 6, "Quick Reference — Stool Exams," p. 150; if positive for parasites see the same page.) For chronic insomnia obtain medical evaluation.

Returning Home

20

Following even a brief visit out of the country, travelers with symptoms of illness may require medical evaluation. Get medical attention for the following:

1. Any recurrent fever. This requires immediate evaluation. Fever accompanied by jaundice, or which occurs after handling parrots or ingesting unpasteurized milk products, also requires immediate attention.

2. Diarrhea or other intestinal problems such as bloating, abdominal cramping, nausea, vomiting, and constipation. These symptoms require stool tests for parasites (stool O & P) and bacteria (stool C & S — culture and sensitivity). You may also need a blood test for hepatitis.

3. Any other symptom of illness, including a skin rash, requires evaluation.

Notify your medical provider of your travel itinerary, especially after visiting areas of risk for malaria, schistosomiasis, or other diseases. If you took any medication prophylactically (preventively), or received treatment or medications for any illness while traveling, provide this information to your physician.

Routine Tests

Even if symptoms of illness aren't present, some routine tests are desirable to make sure you weren't accompanied by unwanted stowaways.

For Brief Travel up to 3–4 weeks

No tests are necessary in the absence of any symptoms.

For Travel of 1–6 Months

The following routine tests are recommended:

1. stool test for parasites (O & P);
2. TB skin test (PPD) 2–3 months after returning home. If positive, a chest x-ray should then be done to ensure there is no active disease.

   If there were any casual sexual contacts, a blood test (RPR) for syphillis is also recommended.

For Travel of 6 Months or More

In addition to the above routine tests, we recommend a physical exam as well as the following:

1. blood tests — a complete blood count (CBC) and liver enzymes;
2. urinalysis;
3. dental checkup.

For Travel of More Than 1 Year:

1. If over age 50, a stool test to check for blood;

   For women:

1. a pap smear and breast exam;
2. if over age 50, a mammogram.

Reentry Shock:
Returning Home After Extended Travel

Coming home to familiar surroundings may seem mundane compared to the challenge of living in a foreign culture. Surprisingly, it can be just as demanding. Some studies suggest that the easier it is adjusting to life in a foreign country, the more difficult it may be readjusting to life back home. This phenomenon is called "reentry shock."

Some symptoms are remarkably similar to culture shock. These include feelings of frustration, isolation, depression, or anger, often directed at your own culture. As with culture shock, symptoms develop slowly and may intensify over time.

One source of frustration is the difficulty others, including family and friends, are likely to have relating to your experiences. No matter how intense and important these seem, they may simply strike others as irrelevant. People may treat time spent outside the country as an interruption in your life, rather than as an integral part of it.

New perceptions about your homeland and other countries are apt to be met with polite tolerance, routine indifference, or outright hostility. People may also simply fail to understand. It may be that it is inherently difficult to share the ways in which you have outgrown your own culture's biases with people who haven't.

You may also have returned to a land less familiar than anticipated. It's not uncommon to see your own culture in a new, perhaps profoundly different light. This too can produce a sense of isolation and alienation, especially if there's no one with whom to share thoughts and feelings.

As perceptions of your own culture change, so may your role within it. Returned travelers frequently redefine their goals and priorities, or reevaluate their educational and career choices.

It is easy to mourn for the loss of a foreign country as if for a good friend, which it may well have become. The loss of excitement and adventure, freedom and independence, responsibilities or lack thereof, may seem at first inconsolable. Thoughts of return to the foreign country are common. In fact, return trips often prove cathartic, providing a needed perspective.

As with culture shock, coping with reentry shock requires patience. It takes time to integrate "foreign" experiences, to realize the meaning of those experiences within the context of your own culture. It takes time to assimilate new perceptions, reorder priorities, gain perspective.

The discomfort of reentry shock is one measure of the magnitude of change that has taken place. It is also an integral part of an ongoing process of change and growth.

Part III

Medications and How To Use Them

None of the medications listed here should be taken unless under the direction of a physician, except when medical care is unavailable and circumstances warrant. General guidelines are provided in this section for medications mentioned in Parts I and II. The prescribed doses are only for acute illness in adults. They are not intended for long term use. Know the proper use and administration of any medication taken while you're traveling. Be familiar with contraindications and side effects. Follow any special instructions.

When possible the generic name of a drug has been provided along with the trade or brand name. Trade names are capitalized, generic names are not. The trade names of drugs in foreign countries often differ from U.S. trade names. If trouble is encountered finding a particular medicine, show the pharmacist or doctor the generic name. With this information it is often possible to obtain the correct medication.

How To Use Part III

Four categories of information are provided on each medication:

1. **Uses** A single medication can often be used for a variety of conditions.

The uses covered here are only for those illnesses discussed in Parts I and II.

2. **Side effects** The side effects mentioned are the most common ones associated with the medication. They may or may not occur. **For any unusual or severe reaction, stop the medication and seek medical advice.**

3. **Contraindications** If a condition listed under contraindications applies to you, don't take the medication.

4. **How To Take** Information is provided on the best way to take the medication for the maximum benefit with the fewest possible side effects.

Important Considerations

Dosages

All dosages are for adults only. When one medication is used to treat several different illnesses, dosages may vary. Check the specific illness in Parts I and II for the exact dosage.

In some cases, dosages must be calculated according to body weight. These dosages are usually given as milligrams per kilogram of body weight. To determine weight in kilograms, divide your weight in pounds by 2.2 (there are 2.2 pounds per kilogram). A pound-kilogram conversion table can be found in Appendix D, p. 321. If you're unsure of a dosage or dosage calculation, get help before taking the medication.

Most of the medications discussed in the book are taken by mouth; instructions read "take orally." A few medications and vaccinations must be given by intramuscular injection, abbreviated "IM."

Use of Multiple Medications

As a general rule, don't use more than one medication for the treatment of an illness or its symptoms, unless prescribed by a doctor or explicitly recommended in the book. This is especially true for antibiotics. Drugs taken together may interact harmfully. If a drug reaction does occur there is no way to tell which drug was responsible — all must be discontinued.

When taking medications regularly for chronic conditions, check with your doctor before departure. Find out if there are any drugs which shouldn't be taken in combination with your regular medications.

Routine Contraindications

Contraindications listed as "routine" for any drug in this section include the following:

History of allergic reaction

Prior to treatment, inform the medical practitioner, dentist, or pharmacist of any food and drug allergies you have. Read the ingredients in every medication before taking it. If you have ever had an allergic reaction to a medication or to any of its ingredients, **don't** use it!

Pregnancy

Inform any doctor, dentist, or pharmacist you consult that you're pregnant. Avoid all medications unless specifically prescribed by a doctor. Definitive answers about drug safety during pregnancy and breastfeeding are frequently unavailable. Under medical supervision a medication may be prescribed when the practitioner judges that it is safe or the benefits outweigh the potential risks.

Breastfeeding

Avoid all medications unless specifically prescribed by a doctor.

Allergic and Other Adverse Reactions

Allergic or other adverse drug reactions can take many forms. If a skin rash or any unexpected or severe side effect occurs while taking a medication, **stop taking it immediately. Obtain medical evaluation.**

Photosensitivity Reactions

Some topical and oral medications sensitize the skin to react strongly when exposed to sunlight. There are 2 common reactions:

1. **severe sunburn** (phototoxicity) — with redness, swelling, blisters, peeling, and increased pigmentation only on light-exposed areas of skin, usually within 6 hours of exposure; or

2. **allergic skin rash** — either hives, or a red, raised, scaly or blistery rash which can occur anywhere on the body, usually within 24–48 hours of sun exposure.

Don't stop a medication because of a photosensitivity reaction. Stay out of the sun to prevent the rash from becoming worse. Photosensitivity reactions can be prevented or decreased by using a sunscreen which blocks out ultraviolet "A" (UV-A) sunlight. See Part I, "Sunscreens."

Treatment of photosensitivity reactions — Use cool compresses or cool baths, topical steroid ointments (hydrocortisone), or Itch Balm Plus. For severe reactions, get medical attention for possible oral steroid therapy.

Photosensitizing medications — The following is a partial list of medications that may cause a photosensitivity reaction.

Antibiotics:
doxycycline
nalidixic acid
sulfa drugs (Fansidar, Bactrim, Gantrisin)
tetracyclines

Anti-inflammatory drugs (nonsteroid):
Clinoril (sulindac)
Feldene (piroxicain)
Naprosyn (naproxen)

Antiparasitic drugs:
Bitin (bithionol)
Povan (pyrvinium pamoate)
quinine

Sunscreens:
Some sunscreens may cause photo-sensitivity reactions!

Other medications:
Some anticancer drugs, diuretics, and diabetic (oral hypoglycemic) medications may cause photo-sensitivity reactions. If you're taking regular medications for hypertension, diabetes, or cancer, check with your doctor prior to any intense or prolonged sun exposure.

Index of Part III Medications by Category

The following is a list of all medications discussed in Part III, grouped according to usage.

Spectinomycin
Sulfa drugs (sulfonamides)
    Bactrim/Septra (trimethoprim
      and sulfamethoxazole)
    Gantrisin
Tetracycline and doxycycline

Antidiarrheals, p. 281
Diabismul
Donnagel PG
Imodium(loperamide HCl)
Lomotil
Paregoric
Parepectolin
Pepto-Bismol

Antiemetics (to prevent or treat nausea, vomiting), **p. 282**
Antivert/Bonine/Marezine
Compazine (prochlorperazine)
Dramamine (dimenhydrinate)
Pepto-Bismol (see antidiarrheals)
Phenergan (promethazine HCL)
Tigan (trimethobenzamide HCl)
Transderm-Scop (scopolomine)

**Antihistamines and decongestants,
  p. 284**
Actifed
Atarax (hydroxyzine HCl)
Benadryl (diphenhydramine HCl)
Chlor-Trimeton (chlorpheniramine
    maleate)
Drixoral
Dimetapp
Entex LA
Seldane (terfenadine)
Sudafed (pseudoephedrine HCl)

**Anti-inflammatories (Oral,
  nonsteroid), 285**
Aspirin
Clinoril (sulindac)
Dolobid (diflunisal)
Feldene (piroxicam)
Indocin (indomethacin)
Motrin (ibuprofen)

Naprosyn (naproxen)
Tolectin (tolmetin sodium)

Antimalarials, p. 286
Aralen (chloroquine)
Doxycycline
Fansidar
Lariam (mefloquine)
Primaquine phosphate
Quinine sulfate

Antiparasitics, p. 287
Atabrine HCl (quinacrine HCl)
Antepar/Vermizine (piperazine citrate)
Antiminth (pyrantel pamoate)
Biltricide (praziquantel)
Diethyl carbamazine citrate (Hetrazan)
Diodoquin, Floraquin, Yodoxin (diio-
    dohydroxyquin or iodoquinol)
Fasigyn (tinidazole)
Flagyl (metronidazole)
Humatin (paromoycin)
Mintezol (thiabendazole)
Vermox (mebendazole)
Yomesan/Niclocide (niclosamide)

Antispasmodics, p. 289
Belladenal
Donnatal

Antivirals, p. 290
Zovirax (acyclovir)

Bronchial dilators, p. 290
Alupent (metaproteranol sulfate)
Brethine (terbutaline sulfate)
Proventil/Ventolin (albuterol)

Contraceptives — Oral, 291
Combination pill
Progesterone-only pill

Dental preparations, p. 292
Cavit
Oil of cloves

Ear medications, p. 292
Cortisporin otic drops

Emetics (to induce vomiting), **p. 292**
Ipecac

Eye medications, p. 292
Bleph 10 (sulfacetamide sodium)
Garamycin ophthalmic (gentamicin sulfate)
Naphcon-A (naphazoline HCl and pheniramine maleate)

Hemorrhoid medications, p. 293
Anusol HC

Menstrual cramping medications, p. 293
Motrin, Advil, Nuprin (ibuprofen)
Naprosyn (naproxen)

Muscle relaxants, p. 294
Flexeril
Parafon Forte
Robaxisal/Robaxin

Nasal medications, p. 294
Afrin

Skin medications (topical) , p. 295
Antibacterials
Antifungal preparations
Antiparasitics (Kwell, Eurax)
Medications for itching (Itch Balm Plus, Domeboro's solution, Calamine)
Steroid creams
Vioform 1%HC (clioquinol and hydrocortisone)

Sleep Medications, p. 297
Benadryl
Halcion (triazolam)
Restoril (temazepam)

Vaginal medications, p. 298
Antifungal creams
Cleocin (clindamycin HCl)
Flagyl (metronidazole)

Altitude Sickness Medications

◆ **Diamox (acetazolamide sodium)**
Use of this medication doesn't eliminate the need for an immediate descent if severe symptoms of altitude sickness occur, such as pulmonary edema (HAPE).

Uses — prevention of altitude sickness

Side effects

cramping in hands and feet	drowsiness
decreased appetite	fatigue
nausea, vomiting, diarrhea	skin rashes
	tingling in extremities
taste alteration, especially carbonated beverages	

Contraindications – routine (see p. 271)
adrenal insufficiency
allergy to sulfa medications
electrolyte imbalance
hypersensitivity to thiazide diuretics
kidney disease
liver disease
lung disease, pulmonary obstruction
use cautiously if taking digoxin or other digitalis medications

How to take — Take orally, with food if stomach upset occurs. Don't take with aspirin, Pepto-Bismol, or sedatives.

Analgesics (Pain-killers)

◆ Aspirin (acetylsalicylic acid)

Aspirin is one of the most useful and underrated of medications. In addition to being a pain killer, it helps reduce swelling — which is frequently one of the causes of pain. It's also an antipyretic (works to bring down fevers).

Aspirin will also slow down the blood clotting mechanism. It should not be used when bleeding or bleeding disorders are present. It should not be used concurrently with other anticoagulants ("blood thinners").

Uses — mild pain relief
reduce fever
reduce inflammation

Side effects — stomach burning (mild to severe)
stop immediately if ringing in the ears occurs while taking aspirin

Contraindications – routine (see p. 271)
ulcers, history of ulcers
use of other anticoagulants such as Coumadin
Aspirin should not be used by children under age 18 either during or immediately following any viral infection (may cause Reyes syndrome)

How to take — Take orally with food or milk to reduce GI side effects. If side effects occur, stop the medication.
Studies have shown that the caffeine in some aspirin preparations may increase the effectiveness of aspirin.

◆ Pyridium (phenazopyridine HCl)

Uses — to stop painful burning sensations in urinary tract infections

Side effects — mild nausea or vomiting (occasionally)
turns urine bright orange (color may stain clothing)

Contraindications – routine (see p. 271)
impaired kidney function

How to take — Take orally with lots of fluids.

◆ Tylenol (acetaminophen)

Uses — mild pain relief
reduce fever

Side effects — liver damage in high doses or prolonged therapy (especially with extra-strength preparations).

Contraindications – routine (see p. 271)
liver disease (hepatitis) or impaired liver function

How to take — Take orally.

◆ Tylenol With Codeine

Uses — moderate to severe pain relief

Side effects — constipation

Contraindications – routine (see p. 271)
liver disease (hepatitis) or impaired liver function

How to take — Take orally with lots of fluids. You may wish to take with prune juice or another natural laxative.

◆ Vicodin (acetaminophen and hydrocodone bitartrate)

Uses — moderate to moderately severe pain

Side effects — anxiety
decreased alertness and coordination
drowsiness
mood changes
nausea, vomiting
sedation

Contraindications – routine (see p. 271)
use cautiously with impaired liver or kidney function, hypothyroidism, or prostate enlargement

How to take — take orally
avoid alcohol
avoid prolonged use as physical and psychological dependence may occur

Antacids

◆ Amphojel, Mylanta, Riopan, Maalox, Tums and Many Others

Uses — Relief of acid indigestion, especially from hot spicy foods. Maalox Plus and Mylanta both contain simethicone, which also makes them useful for flatulence (gas).

Side effects — Antacids with aluminum hydroxide, aluminum carbonate and calcium carbonate may be constipating. Antacids containing primarily magnesium compounds tend to work as a laxative. Read carefully all ingredients before buying.

Contrandications — Anyone on a low salt diet should be careful to avoid antacids containing large amounts of sodium, including Alka Seltzer. Those with low amounts of sodium are Maalox, Mylanta, Riopan and Tums.

How to take — Take orally.

Antibiotics

Antibiotics treat only bacterial infections. They are useless for illnesses due to viruses and other causes. **Never** take antibiotics for routine colds or trivial infections! Even for bacterial infections, antibiotics are **never** to be taken casually. Besides killing bacteria which cause infection, they frequently also kill beneficial bacteria. This sometimes results in still other infections.

Vaginal yeast infections are a common occurrence following use of antibiotics. Women prone to yeast infections may wish to add vaginal yeast medications to their first aid kit.

All broad spectrum antibiotics are capable of causing a potentially serious inflammation of the intestines called pseudomembranous colitis. The condition ranges from minor to life-threatening. It may be indicated by diarrhea which develops either during or immediately following the use of antibiotics, and which fails to respond to treatment for traveler's diarrhea. If this occurs, obtain immediate medical evaluation.

Overuse or misuse of antibiotics can also result in the creation of organisms resistant to the antibiotic — rendering it ineffective. At best, this will complicate or delay treatment. At worst, it may result in serious illness or death.

Use of Antibiotics

Once an antibiotic is started, always take it for the full length of time prescribed. **Finish it!** This helps prevent both recurrence of illness and creation of organisms resistant to the medication. It's dangerous to stop taking antibiotics just because you're feeling better. Stop antibiotics if an allergic reaction occurs.

◆ Cephalosoporins

These are broad-spectrum antibiotics that resemble the penicillins.

Keflex (cephalexin)
Velosef (cephadrine)

Uses — bacterial skin infections

bladder infections
  (cystitis)
pneumonia

bronchitis
otitis media

Side effects

diarrhea

nausea

pseudomembranous
  colitis

upset stomach
vomiting

Contraindications – routine (see p. 271)

If allergic to penicillin, take cephalosporins only under the care of a physician.
Don't take if you had an anaphylactic reaction to penicillin.
Use cautiously in cases of impaired kidney function.

How to take — Take orally. Velosef may be taken with food to decrease stomach irritation.

Rocephin (ceftriaxone sodium)

Uses — gonorrhea
pelvic inflammatory disease (PID)

Side effects

pain and swelling at injection site	diarrhea rash

Contraindications — hypersensitivity allergy to penicillin (see Keflex, Velosef)

How to take — intramuscularly (IM) only under the care of a physician
Apply ice to injection site to treat severe discomfort, or take aspirin or Tylenol for pain

◆ Chloromycetin (chloramphenicol)

This antibiotic should **never** be used in any form for the treatment of trivial or routine infections (cold, influenza, upper respiratory diseases, diarrhea or intestinal disturbances), as a prophylactic agent to prevent infections, or for undiagnosed disorders. **Refuse this medication if prescribed for any of these conditions.** Chloramphenicol can cause a serious or fatal blood disease. **Take this medication only under direct medical supervision.**

◆ Erythromycin

This is a broad-spectrum antibiotic.

Uses — Erythromycin is an alternative to oral penicillin when penicillin allergies are present. It's also an alternative to tetracycline when tetracycline is contraindicated (e.g., during pregnancy or breast-feeding). It's also the antibiotic of choice for mycoplasma pneumonia and campylobacter jejuni. It's also an alternative treatment for vibrio cholerae.

Side effects — nausea, vomiting, diarrhea

Contraindications – routine (see p. 271), concurrent use of Seldane

How to take — Take orally, preferably on an empty stomach. If nausea, vomiting, or diarrhea occur, take with food or milk. **Don't** take Seldane with this antibiotic.

◆ Flagyl (metronidazole)

Flagyl is used mainly for infections by protozoa, but can be used for some bacterial infections.

Uses

bacterial vaginosis	blastocystis hominis
entamoeba histolytic (amoeba)	giardia
Guinea worm (Dracunculus medinensis)	trichomonas vaginitis

Side effects

abdominal cramping	dark urine
gastrointestinal upset	alcohol reaction
headache, dry mouth	metallic taste in
nausea, vomiting, diarrhea	the mouth

stop the medication and obtain medical help for unusual side effects, such as a rash or severe nausea.

Contraindications – routine (see p. 271) active liver disease

How to take — Take orally with food or milk to minimize side effects if necessary.
Don't drink alcohol. Combining alcohol with Flagyl may cause cramps, nausea, vomiting, and severe headache. It's best not to drink alcohol for 24 hours before taking Flagyl and for 48 hours after finishing the medication. Be sure to check for alcohol in other liquid medications such as cough syrups, vitamins, or pain relievers.

◆ Macrodantin (nitrofurantoin macrocrystals)

Uses — bladder infections, especially during pregnancy

Side effects

abdominal pain	decreased appetite
diarrhea	dizziness
drowsiness	headache
nausea, vomiting	

Contraindications – routine (see p. 271)

impaired kidney function	hypersensitivity pregnancy at term
use cautiously with anemia or diabetes	

How to take — take orally with meals or milk to decrease stomach irritation

Penicillins

There are several classes of penicillins, grouped according to what they treat.

1. Penicillin VK, Penicillin G, Bicillin (benzathene penicillin)
2. Ampicillin, amoxicillin
3. Penicillinase-resistant penicillins

Side effects (all penicillins) — nausea, vomiting, diarrhea

epigastric distress, black "hairy" tongue (more likely with Penicillin VK, Procaine, Penicillin G, and Bicillin)

note: diarrhea occurs much less often with amoxicillin than with ampicillin

Stop using **any** penicillin immediately if a rash develops. This is a sign of allergic reaction to the medication. Obtain medical help as soon as possible. An allergic reaction to penicillin can occur at any time, even if you've taken it with no side effects in the past.

Stop using **any** penicillin if severe diarrhea persists.

Stop using **any** penicillin if wheezing or shortness of breath occur. Obtain medical help immediately. This is a life-threatening emergency.

Contraindications (all penicillins)

1. **All** penicillins are contraindicated if you've had an allergic reaction to *any* penicillin.
2. **All** penicillins are contraindicated if you've had a severe allergic reaction to Keflex, Velosef, Anspor, or any of the class of antibiotics known as cephalosporins. Following mild reactions to these medications, seek medical advice before taking any penicillin.

How to take (all penicillins)

Orally — It's preferable to take penicillin on an empty stomach, 1 hour before or 2 to 3 hours after a meal. If mild nausea, vomiting or diarrhea occur, try taking the medication with food.

By intramuscular injection — Take **only** in a medical setting. Wait 20–30 minutes after any penicillin injection to assure there is no allergic reaction. When used to treat gonorrhea, always take Procaine Penicillin G (IM) with 1 gram of Benemid (probenecid) orally. This increases the effectiveness of the medication.

Penicillin VK (Oral), Procaine Penicillin G (IM), Bicillin (IM)

Oral uses

abscessed or infected gums	impetigo strep throat

Intramuscular uses (IM) — gonorrhea of the cervix, urethra, throat, and rectum are sometimes treated with Procaine Penicillin G, although it is not the drug of choice

syphilis is treated with Bicillin

Ampicillin, Amoxicillin

These are wide-range, broad-spectrum antibiotics. Amoxicillin is absorbed twice as efficiently as ampicillin. It's also more expensive.

Uses — bronchitis

gonorrhea	otitis media
shigella	sinutis
urinary tract infection	typhoid fever

Penicillinase-resistant Penicillins

Cloxacillin (Tegopen)	Dicloxacillin
Nafcillin	Oxacillin

These are used for infections from bacteria resistant to other forms of penicillin, usually skin infections from staph aureus and streptococcus.

Uses —

abcess	boils (furuncles)
carbuncle	cellulitis
impetigo	

◆ Quinolones
Cipro (ciprofloxacin)

Uses —

traveler's diarrhea	dysentery
urinary tract infections	skin infections

Side effects — dizziness
lightheadedness
headache
nausea, vomiting, diarrhea
 photosensitivity reactions

Contraindications – routine (see p. 271)
hypersensitivity to quinolones
use cautiously if there is a history of
 seizures
under age 18

How to take — take orally 2 hours after
eating, if possible
drink plenty of fluids while taking Cipro
avoid taking antacids with aluminum or
 magnesium for 2 hours after taking
 Cipro

Noroxin (norfloxacin)

Uses — traveler's diarrhea
urinary tract infections

Side effects

dizziness	headache
lightheadedness	nausea

Contraindications – routine (see p. 271)
hypersensitivity to quinolones, naladixic
 acid
use cautiously in cases of impaired kidney function or a history of seizures
under age 18

How to take — take orally one hour before or two hours after meals with a
 glass of water
don't take with nitrofurantoin
don't take antacids with or for two hours
 after taking norfloxacin
Drink plenty of fluids while taking
 norfloxacin

◆ Spectinomycin

Uses — This antibiotic is used to treat
urethral, cervical, and rectal gonorrhea.
It's usually reserved for people who are
allergic to penicillin or who have penicil-
lin-resistant gonorrhea.

Note: Gonorrhea is increasingly resistant to both penicillin and tetracycline in
Third World countries.

Side effects

fever, chills	hives
insomnia	nausea
pain at the injection site	

Contraindications – routine (see p. 271)

How to take — It's taken intramuscularly in the buttock, only under the care
of a physician.

◆ Sulfa Drugs
Bactrim, Septra (trimethoprim and sulfamethoxazole).

Bactrim and Septra are identical an
very useful medications. Like other sulfa
preparations they may cause allergic
reactions.

Both products are available in double
strength preparations, designated "DS."
As the designation implies, one DS tablet equals two regular strength tablets
Regular or "DS" tablets can be substituted for one another, but be sure to adjust the number you take accordingly.

Uses

bronchitis	otitis media
shigella infections	pneumonia
skin infections	sinusitis
traveler's diarrhea	typhoid fever
yersinia enterocolica (alternative treatment)	urinary tract infections

Side effects — dizziness
nausea, vomiting, diarrhea
ringing in the ears
stop taking immediately at the first sign
of a skin rash, fever, jaundice, sore
throat, or **any** other adverse reaction.
These may be early indications of a life-
threatening drug reaction.

Contraindications – routine (see p.271)
history of allergy to any sulfa medication
use cautiously with impaired kidney or
 liver function

How to take — Take orally with lots of
fluids to help prevent kidney problems.

Gantrisin (sulfisoxazole)
This is also a sulfa medication.

Uses — urinary tract infections

Side effects — headache
nausea, vomiting, diarrhea

Contraindications – routine (see p. 271)
use cautiously in liver or kidney disease,
or G6PD deficiency

How to take — Take orally on an empty
stomach with at least one full glass of
water or other liquid. If gastrointestinal
upset occurs, take with food.

◆ Tetracycline
Tetracycline is a broad-spectrum antibiotic, one that kills many different bacteria.

Uses

bronchitis	brucellosis
campylobactor jejuni	chancroid
(alternative treatment)	chlamydia
cholera	gonorrhea
granuloma inguinale	LGV
nonspecific urethritis	malaria
pelvic inflammatory	pneumonia
disease	relapsing fever
psittacosis/ornithosis	sinusitis
syphillis	tick fever
traveler's diarrhea	typhus
urinary tract infections	vibrio cholerae
vibrio parahaemolyticus	

Side effects — nausea, vomiting,
diarrhea
photosensitivity reactions

Contraindications – routine (see p. 271)
a history of kidney problems (renal
insufficiency)

How to take — Take orally on an
empty stomach with a full glass of liquid.
Don't take with milk or other dairy products, or with antacids, potassium, or
iron. These all interfere with absorption
of the medicine.
Take at least 1 hour before meals or 2
hours after a meal. If using antacids,
take them at least 3 hours after the
tetracycline.

Doxycycline
This is a long-acting form of tetracycline. It can be substituted for tetracycline in the treatment of any disease. It
doesn't need to be taken as often, but is
usually more expensive.
The side effects and contraindications
are the same as for tetracycline, although doxycycline does offer a few advantages. It can be taken with dairy
products, and it's not contraindicated in
cases of impaired kidney functions.

Antidiarrheal or Antimotility Medications

Never take these medications if there is blood, pus, or mucus in stools, or a high fever above 102°F (38.9°C). Never take for more than 2 days. See pp. 133–137.

◆ Imodium AD (loperamide HCl)
A nonopiate antidiarrheal agent.

Uses — diarrhea

Side effects

abdominal distension,	constipation
pain	dizziness
drowsiness	dry mouth
nausea, vomiting	skin rash

Contraindications – routine (see p. 271)
blood in stools
fever above 102°F (38.9°C).
liver disease or impaired liver
functioning

How to take — Take orally. Discontinue
use after 48 hours.

◆ Lomotil (diphenoxylate HCl with atropine sulfate)

An opiate derivative that acts by slowing intestinal motility.

Uses — diarrhea

Side effects

abdominal discomfort	depression
constipation (frequent)	drowsiness
dry mouth	headache
nausea and vomiting	rashes

Contraindications – routine (see p. 271)
blood in stools
fever above 102°F (38.9°C).
hypersensitivity
jaundice

How to take — Take orally.
Don't exceed recommended dosage
Don't take with alcohol, barbiturates, or tranquilizers.
Discontinue use after 48 hours.

◆ Opiate-Containing Antidiarrheals

Diabismul (Suspension Or Tablets)
Donnagel Pg (Suspension)
Paregoric
Parepectolin (Suspension)

Uses

abdominal cramping	diarrhea

Side effects — constipation (very frequent)
large doses can cause symptoms of opiate intoxication and may be habit-forming

Contraindications – routine (see p. 271)

How to take — Take orally with at least one glass of water or other liquid. Discontinue medication when diarrhea subsides. **Don't exceed recommended dosages.**

◆ Pepto-Bismol (bismuth salicylate)

Uses

abdominal cramps	diarrhea
gas pains	nausea
upset stomach	

Side effects — constipation
may temporarily discolor tongue (black)
temporary darkening of stool
stop the medication immediately if you develop ringing in the ears

Contraindications – routine (see p. 271)
aspirin intolerance (or if you should avoid aspirin for any reason)
don't use if taking doxycycline

How to take — Take orally. If using tablets, chew or dissolve them in your mouth — then follow with liquids. Rinse mouth and brush tongue after taking to minimize blackening of tongue.

Antiemetics

These medications are for nausea and vomiting due to illness or motion sickness.

◆ Antivert, Bonine (meclizine HCl) Marezine (cyclizine HCl)

Uses — prevention and treatment of nausea and vomiting due to motion sickness. Meclizine can also be tried for dizziness (vertigo).

Side effects

blurred vision	drowsiness
dry mouth	rashes

Contraindications – routine (see p. 271)
use cautiously with asthma, glaucoma, or enlarged prostate

How to take — Take orally. **Avoid** alcohol and other depressants (may increase drowsiness).

◆ Compazine (prochlorperazine)

Uses — severe nausea and vomiting due to illness or motion sickness

Side effects
blurred vision
dizziness
drowsiness
photosensitivity reaction
pink or reddish-brown colored urine
twitching or spasms of the tongue, head, and neck. If these occur, stop taking the medication immediately and get medical help. If medical help is not available, treat these side effects with 50 mg. of Benadryl orally every 6 hours until they subside, while seeking medical care.

Contraindications – routine (see p. 271)

How to take — Take capsules orally, or use a rectal suppository. **Avoid** alcohol and other depressants. Avoid sunlight as a rash may occur.

◆ Dramamine (dimenhydrinate)

Uses — prevention and treatment of nausea, vomiting, or dizziness due to motion sickness

Side effects
drowsiness (frequent)   headache
insomnia   nervousness

Contraindications – routine (see p. 271)
asthma   enlarged prostate
glaucoma

How to take — Take orally. **Don't** use alcohol while taking this medication. To prevent motion sickness, the first dose should be taken 1/2–1 hour before activity or travel.

◆ Pepto-Bismol see "Antidiarrheals"

◆ Phenergan (promethazine HCl)
Uses — motion sickness
nausea, vomiting   sedation

Side effects
drowsiness
dry mouth

Contraindications – routine (see p. xxx)
asthma attack
cardiovascular disease: use cautiously
concurrent use of MAO inhibitors
hypersensitivity to antihistamines
hypertension
impaired liver function:use cautiously
narrow angle glaucoma

How to take — Take orally. **Don't** take with alcohol or sedatives.
For motion sickness, take one hour before travel.

◆ Tigan (trimethobenzamide HCl)

Uses — severe nausea and vomiting
rectal suppositories are especially useful for symptoms due to hepatitis

Side effects
diarrhea   dizziness
drowsiness   headache

Contraindications – routine (see p. 271)

How to take — Take capsules orally, or use rectal suppositories.

◆ Transderm-scop (scopolamine)

Uses — prevention of nausea and vomiting due to motion sickness

Side effects —
blurred vision (occasionally)
drowsiness
dry mouth
stop the medication if hallucinations, confusion, disorientation, memory loss, or restlessness occur.

Contraindications – routine (see p. 271)
liver disease   glaucoma
(hepatitis)   kidney disease

How to take — Apply disc to a clean area of skin behind the ear 6–8 hours before travel. Avoid placing on hair. You can bathe with the disc, and it may be left in place for up to three days. If it comes off, simply replace it with a new one.
Be sure to wash your hands after touching the disc to remove any scopolamine. If you rub scopolamine into your eye it will cause a painfully dilated pupil. Transderm comes with step-by-step instructions — read them carefully.

Antihistamines and Decongestants

◆ **Actifed (pseudoephedrine HCl and triprolidine HCl)**
Dimetapp (brompheniramine maleate, phenylephrine HCl, phenylpropanolamine HCl)
Drixoral (pseudoephedrine HCl and dexbrompheniramine maleate)

Uses
colds (as a decongestant)
eustachian tube blockage
hay fever symptoms (sneezing, runny nose, watery itchy eyes, itching of the nose or throat)
nasal congestion
other upper respiratory allergies
sinus infection

Side effects — drowsiness
thickening of bronchial secretions
kidney disease

Contraindications – routine (see p. 271)
Medical supervision is required for use with the following chronic conditions:
asthma   diabetes
glaucoma   heart disease
hypertension   thyroid disease

How to take — Take orally. **Don't** use alcohol while taking any of these medications.

◆ **Atarax (hydroxyzine HCl)**

Uses — insomnia
itching due to hives or other causes

Side effects
drowsiness, mild sedation (frequent)
dryness of the mouth (frequent)

Contraindications – routine (see p. 271)

How to take — Take orally. **Don't** use alcohol while taking this medication (may increase drowsiness).

◆ **Benadryl (diphenhydramine HCl)**
Used chiefly to control symptoms of allergies, especially itching, and to decrease nasal secretions.

Uses
hay fever and similar allergic reactions
insomnia (may be used occasionally for its chief side effect, drowsiness)
itchy allergic reactions to medications
itching from insect bites
itchy rashes from scabies and lice
upper respiratory illnesses (as a decongestant)

Side effects — drowsiness (frequent)
dryness of mouth, nose and throat (frequent)
nausea, vomiting, diarrhea (rare)

Contraindications – routine (see p. 271)
narrow angle glaucoma   asthma
prostate enlargement   peptic ulcer

How to take — Take orally. **Don't** use alcohol while taking this medication (may increase drowsiness).

◆ **Chlor-Trimeton (chlorpheniramine maleate)**

Uses — hayfever symptoms

Side effects — drowsiness

Contraindications – routine (see p. 271)

How to take — Take orally. **Don't** use alcohol while taking this medication (may increase drowsiness).

◆ **Seldane (terfenadine)**

Uses — hay fever symptoms

Side effects — (infrequently) drowsiness, headache

Contraindications — routine (see p. 271), impaired liver function; heart disease; concurrent use of ketaconazole (Nizoral) or erythromycin.

How to take — Take orally. **Don't** exceed recommended dosage. Discontinue use if fainting or heart palpitations occur.

◆ Entex LA (phenylephrine HCl and guaifenesin)

Uses — symptomatic relief of sinusitis, bronchitis, colds
eustachian tube blockage
injuries due to changes in pressure (barotrauma), especially of the ear

Side effects

headache	insomnia
nausea	nervousness

Contraindications – routine (see p. 271)
use cautiously with medical conditions such as:

elderly	heart disease
hypertension	hyperthyroidism
peripheral vascular disease	prostate enlargement

How to take — Take orally

◆ Sudafed (pseudoephedrine hydrochloride)

Uses

colds (as a decongestant)	serous otitis blockage
otitis media with eustachian tube	bronchitis sinusitis

Side effects — possible mild stimulant

Contraindications – routine (see p. 271)
use with caution for the following:
hypertension
taking antidepressive medications

How to take — Take orally.

Anti-inflammatory Medications (Oral, Nonsteroid)

◆ Aspirin — see "analgesics"
Clinoril (sulindac)
Dolobid (diflunisal)
Feldene (piroxicam)
Indocin (indomethacin)
Motrin (ibuprofen)
Naprosyn, Anaprox (naproxen)
Tolectin (tolmetin sodium)

Uses — mild to moderate pain from menstrual cramps, muscle spasms, strains and sprains

Side effects

constipation	dizziness
drowsiness	headache
nausea, vomiting, diarrhea	

stop the medication if any of the following occur:

black tarry stools	itching
edema (swelling from fluid accumulation in the extremities)	persistant headache
	rash
severe nausea, vomiting, diarrhea, or abdominal pain	visual disturbances

Contraindications – routine (see p. 271)
allergy to aspirin or when aspirin is contraindicated
history of asthma
history of ulcers
hypertension (use cautiously)
impaired kidney function
runny nose, or other allergic reaction from aspirin or other nonsteroid anti-inflammatory medications
ulcers

How to take — Take orally. Don't take aspirin along with these medications. Take with food, milk, or antacids if gastrointestinal upset occurs.

Antimalarial Medications

◆ Aralen (chloroquine phosphate)

This is the primary antimalarial medicine for nonchloroquine-resistant areas. It's one of the most important medicines a traveler may need.

Uses

prevention of malaria caused by Plasmodium ovale and Plasmodium vivax, as well as nonresistant P. falciparum

Side effects

itching, especially in blacks	dizziness
	headache
nausea, vomiting, diarrhea	rashes
	weight loss

possible worsening of psoriasis, eczema, and other rashes

Contraindications — hepatitis hypersensitivity

How to take — Take orally once a week on the same day (we suggest you take it religiously, on Sundays). There are no restrictions on food or liquids.

Start one to two weeks before entering a malaria area. Continue taking while in the malarial area, and for four weeks after leaving the area.

◆ Doxycycline (see "Antibiotics")

◆ Fansidar (pyrimethamine and sulfadoxine)

Uses — treatment of chloroquine-resistant P. falciparum malaria

Side effects

abdominal cramps	headache
nausea, vomiting, diarrhea	hepatitis

Contraindications – routine (see p.271) anyone with severe allergies or bronchial asthma should consult their doctor before taking this medication.
history of allergic reaction to sulfa drugs

How to take — Take orally. Drink lots of fluids to help prevent kidney stones.
Don't take other sulfa drugs (Septra, Bactrim) while taking Fansidar
Take as a single dose (3 tablets) for febrile illnesses that occur while taking chloroquie (during short stays in areas of chloroquine-resistant P. falciparum).
If Fansidar is used once a week for the prevention of chloroquine- resistant malaria, it should be discontinued immediately if any of the following develop:
any abnormality of the skin or mucous membranes, including

itching	rash
redness	sore throat
mouth or genital lesion(s)	

◆ Lariam (mefloquine HCl)

Uses

prevention of malaria

Side effects

The following may occur briefly but usually resolve quickly:

dizziness	headache
lightheadness	nausea/vomiting
upset stomach	

More serious side effects

convulsions (seizures)
mental distrubances, including psychosis

Contraindications – routine (see p. 271)
history of seizures, psychosis, or depression.
work requiring fine coordination and spacial discrimination – airline pilots, heavy equipment operators
concurrent use of quinine or quinidine
concurrent use of heart medications that prolong or alter electrical conduction, including beta blockers and calcium channel antagonists

How to take — Take orally.

◆ Primaquine Phosphate

Uses — prevention of malaria caused by P. ovale and P. vivax

Side effects — abdominal cramps
hemolytic anemia in G_6PD defiencies
nausea, vomiting
stop the medication if jaundice develops, or if urine turns dark or red, and obtain medical help.

Contraindications – routine (see p. 271)
G6PD blood deficiency (requires blood test to determine)
rheumatoid arthritis   lupus

How to take — Take orally. Take daily during the last 2 weeks of chloroquine or other antimalarial treatment.
  Always try to take this medication under medical supervision, after you have returned home.

◆ Quinine Sulfate

Uses — Treatment of chloroquine-resistant P. falciparum malaria, in combination with either Fansidar or tetracycline/doxycyline.

Side effects

abdominal pain	dizziness
ringing in the ears	headache
visual disturbances	nausea

Contraindications – routine (see p. 271)
history of blood disorders from previous quinine therapy
hypersensitivity
G6PD deficiency (requires a blood test to determine)
ringing in the ears

How to take — Take orally with food or after meals
Don't take with antacids

Antiparasitic Medications

◆ Antepar, Vermizine (piperazine citrate)

This medication paralyzes worms, allowing them to be expelled.

Uses — an alternative medication for roundworm infections (Ascaris)

Side effects — The following occur occasionally:

abdominal pain	cramps
dizziness	hives
nausea, vomiting, diarrhea	

Contraindications – routine (see p. 271)
epilepsy
impaired kidney or liver function

How to take — Take orally on an empty stomach

◆ Antiminth (pyrantel pamoate)

Uses — roundworms (Ascaris)
pinworms   hookworms

Side effects — The following occur occasionally:

abdominal pain	dizziness
decreased appetite	fever
headache	insomnia
nausea, vomiting, diarrhea	rash

Contraindications – routine (see p.271)

How to take — Take orally on an empty stomach.

◆ Atabrine HCl (quinacrine HCl)

Uses — Giardia lamblia

Side effects

abdominal cramps	diarrhea
decreased appetite	dizziness
headache	nausea

yellowing of skin and urine (temporary)
stop the medication if any visual disturbances occur.

Contraindications – routine (see p. 271)
porphyria   psoriasis

How to take — Take orally on an empty stomach with a full glass of liquid.

◆ Biltricide (praziquantel)

Uses

liver flukes   schistosomiasis

Side effects — Usually mild and transient, but may be more severe when large numbers of worms are present.
abdominal discomfort
dizziness
drowsiness (may interfere with driving or other tasks requiring alertness)
headache
malaise

Contraindications – routine (see p. 271)
don't treat cysticercosis with this medication if symptoms of eye involvement are present

How to take — Take orally with liquids during meals.
Don't chew tablets.
Swallow quickly as bitter taste may produce gagging and vomiting

◆ Diodoquin, Floraquin, Yodoxin (diiodohydroxyquin or iodoquinol)

Uses — Blastocystis hominis
Dientamoeba fragilis
Entamoeba histolytica (amoebas)

Side effects

nausea, vomiting, diarrhea	constipation
	gastritis
skin rashes, including hives and generalized itching	headache
	malaise

Contraindications – routine (see p. 271)
iodine sensitivity
liver damage (including active or chronic hepatitis)
thyroid disease: use with caution

How to take — Take orally. If gastrointestinal symptoms occur, take with food. If diarrhea continues, stop the medication.

◆ Fasigyn (tinidazole)

This drug is available in many countries outside the U.S. It hasn't yet been approved for use in the U.S.

Uses

Entamoeba histolytica (amoebas)
Giardia lamblia (giardiasis)
Trichomonas vaginalis ("trich")

Side effects — alcohol reaction less severe than with Flagyl
decreased appetite
metallic taste in the mouth
nausea, vomiting, diarrhea

Contraindications – routine (see p. 271)
history of blood disorders
history of central nervous system disease

How to take — Take orally with food to help minimize side effects. **Don't consume any alcohol while using this medication** Avoid alcohol for 24 hours before starting and 48 hours after finishing the medication. Be sure to check for alcohol in other liquid medicines such as cough syrups, vitamins, or pain relievers.

◆ Flagyl (see "Antibiotics")

◆ Hetrazan (diethylcarbamazine citrate)

Used for some ascaris and onchocerciasis infections. Must only be taken under medical supervision as severe allergic reactions can occur after a single dose.

◆ Humatin (paromomycin sulfate)

Uses — amoebas, both acute and chronic infections

Side effects

nausea, vomiting, diarrhea	cramps
	headache
vertigo (spinning sensation)	rash

stop taking the medication and notify the doctor if hearing impairment, ringing in the ears, or dizziness occur.

Contraindications – routine (see p. 271)
intestinal obstruction

How to take — Take orally with food.

◆ Mintezol (thiabendazole)

Uses — Capillaria phillippinensis (alternative treatment, drug of choice is mebebendazole)

creeping eruption (cutaneous larva migrans)

Guinea worm (alternative treatment, as drug of choice is Flagyl)

hookworm (Necator americanus) (an alternative treatment, as the drug of choice is mebendazole)

threadworm (Strongyloides)

Side effects — any of the following may occur, usually 3–4 hours after taking the drug:

decreased appetite   dizziness
nausea, vomiting

Contraindications – routine (see p. 271)

How to take — Take with food to decrease gastrointestinal side effects. Chew tablets thoroughly before swallowing.

◆ Vermox (mebendazole)

This medication is very effective and has few side effects. It kills worms by blocking their sugar intake.

Uses
Capillaria phillippinensis
hookworms (Ancylostoma duodenale)
pinworms (Enterobius vermicularis)
roundworms (Ascaris lumbricoides)
whipworms (Trichuris trichiura)

Side effects — If there are many worms, there may occasionally be transient symptoms of abdominal pain and/or diarrhea.

Contraindications – routine (see p. 271)

How to take — Take orally.

◆ Yomesan, Niclocide (niclosamide)

This medication is used primarily for intestinal tapeworms and some flukes.

Uses — beef tapeworm (Taenia saginata)

dwarf tapeworm (Hymenolepis nana) (alternative drug, drug of choice is praziquantel)

fish tapeworm (Diphyllobothrium latum)
intestinal fluke (Fasciolopsis buski)
pork tapeworm (Taenia solium)

Side effects
constipation   dizziness
drowsiness   headache
nausea, vomiting,   rectal bleeding
  diarrhea

Contraindications – routine (see p. 271)

How to take — Take orally with food to minimize side effects. Chew tablets, then swallow with a small amount of water. Use a mild laxative if necessary to relieve constipation.

Antispasmodics

◆ Belladenal (phenobarbital and belladona)

May be habit forming due to phenobarbital (a barbiturate).

Uses — relief of abdominal cramps caused by diarrhea

Side effects
blurred vision   drowsiness
dry mouth   flushed skin
urinary retention

Contraindications – routine (see p. 271)
advanced kidney disease
glaucoma

How to take
Take orally.

◆ **Donnatal (phenobarbital, hyoscyamine sulfate, atropine sulfate, and scopolamine hydrobromide; in addition, the elixir contains alcohol)**

Uses — relief of abdominal cramps caused by diarrhea

Side effects

blurred vision	dry mouth
flushed skin	skin dryness
urinary retention	

Contraindications – routine (see p. 271)
glaucoma   liver impairment
kidney impairment

How to take — Take orally.

Antiviral Medications

◆ **Zovirax (acyclovir)**

Uses – initial or recurrent herpes simplex

Side effects

fatigue	headache
menstrual	insomnia
abnormalities	joint pain
nausea, vomiting,	rash
diarrhea	vertigo

Contraindications – routine (see p. 271)

How to take — Tablets — take orally. Avoid sexual contact while lesions are present.

Bronchial Dilators

How To Use an Oral Inhaler
The assembled inhaler should form an "L" shape. Put the inhaler next to your mouth, not inside it. Don't seal your lips around it. Exhale, then squeeze the inhaler and breathe in the medicine. The extra air inhaled with the medicine helps drive it deeply into the lungs. Hold the medication in for 10–20 seconds, then breathe out. Wait 5–10 minutes and repeat the procedure.

◆ **Alupent (metaproterenol sulfate), inhalant or tablets**

Uses — reversible wheezing associated with bronchitis, bronchial asthma, or emphysema

Side effects

increased heart rate	nausea
nervousness	tremors

Contraindications — abnormally rapid heart rhythms (tachycardia)

How to take — inhalant — see above
tablets — take orally
don't overuse the medication

Side effects

apprehension	nausea, vomiting
rapid heart rate	restlessness

Contraindications – routine (see p.271)
abnormally rapid   tachycardia caused
heart rhythms   by digitalis
(tachycardia)   medications
use cautiously with the following conditions:

cardiac rhythm	heart disease
disturbances	history of stroke
diabetes	hyperthyroidism
history of seizures	prostate
hypertension	enlargement

How to take — inhalant— see above.
tablets— take orally
don't exceed recommended dosage, as excessive use decreases effectiveness and may lead to adverse effects
don't use long term unless under medical supervision

◆ **Brethine (terbutaline sulfate), inhalant or tablets**

Uses — reversible wheezing associated with bronchitis, bronchial asthma, or emphysema

◆ Proventil, Ventolin (albuterol/salbutanol), inhalant

Uses
reversible wheezing associated with bronchitis, bronchial asthma, or emphysema

Side effects
apprehension
insomnia
nausea
palpitations
rapid heart rate (tachycardia)
restlessness
tremor

Contraindications – routine (see p. 271)
abnormally rapid heart rhythms (tachycardia)
use cautiously with the following conditions:
  diabetes
  heart disease
  hyperthyroidism

How to take — see "how to use an inhaler"on previous page.
don't exceed recommended dosage, as excessive use decreases effectiveness and may lead to adverse effects

Contraceptives — Oral

◆ Combination Pills (estrogen and progesterone)

These work by inhibiting ovulation and implantation of a fertile egg, and by creating a thick cervical mucus. There are many different types. Try to use only low-dose pills (those with 50 micrograms or less of estrogen).

Uses — preventing pregnancy

Side effects — multiple (beyond the scope of this book)

Contraindications – routine (see p. 271)
coronary artery disease
history of heart problems
history of or active breast or reproductive system cancer
history of embolus or thrombosis (material blocking a blood vessel)
impaired liver function including hepatitis, liver cancer
pregnancy

How to take – Take orally, 1 pill each day at approximately the same time of day.

Diarrhea which occurs while using the pill may have the same effect as missing one or more pills.

If you miss 1 pill, take 2 the next day. If you miss 2 pills, take 2 pills the next day and 2 pills the day after that. Use a backup form of birth control for the rest of the month. If you miss 3 pills, stop taking them altogether. Throw away the package with the remaining pills. Start a new package on the first day of bleeding or on the Sunday after your next period or 5 days after the bleeding begins. Use a backup form of birth control (condoms, foam, sponge) for one month.

If you miss a pill or pills while sexually active and have no period for 45 days, get a pregnancy test (see pp. 236–238).

◆ Progesterone Only Pill ("mini-pills," Micronor, Nor, Q-D Ovrette)

These are primarily used by people who can't use the combination pill due to hypertension, headaches, breast feeding, or any other reason.

Uses — preventing pregnancy

Side effects
absence of periods
bleeding between periods
irregular periods

Contraindications — pregnancy
coronary artery disease
history of heart problems
history of an active breast or reproductive system cancer
history of embolus or thrombosis (material blocking a blood vessel)
impaired liver function, including hepatitis, liver cancer

How to take — Take orally, one each day. **Never** miss a pill as you may ovulate and become pregnant. If you miss a period, obtain a pregnancy test.

Dental Preparations

◆ Cavit

Uses — a temporary filling for cavities when dental care is not available

Side effects — none

Contraindications — none

How to take — See Chapter 12, "Dental Problems."

◆ Oil of Clove

Important dental anesthetic for travelers. It works as a "counter-irritant," irritating the nerve ending to the point of deadening it.

Uses — painful cavities due to cracked or missing fillings new cavities

Side effects — none

Contraindications — none

How to take — Dab onto tooth with a Q-tip, or use a dropper to apply 1–2 drops to tooth and gum prior to sealing tooth (see Chapter 12, "Dental Problems," pp. 188–189). Don't swallow or ingest this medication.

Ear Medications

◆ Cortisporin Otic Drops (polymyxin B sulfate, neomycin sulfate, and hydrocortisone)

This medication combines two antibiotics with an anti-inflammatory agent.

Uses — external infections of the ear canal (otitis externa)

Side effects — neomycin may be sensitizing; if rash/redness occurs, discontinue use

Contraindications — herpes infections (including chickenpox)

How to take — After putting drops in the ear, keep head tilted for 3–5 minutes. This allows the medication to work all the way down the canal. **Don't** get water in the affected ear(s) during the course of treatment.

Emetics

Emetics are used to induce vomiting in cases of accidental poisoning. Emetics should **not** be given to unconscious victims, or when poisoning is due to petroleum-based products, acids or alkalis, or strychnine.

◆ Ipecac Syrup

Uses — accidental poisoning

Side effects — none

Contraindications — as indicated above

How to take — Take orally with lots of fluids (7-Up works especially well). Repeat dosage in 20 minutes if vomiting does not occur.

Eye Medications

◆ Bleph 10/Sodium Sulamyd Antibiotic Eye Drops (sulfacetamide sodium)

Uses — conjunctivitis (pink eye)

Side effects — none

Contraindications – routine (see p. 271) history of allergic reaction to sulfa drugs

How to take — See instructions for ophthalmic solutions on the next page.

◆ Garamycin Ophthalmic Eye Drops and Ointment (Gentamicin sulfate)

Uses — conjunctivitis (pink eye)

Side effects — burning and stinging of the eyes (occasionally)

Contraindications – routine (see p. 271)

How to take

Ophthalmic solution:
Lie down or tilt head backward, hold dropper above eye and put drops inside lower lid. **Don't** touch dropper to eye, fingers, or any surface. Keep eye open, avoid blinking for 30 seconds. After instillation, don't close eyes tightly. Try not to blink excessively.

Ophthalmic ointment:
Hold tube in hands for several minutes to warm it before use. Tilt head back or lie down. Squeeze a small amount of the ointment (1/4inch to 1/2 inch) inside the lower lid. **Don't** touch tip of tube or cap to eye, finger, or any surface. Close eye gently and roll the eyeball in all directions while eye is closed. Temporary blurring may occur.

◆ Naphcon-A (naphazoline HCl and pheniramine maleate)

Uses — eye irritation from allergies

Side effects — mild transient stinging, burning, tearing

Contraindications – routine (see p. 271)
concurrent use of MAO inhibitors
narrow angle glaucoma
use cautiously with the following
  conditions:
cardiac rhythm disturbances
diabetes
hypertension
hyperthyroidism

How to take — apply 1 drop in each eye every 3–4 hours

Hemorrhoid Medications

◆ Anusol HC (hydrocortisone acetate, bismuth subgallate, bismuth resorcin compound, benzyl benzoate, peruvian balsam, zinc oxide)

Uses — symptomatic relief of pain and discomfort from hemorrhoids

Side effects — local irritation

Contraindications – routine (see p. 271)

How to take
suppository — insert rectally
cream — fill tube with cream and insert into anus, squeezing tube to push cream inside. For external use put cream on fingers and rub in gently.

Menstrual Cramping (Dysmenorrhea) Medications

◆ Motrin, Advil, Nuprin (ibuprofen) Naprosyn (naproxen)

Uses — to relieve or reduce the pain of menstrual cramps

Side effects

blurred vision	dizziness
edema	rash
nausea, vomiting, diarrhea	

Contraindications – routine (see p. 271)
hypersensitivity to other nonsteroid antiinflammatory medications (see p. 285)

How to take
Take orally. Begin taking the medication either before cramps start or just as they begin. Take with food to help minimize side effects.

Muscle Relaxants

◆ Flexeril (cyclobenzaprine HCl)

Uses — severe muscle spasms only

Side effects — dizziness
drowsiness   dry mouth

Contraindications – routine (see p. 271)

How to take — Take orally. **Don't** use
alcohol while taking this medications.
Don't take for longer than 2 weeks.

◆ Parafon Forte DSC (chlorzoxazone and acetaminophen)

Uses
mild to severe muscle-skeletal discomfort
muscle spasms

Side effects — gastrointestinal upset
(rare)

Contraindications – routine (see p. 271)
liver impairment, including hepatitis

How to take — Take orally. **Don't** use
alcohol while taking this medication.
Don't overuse due to the possibility of
liver damage.

◆ Robaxisal (methocarbamol and aspirin), Robaxin (methocarbamol)

Uses

mild to severe	muscle spasms
muscle-skeletal	sprains and
discomfort	strains

Side effects

dizziness	drowsiness
light-headedness	nausea

Contraindications – routine (see p. 271)
aspirin allergy (Robaxisal)
ulcers, history of ulcers

How to take — Take orally. Take with
food if nausea occurs.
Don't use alcohol with this medication.

Nasal Medications

◆ Afrin Nasal Spray
This medication constricts the smaller
arterial blood vessels of the nasal
passages.

Uses — relief of nasal congestion due
to allergic or infectious disorders of the
nose (hayfever, colds, sinusitis)

Side effects
headache
sneezing
possible burning, stinging and dryness
   of nasal membranes
"nasal rebound" — a reaction that occurs when you stop using the spray.
   The nasal membranes puff right back
   out worse than before starting the
   medication. Be very aware of this important side effect.

Contraindications – routine (see p. 271)

How to take
Drops or spray are put in one or both
nostrils. **Don't** use more often than the
instructions indicate. To avoid nasal rebound, **don't** use for more than 3 days
at a time.

◆ Other Nasal Decongestants—see "Antihistamines and Decongestants"

Skin Medications, Topical

These medications are applied to the skin. In Third World countries, many topical medications are combined with antibiotics. Don't use these products. They frequently cause allergic reactions. Almost all topical medicines are available without prescription in Third World countries. Be careful not to overuse them.

◆ Antibacterial Ointments

Bacitracin
Neomycin Triple Antibiotic (polymyxin b, bacitracin, neomycin)
Neosporin

These are the most common. Always read the ingredients on the label. If allergic to any of them (particularly neomycin), don't use the medication.

Uses — minor skin infections (folliculitis, infected insect bites, cuts, abrasions)

Side effects — none

Contraindications – routine (see p. 271)

How to take — Rub in lightly and gently on the affected area. **Don't** use in eyes.

◆ Antifungal Preparations (Creams, Powders, and Lotions)

Desenex (undecylenic acid)
Monistat Derm (miconazole nitrate)
Mycelex, Lotrimin (clotrimazole)
Mycolog (nystatin, triamcinolone)
Nizoral (ketaconazole)
Nystatin, Mycostatin (nystatin)
Tinactin (tolnaftate)

All of the above can be used more or less interchangeably. However, some preparations may be more effective than others for specific disorders. Check treatment recommendations (Chapter 5).

Uses

fungal rashes:	athlete's foot
heat rash	ringworm
tinea versicolor	

Side effects — possible skin irritation with redness, blistering, stinging, swelling or itching (infrequent)

Contraindications – routine (see p. 271)

How to take — Spread thinly and rub in lightly to the area of rash. **Don't** overuse.

Selsun Solution (selenium sulfide)

Uses — tinea versicolor

Side effects — possible oiliness or dryness of the skin

Contraindications – routine (see p. 271)

How to use — Apply to rash, rubbing in gently. Leave on 15 minutes, then wash off. Repeat daily for 2 weeks.

◆ Antiparasitic Preparations

Eurax (crotamiton)
This is an alternative to Kwell and Elimite, usually preferrable during pregnancy and breastfeeding.

Uses — scabies

Side effects — skin irritation

Contraindications — history of allergic reaction to the ingredients

How to use — **Don't** use near the eyes or mouth. Rub in thoroughly on entire body from the neck down, but avoid use on the nipples when breastfeeding. Repeat application in 24 hours. Don't wash off until 48 hours after the second application.

◆ Kwell Lotion And Shampoo (lindane or gamma benzene hexachloride)

This medication is a derivative of the pesticide DDT — handle with care. Avoid use on children or infants and overuse by adults.

Uses

Lotion — scabies, crabs, and body lice

Shampoo — crabs and head lice

Side effects — rash (usually occurs only from overuse)

Contraindications – routine (see p. 271) Use Eurax instead during pregnancy and breastfeeding.

How to take — **Don't** take orally. **Don't** use near the eyes. **It's very poisonous.**

Lotion — **Don't** bathe before use. Shake the bottle well and apply lotion to entire body below the neck. Leave on for 8 hours, then wash off thoroughly (the lotion can't be seen or smelled when on the skin).

Shampoo — Apply to hairy areas of the body, add a little water, and lather thoroughly. Leave on for 4 minutes, then rinse off even more thoroughly.

◆ Rid (pyrethrins)

Uses — head and body lice, crab lice (including eggs)

Side effects — none

Contraindications — Don't use if allergic to ragweed.

How to use — Apply to affected areas undiluted (no water) until entirely wet. Allow to stay on for 10 minutes **only**. Then wash off thoroughly with water and either soap or shampoo. Repeat treatment in 7–10 days.
   Don't use on eyebrows or eyelids.

◆ Medications For Itching

Domeboro's Solution (aluminum sulfate and calcium acetate)

Uses
athlete's foot
contact dermatitis
insect bites

Side effects — none

Contraindications — none

How to use — Don't take orally.
   Don't apply to blistered, raw, or oozing areas of the skin.
   Add the medicine to bath water before bathing. An alternative method is to soak a towel or cloth in the Domeboro's solution, then wrap the cloth around the irritated area.

◆ Calamine Lotion (also available as Caladryl with the antihistamine Benadryl 1% and camphor)

Uses
athlete's foot
contact dermatitis (including poison oak, ivy, or other poisonous plants)
insect bites

Side effects — stop the medication if a rash develops or a burning sensation occurs

Contraindications – routine (see p. 271)

How to take — Don't take orally. Keep away from the eyes.
   Don't apply to blistered, raw, or oozing areas of the skin.
   Shake the bottle well before using. Cleanse the area with soap and water before each application. Apply to affected areas 3–4 times a day.

◆ Steroid Creams

Aristocort .1% or .5%
Kenalog .1%
Halog .1%
Lidex
Valisone .1%
Hydrocortisone 0.5 or 1%

There are many more. These are some of the most widely used.

Uses

inflammation and itching due to insect bites, contact dermatitis (see pp. 114–115).

Side effects

burning, itching, dryness of the skin
folliculitis
secondary bacterial infection

Contraindications — Don't use on any rash caused by a virus (herpes, chickenpox).

How to take

Apply thinly to skin and rub in lightly.
Don't put in or around the eyes.
Don't use on the face.
Don't use in genital region for more than three days.

◆ Vioform HC 1% (Clioquinol and hydrocortisone)

If unable to determine if a rash is due to an allergy, contact dermatitis, or a fungal infection, this is a good medication to use.

Uses — contact dermatitis
fungal skin infections   eczema

Side effects — rash
burning, itching, and dryness of the skin

Contraindications – routine (see p. 271)
tuberculosis of the skin
viral skin infections including herpes

How to use — apply thinly to the skin 2–3 times a day

Sleep Medications

◆ Benadryl (see "Antihistamines")

◆ Halcion (triazolam)

Uses – short-term treatment of insomnia

Side effects

dizziness, light-headedness	confusion
	drowsiness
memory impairment (retrograde amnesia)	nausea, vomiting
	nervousness
	tiredness

sleep disturbances, especially first day of treatment and after discontinuing use

Contraindications – routine (see p. 271)
hypersensitivity to triazolam or other benzodiazepines
use cautiously with following conditions:

kidney disease	liver disease
lung disease	elderly people use cautiously

How to take — Take orally.
Don't exceed the prescribed dose.
Don't take with alcohol. Take only short-term as physical and psychological dependency may occur.

◆ Restoril (temazepam)

Uses — short-term treatment of insomnia

Side effects

confusion	diarrhea
decreased appetite	
dizziness	drowsiness
sleep disturbances for 1–2 days after discontinuing use	lethargy
	weakness

Contraindications – routine (see p. 271)
elderly people use cautiously

How to take — Take orally.
Don't exceed the prescribed dose.
Don't take with alcohol, antihistamines, or tranquilizers. Take only short-term as physical and psychological dependency may occur.

Vaginal Medications

◆ Cleocin (clindamycin)

Uses — bacterial vaginosis

Side effects

appetite loss	diarrhea
fatigue	headache
nausea, vomiting	rash, itching
pseudomembranous colitis	sore throat

Contraindications – routine (see p. 271) use cautiously with
 impaired kidney or liver function
 stomach or intestinal disorders
 history of asthma

How to take — Take orally with a full glass of water

◆ Flagyl — see "Antibiotics"

Uses — bacterial vaginosis
trichomonas vaginitis

◆ Vaginal Antifungal Creams

Femstat (butaconazole)
Monistat (miconazole)
Mycelex, Gynelotrim (clotrimazole)
Mycostatin (nystatin)
Terazol 7 (teraconazole)

Uses — vaginal yeast (monilial) infections

Side effects — none

Contraindications – routine (see p. 271) don't use in pregnancy after membranes have ruptured

How to take

Cream: use the applicator to place the cream as high up and far back in the vagina as possible

Suppository: place the suppository as far back in the vagina as possible. The medication should be applied or re-applied following intercourse. Otherwise, it gets squashed out and does you no good. If there is any irritation on the outside of the vaginal opening, spread some cream thinly over the irritated area twice a day.

Immunizations

Precautions When Obtaining
Any Injection in a Foreign Country

If you require vaccinations or any other injectable medication while traveling, the syringes used must be sterile beyond question. Do not risk infection with AIDS, hepatitis B, or other diseases from contaminated equipment. Insist on **sterile, disposable** syringes for any injection you receive while traveling.

How do you tell? Syringes should be made of plastic, not glass, and come in an unopened protective wrapper with no tape around the outside. For extended travel, you may even want to ask your medical provider for syringes and needles to add to your first aid kit. If so, you must carry a written prescription for these items.

In developing countries, many injectable medications are available at pharmacies without a prescription. Frequently the pharmacist or an assistant will offer to give the injection. Do not take advantage of this service **unless you can assure yourself that sterile syringes are used and sterile technique is employed.**

Several years ago, a Peace Corps Volunteer, stationed alone in a remote area of Honduras, managed to crawl to the local pharmacy after 5 days of intense illness. He was desperately sick, and the shopkeeper had just the thing. "Medicina fuerte — strong medicine," he promised. Obligingly, the injection was given. Too weak to protest, the unfortunate volunteer barely registered a vision of the needle being wiped off with a grubby handkerchief. He soon recovered from the original illness and, much later, from hepatitis B, which he contracted from the contaminated syringe.

Cholera

Cholera is a bacterial illness transmitted through contaminated food and water. The vaccine, given intramuscularly, isn't recommended for travelers under normal circumstances. It may occasionally be required for crossing borders into certain countries. Recently, it has found use in some refugee camps to control outbreaks of cholera. Vaccination may be desirable for people working with refugees in these areas.

The vaccine may also be recommended for travelers with certain stomach problems. Unfortunately the vaccine is only 50% effective, and lasts for only 3–6 months. The best protection is to rigorously follow food and water precautions. An oral vaccine is under development.

Side Effects

Pain, redness, and swelling at the injection site can last 1–2 days. There may also be fever, headaches, and fatigue. Two aspirin or acetaminophen (Tylenol) 4 times a day, with cold packs to the injection site, will help relieve symptoms.

Contraindications

The vaccine should be avoided if there has been a previous severe reaction.

German Measles (Rubella)

If you've had your childhood immunizations or a blood test showing immunity, vaccination isn't required. If you don't have immunity, a single injection provides lifelong protection.

Side Effects

Occasionally there may be a rash with swollen lymph nodes, joint pain, or pain in the hands and feet. Take 2 aspirin every 4–6 hours as needed for relief of symptoms.

Contraindications

Don't take rubella vaccine during pregnancy. Avoid pregnancy for 3 months after vaccination because of possible harm to the fetus.

The vaccine should be avoided by anyone with a history of severe allergic reaction to topical or injected neomycin. It should not be taken by anyone whose immune system is supressed by drug or radiation therapy, steroids, or cancer. The vaccine is safe for people who are HIV positive.

Rubella vaccine shouldn't be taken concurrently with immune globulin (IG). It should be taken at least 14 days before or 6 weeks and preferrably 3 months after receiving IG.

Hepatitis B

Vaccination prevents hepatitis B if you obtain it sufficiently in advance of exposure, and is recommended for people at increased risk. This includes gay men, IV drug users, household and sexual contacts of known hepatitis B carriers, and anyone with occasional or habitual contact with prostitutes. Health care workers who are frequently exposed to blood, blood products, or to people who require transfusions or hemodialysis are also at risk.

In addition, hepatitis B vaccine is recommended for people who plan to reside 6 months or more in high risk areas, working or living in close contact with the local population. The areas of highest risk are eastern Asia and subSaharan Africa. The vaccine is also recommended for short stays in these areas, for potential exposure to blood or high risk sexual contact.

Side Effects

There may be mild pain, redness, and swelling at the injection site. Take 1–2 aspirin or acetaminophen (Tylenol) up to 4 times a day as needed. Ice packs can be applied locally up to 3–4 times a day to relieve discomfort.

Contraindications — Essentially none. The vaccine is safe during pregnancy.

Dose — The vaccination consists of three shots over a six month period.

Immune Globulin (Ig)

Formerly called immune serum globulin or gamma globulin, immune globulin provides protection against hepatitis A (infectious hepatitis). This is a common traveler's illness in developing countries. Immune globulin should be your last shot, given as close to departure as possible.

Side Effects — There may be mild pain at the injection site.

Contraindications

Don't take immune globulin in conjunction with live vaccines, especially measles, mumps, rubella, yellow fever, or polio. If a live vaccine is needed, it should be taken 14 days before or 6 weeks and preferrably 3 months after immune globulin. When time does not permit this scheduling, polio and yellow fever vaccines may be taken with IG.

All other vaccines can be taken in conjunction with IG, and immunization is safe during pregnancy. Immune globulin may be contraindicated if you're allergic to Thimersol, the preservative contained in some contact lens solutions. If you're obtaining IG outside of the United States, see "Precautions" below.

Precautions when getting IG in a foreign country. If you'll be gone more-than 5 months, first obtain a hepatitis A IgG test. A positive test indicates immunity to hepatitis A. No immune globulin injections are needed.

Otherwise, during extended travel, repeat shots are needed at 5 month intervals for ongoing protection against hepatitis A. Immune globulin is widely available through private doctors, hospitals, pharmacies, and public health clinics.

When revaccinated in a foreign country, make sure any immune globulin you receive is manufactured in the U.S. Immune globulin produced elsewhere may not be adequately screened or processed against contamination with HIV, the virus which causes AIDS. If necessary, verify the place of manufacture by asking to see the bottle. If you can't verify U.S. manufacture, don't get this shot! It's simply not worth risking AIDS, which will kill you, to prevent hepatitis A, which will not.

Influenza

This vaccine is recommended only for some people, including:

1. adults with chronic disorders requiring regular medical care, such as heart, lung, or kidney disease, asthma, anemia, HIV infection, immunosuppressive therapy, or metabolic disorders;

2. healthy adults over age 65;

3. medical personnel who will be exposed to influenza patients.

Side Effects

There may be redness and swelling at the injection site for 1 to 2 days. Apply ice or cold packs 3–4 times a day if necessary. Fever, fatigue, and body aches may be present. Take 1–2 aspirin or acetaminophen (Tylenol) every 4–6 hours as needed for these symptoms.

Contraindications

Don't take this vaccine if you're allergic to eggs. Don't take it during the first 3 months of pregnancy, or with an acute illness accompanied by fever.

Japanese B Encephalitis

This viral disease is spread by mosquitos. In the cooler climates of Asia the virus is inactive in winter. It surfaces in epidemics during the summer months (June through October) in the temperate and nothern tropical zones of India, Bangladesh, China, Nepal, Burma, Thailand, Vietnam, Laos, Kampuchea, Malaysia, Indonesia, Korea, Japan, and the eastern USSR. Risk is present throughout the year in the tropical and subtropical zones of southern India, Sri Lanka, Indonesia, Malaysia, Singapore, Taiwan, the Philippines, and southern Thailand. The disease can reach epidemic proportions during the rainy season, and the death rate may be 20%.

Vaccination is desirable for anyone living or working in high risk areas. It's also suggested for any rural travel of 3 weeks or more in these areas. If travel is required during the high risk season, or your activities will expose you to mosquitos, vaccination is recommended regardless of length of stay.

Travelers already overseas who need the vaccine should contact their embassy or consulate, or local public health departments in countries where the disease is present. In Bangkok obtain vaccine at the "Red Cross Immunization Clinic," in the same building as the Snake House. In Nepal, obtain vaccine at the Kalimati Clinic in Kathmandu.

Side Effects

There may be mild pain, redness, and swelling at the injection site. Fever, headache, and malaise occur infrequently. Two aspirin or acetaminophen (Tylenol) every 4–6 hours will help relieve symptoms.

Contraindications

Don't take the vaccine if you've had a previous hypersensitivity reaction to it. During pregnancy, when travel to high risk areas is unavoidable, travelers should be vaccinated only under medical supervision. The same is true for those with heart, kidney, or liver disease, leukemia, lymphomas, or other generalized cancers.

Measles (Rubeola)

Measles is a viral illness of high incidence in developing countries. In 1982, 36% of all recorded cases in the U.S. originated outside the country, and this figure averaged 20% between 1981-1987. The majority of these were U.S. citizens returning from trips abroad. Anyone born between 1956–1980 should obtain a single vaccine shot before traveling to a Third World country.

Side Effects

Initial vaccination may cause a mild fever and transient rash about six days later. Symptoms can last 1–2 days, and in a small percentage of people (5- 15%) the temperature may reach 103°F (39.4°C). Take 1 or 2 aspirin or acetaminophen (Tylenol) every 4–6 hours as needed for fever.

Contraindications

Don't take during pregnancy. Avoid pregnancy for three months after injection because of possible harm to the fetus.

Anyone with a history of severe allergic reaction to eggs, or to topical or injected neomycin should avoid measles vaccine. It shouldn't be taken by anyone whose immune system is supressed by drug or radiation therapy, steroids, or cancer. The vaccine is safe for people who are HIV positive.

Measles vaccine should be taken at least 14 days before or 6 weeks and preferrably 3 months after receiving immune globulin.

Meningococcal Meningitis

Meningococcal bacterial infections are contracted following the inhalation of infectious air droplets from people coughing and sneezing. Vaccination is currently recommended at least 10–14 days prior to arrival in high risk areas. These include Kenya, Tanzania, Nepal, New Delhi, Saudi Arabia, and subSaharan

Africa during the dry season from December to June, particularly in the savannah area extending from Mali eastward to Ethiopia (see map in Appendix B, p. 309). Vaccination is mandatory for visitors and pilgrims to Mecca during the annual Haj. In Nepal, the vaccine can be obtained at the Epidemiology Division, Department of Health Services, Teku, Kathmandu.

Side Effects
There may be local redness and soreness at the injection site for 1–2 days. Take 2 aspirin or acetaminophen (Tylenol) every 4–6 hours as needed to help relieve symptoms. Ice packs can also be applied to the injection site. A small percentage of young children develop a transient fever following vaccination.

Contraindications
Don't take the vaccine if you've had a prior hypersensitivity reaction to it.

Plague

This vaccine is recommended for travelers in rural areas who anticipate handling wild animals, particularly rabbits or other rodents. It's also recommended for people living or working in plague zones where protection from fleas and rodents isn't possible. Plague is especially prevalent in interior regions of Vietnam, Democratic Kampuchea (formerly Cambodia) and Laos. Elsewhere it isn't currently a significant problem for travelers.

Side Effects
There may be mild pain, redness, and swelling at the injection site. Fever, headache, and malaise can occur after repeated doses.

Pneumococcal Pneumonia

This vaccine is recommended only in special cases. It's considered for travelers with heart, lung, liver, or kidney disease, sickle cell anemia, or who have had their spleen surgically removed. A single vaccination provides lifelong immunity.

Polio

Polio vaccine is highly recommended for travel in developing countries, which have a high incidence of the disease. In 1984, 24,275 cases were reported. The breakdown:

Southeast Asia 63%   Western Pacific 19%
East Mediterranean 8%   Africa 8%
Central and South America 2%

In the period 1969–1981, 19 US citizens acquired polio in Mexico.

Adults who have had their complete childhood polio immunization of Trivalent Oral Polio Vaccine (OPV) need only a single booster for lifetime immunity. Travelers who have not had a complete childhood vaccination series should con-ult their medical provider. The recommended primary series for adults is the Enhanced Inactivated Polio Vaccine (eIPV).

Side Effects

There is a very small risk of vaccine-associated paralysis from OPV. Minor pain and swelling may occur at the site of eIPV injection for about 24 hours.

Contraindications

Don't take either polio vaccine during pregnancy unless there is substantial risk of exposure to polio. In this case Oral Polio Vaccine (OPV) is the preferred vaccine. OPV is not recommended for anyone whose immune system is supressed by chemotherapy, steroids, cancer, or HIV infection. If living with an immune-suppressed person, or in a household with adults who have never had their childhood immunization against polio, eIPV is the preferred vaccine.

Anyone who has had an anaphylactic reaction (severe or life-threatening allergic reaction) to neomycin or streptomycin should not receive eIPV. Minor allergic reactions to neomycin or streptomycin are not contraindications, and eIPV can be taken safely.

Rabies (HDCV, Human Diploid Cell Vaccine): Pre-exposure

Pre-exposure vaccine is recommended for travelers (veterinarians, field biologists, cave explorers, etc.) anticipating contact with animals that might carry rabies. It's also advisable for travelers, especially children, who will spend more than 4 weeks in areas of increased risk where the disease is endemic in the dog population. Unfortunately, this is the case throughout the Third World countries of Africa, Asia, and Latin America. Risk is highest in, but not limited to, Mexico, Guatemala, El Salvador, Colombia, Ecuador, the Philippines, Thailand, Vietnam, India, Sri Lanka, and Nepal.

The pre-exposure vaccine doesn't eliminate the need for rabies treatment — additional vaccine — if you're exposed to rabies through a bite or saliva. It does provide an extra margin of safety and it reduces the number of post-exposure vaccinations. It also eliminates the need for rabies immune globulin.

Comment

It's crucial to obtain rabies treatment as soon as possible after any animal bite — with or without pre-exposure rabies vaccine (see Chapter 7, "Rabies", pp. 167–70). A 23-year old agricultural volunteer from the US, working in Kenya, was bitten by her puppy. She died 3 months later of rabies. She had had her pre-exposure rabies vaccine, but failed to obtain followup treatment after the bit

Side Effects

There may be mild pain, redness, swelling, or itching at the injection site. Headache, nausea, abdominal pain, muscle aches, and dizziness can also occur. About 6% of those receiving booster shots experience a reaction with hives, itching, and malaise.

Take 2 aspirin every 4–6 hours as needed for relief of symptoms. Ice pack can be applied to the injection site.

Contraindications

The vaccine is considered safe for use during pregnancy. History of a severe allergic reaction to the vaccine requires medical evaluation before further injections can be taken.

Dose

The pre-exposure series of HDCV (Human diploid cell vaccine) consists of shots given over a 21 to 28 day period. The intradermal vaccine, which is cheaper, must be completed 30 or more days before departure and prior to initiation of the antimalarial medications chloroquine or mefloquine. If that is not possible, the vaccine must be given IM. A booster is recommended every 2 years for those who continue to be at significant risk for rabies exposure.

Smallpox

Smallpox no longer exists, except in the research or germ warfare laboratories of a few countries. In May 1980 the World Health Organization declared the world free of smallpox. Vaccination is no longer required for entry into any country.

Tetanus-diphtheria (Td)

The organisms that cause these diseases are found throughout the world. Tetanus may be transmitted by a cut, abrasion, or puncture wound (see Chapter 4). Diphtheria is spread in food or milk contaminated with infectious secretions from the nose and mouth.

Almost everyone will have had their basic tetanus-diphtheria series in childhood but a booster shot is recommended every 10 years for travel. If you can't remember when you had the last one and have no record of it, get one before departure. If you never had your childhood series, see a medical provider to get started.

Side Effects

There may be a local reaction, with redness, swelling, and occasionally tenderness at the injection site for about 24–48 hours. Take 2 aspirin or acetaminophen (Tylenol) every 4–6 hours as needed. A cold compress can also be applied directly to the site.

Indications and Contraindications

Following a puncture wound, or any deep or dirty wound or other injury with potential tetanus exposure, you'll need a Td booster if you haven't had one within the preceeding 5 years. If you're allergic to the vaccine or have never been vaccinated, you'll need to obtain a shot of tetanus immune globulin.

The vaccine is considered safe during pregnancy. The only contraindication is history of a prior severe reaction.

Tickborne encephalitis

This viral infection affects the central nervous system. It is transmitted by ticks in forested areas of Central and Eastern Europe and the USSR from April through August. The virus can also be transmitted through unpasteurized dairy products from cows, goats, or sheep.

Vaccination is not recommended for routine travel. It is suggested for residents or those visiting or hiking through forests in high risk areas, especially in Hungary and around Vienna. Tick precautions (see pp. 19–21) will also help prevent infection. Vaccination, not available in the U.S., can be obtained from Immuno, Vienna, Austria.

Typhoid

Typhoid is a bacterial disease transmitted by contaminated food and water. The vaccine is recommended for visitors to all developing countries who travel outside the usual tourist destinations. Countries of particularly high risk include Mexico, Peru, and India. Vaccination isn't required for short trips to most major cities.

Side Effects

1. **oral** — infrequent, but can include nausea, vomiting, abdominal cramping, rashes and diarrhea.

2. **injectable** — possible reactions include soreness for 1–2 days at the injection site, fever, malaise, and headache. Cold packs applied to the site will help relieve any local discomfort. For other symptoms, take 2 aspirin or acetaminophen (Tylenol) every 4–6 hours as needed.

Contraindications

1. **oral** — hypersensitivity, pregnancy, immune-suppression, or HIV positive status. Don't take the vaccine during any illness with fever, diarrhea, or vomiting, or while being treated with antibiotics.

2. **injectable** — don't take the vaccine if there has been a previous severe reaction to it. Avoid vaccination during pregnancy if a previous reaction produced high fever.

Dose

1. **oral** — take 1 capsule every other day for 4 doses. The capsule should be swallowed approximately 1 hour before a meal with a cold or lukewarm drink, but not with hot liquids exceeding body temperature (98.6°F (37°C)). Do not chew the capsule. A booster dose of 4 capsules is recommended every 5 years.

2. **injectable** — two vaccine doses are required. These are obtained 4 or more weeks apart. The vaccine is effective for 3 years, after which a booster is recommended for continued protection. If there's insufficient time for the 2 doses

as specified, take at weekly intervals for a total of 3 doses. This schedule may not provide as high a level of protection.

Typhus

This vaccine isn't required for entry into any country. There have been no reported cases in North American travelers since 1950. Unless you'll be working in direct contact with animals that may have typhus, the vaccine isn't recommended. Production of the vaccine in the U.S. has been discontinued.

Vaccines for HIV Positive Individuals

All vaccines are safe for individuals who have tested positive for the AIDS or human immunodeficiency virus (HIV), with the exception of oral polio (OPV) and oral typhoid. Yellow fever vaccine is contraindicated in persons who have symptoms of HIV infection. HIV positive individuals without symptoms who cannot avoid potential exposure to yellow fever should consider vaccination.

Yellow Fever

Most of equatorial Africa between 15°N. and 15°S. latitude is a high risk zone for yellow fever. So, too, are parts of Central and South America, including Panama, Venezuela, Surinam, Guyana, French Guiana, Colombia, northwest Brazil, eastern Peru, Bolivia, and Ecuador.

Side Effects
There may be pain at the injection site for about 24 hours. A small percentage (2–5%) of those vaccinated experience mild headache, muscle aches, and low grade fever 5–10 days after vaccination. Two aspirin or acetaminophen (Tylenol) every 4–6 hours as needed will help relieve symptoms.

Contraindications
The vaccine shouldn't be taken during pregnancy unless travel in a high risk area is unavoidable.

Anyone with a history of allergic reaction to eggs should avoid yellow fever vaccine. It shouldn't be taken by anyone whose immune system is supressed by drug or radiation therapy, steroids, or cancer.

Dose
Single injection. A booster shot is recommended every 10 years.

Geographic Distribution of Potential Health Hazards

B

The maps in this Appendix provide a quick visual reference of the potential of encountering the indicated health hazards in a particular area of the world. Once your destination is determined, it's also a good idea to check with the travel clinic nearest you for more details.

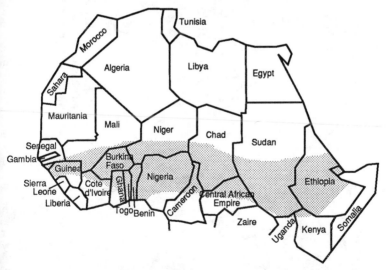

Meningococcal meningitis — Areas of Africa with frequent epidemics of meningococcal meningitis.

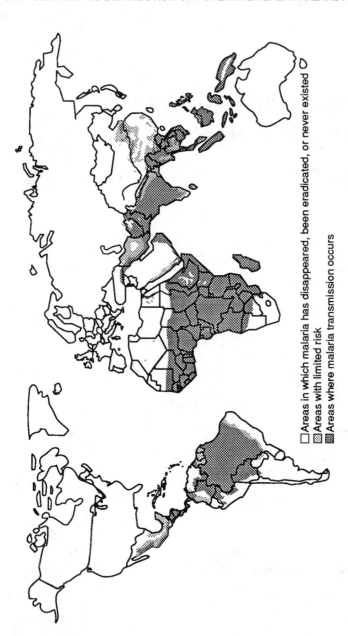

Areas in which malaria has disappeared, been eradicated, or never existed

Areas with limited risk

Areas where malaria transmission occurs

Malaria — Worldwide Distribution

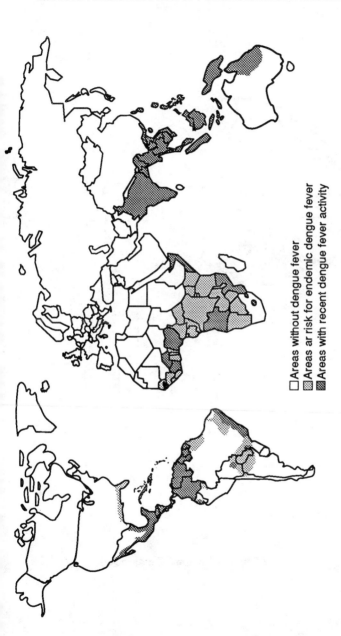

☐ Areas without dengue fever
▨ Areas ar risk for endemic dengue fever
▓ Areas with recent dengue fever activity

Worldwide Distribution of Dengue Fever

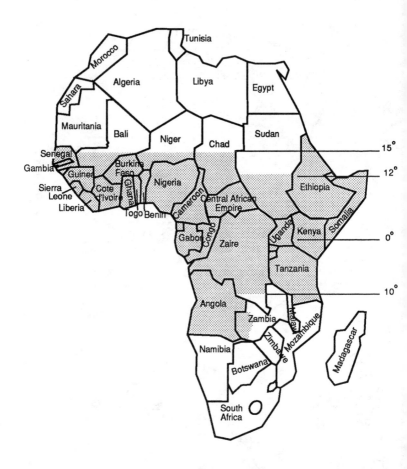

Yellow Fever — Endemic Zones in Africa.

Yellow Fever — Endemic Zones in South America.

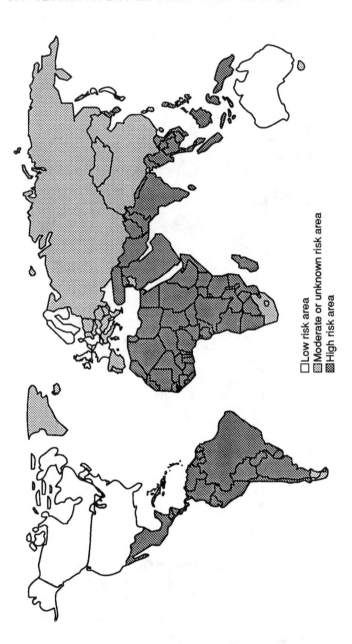

Traveler's Diarrhea — Relative Risk of Acquiring

☐ Low risk area
▦ Moderate or unknown risk area
▓ High risk area

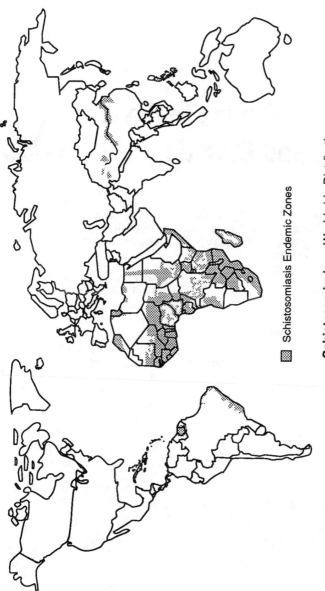

Schistosomiasis Endemic Zones

Schistosomiasis — Worldwide Distribution

Travel Clinics in the U.S. and Canada

C

The American Society of Tropical Medicine and Hygiene maintains a list of travel clinics in North America, from which most of the following addresses were gathered. Check locally with the public health department for information on other travel clinics in your area.

Arizona
Travel Clinic
5757 West Thunderbird
Suite W212
Glendale, AZ 85306
(602) 439-0274

University of Arizona Health Sciences
Center
1450 N. Cherry, Annex 2
Tucson, AZ 85724
(602) 626-7900

The Scottsdale Clinic
9220 E. Mountain View
Scottsdale, AZ 85258
(602) 3911805

California
International Travelers' Clinic
2301 El Cajon Blvd.
San Diego, CA 92104
(619) 698-6736

Sharp Rees-Stealy
16870 W. Bernardo Dr.
San Diego, Ca. 92127
(619) 673-2300

Tropical Disease and Travelers' Clinic
University of California
San Diego Medical Center
San Diego, CA 92103
(619) 543-5787

Palo Alto Medical Clinic
920 Bryant
Palo Alto, CA 94301
(415) 964-2110

Travelers Immunization Center
12311 Ventura Blvd.
Studio City, CA 91604
(818) 762-1167

UCLA Travelers' and Tropical Medicine Clinic
10833 Le Conte Ave.
Los Angeles, CA 90024-1688
(213) 825-9711

Travelers' Clinic
350 Parnassus St.
San Francisco, CA 94143-0560
(415) 476-5787

The Immunization Center
19234 Van Owen St.
Reseda, CA 91335
(818) 705-1115

Colorado
Denver Disease Control Center
605 Bannock St.
Denver, CO 80220
(303) 893-6171

Connecticut
Mansfield Professional Park
Storrs, CT 06268
(203) 487-0002

Tropical Medicine & International Travelers Clinic
Yale University School of Medicine
20 York St.
New Haven, CT 06504
(203) 785-2476; after 5 p.m. 785-2471

Internat'l Travelers Medical Service
Univ. of Connecticut Health Center
Farmington, CT 06032
(203) 674-3245

District of Columbia
Traveler's Clinic
George Washington Univ. Hospital
22nd and Eye St.
Washington, DC 20037
(202) 699-4846

Travelers Medical Service
2141 K Street NW, Rm. 408
Washington, D.C. 20037
(202) 466-8109

Humed Travel Clinic
6323 Georgia Ave, NW
Washington, DC 20011
(202) 291-2005

Florida
Tropical Medicine & Travelers' Clinic
3741 Lejeune Rd. SW
Miami, FL 33146-2809
(305) 663-9666

Georgia
Morehouse Family Practice Center
720 Westview Dr. SW
Atlanta, GA 30331
(404) 699-3200

Emory University School of Medicine
Travel Well International Travelers' Medical Center
20 Linden Ave.
Atlanta, GA 30365
(404) 686-8114/5885

Hawaii
Travel Medicine Clinic/Kaiser Permanente
Honolulu Clinic
1010 Pensacola St.
Honolulu, HI 96814
(808) 529-2394

Straub Clinic & Hospital, Inc.
888 South King St.
Honolulu, HI 96813
(808) 522-4511

Illinois
Travelers Clinic
333 E. Ontario St., Ste. 3211
Chicago, IL 60611
(312) 751-0543

Univ. of Chicago Hospitals & Clinics
Travel Clinic
5841 South Maryland
Chicago, IL 60637
(312) 702-6757

Travel Immunization Center
Northwestern Memorial Hospital
251 East Chicago Ave., Room 168
Chicago, IL 60611
(312) 908-3155

Iowa
Travel & Tropical Medicine Clinic
Univ. of Iowa Hospitals C41GH
Iowa City, IA 52242
(319) 356-1606

Kansas
Internal Medicine/Infectious Disease
Medical Consultants, PA
631 SW Horne, Suite 420
Topeka, KS 66606
(913) 234-8405

Louisiana
Consultant in Tropical Medicine
3600 Chestnut St.
New Orleans, LA 70115
(504) 895-2007

Louisiana State Univ. School of Med.
P. O. Box 33932
Shreveport, LA 71130-3932
(318) 674-5190

Maine
Spurwink Internal Medicine Assoc.
155 Spurwink Ave.
Cape Elizabeth, ME 04107
(207) 767-2174

Maryland
International Travel Clinic
550 N. Broadway, Room 107
Baltimore, MD 21205
(301) 955-8931

Travelers' Health Service
Univ. of Maryland Hospital
419 W. Redwood St., Suite 600
Baltimore, MD 21201
(301) 328-5196

Massachusetts
Northampton Health Center
70 Main St.
Florence, MA 01060
(413) 586-8400

Traveler's Advice & Immunization Ctr
Massachusetts General Hospital
Wang ACC 428
7 Fruit St., Ste. 037
Boston, MA 02114
(617) 726-2748

Travelers Health & Immunization
Services
148 Highland Avenue
Newton, MA 02160
(617) 527-4003

Division of Geographic Medicine & Infectious Diseases
N.E. Medical Center Hospitals
750 Washington St., Box 041
Boston, MA 02111
(617) 956-0162

Michigan
Travel Health Clinic
Henry Ford Hospital
2799 W Grand Ave.
Detroit, MI
(313) 876-2573

Interhealth/Health Care for International Travelers
3535 West Thirteen Mile Rd.
Royal Oak, MI 48072
(313) 551-0496

Missouri
Washington Univ. School of Medicine
660 S. Euclid Ave.
St. Louis, MO 63110
(314) 362-2998

Nebraska
Travelers' Clinic
4102 Woolworth Ave.
Omaha, NE 68105
(402) 444-7207

New Hampshire
Hitchcock Clinic
Dartmouth Hitchcock Medical Center
Hanover, NH 03756
(603) 646-8840

New York
International Health Care Service
440 E. 69th St.
New York, NY 10021
(212) 472-4284

Travel & Immunization Center
Long Island Jewish
Hillside Medical Ctr
New Hyde Park, New York 11040
(718) 470-4415

Tropical Disease Center
Lenox Hill Hospital
New York, New York 10021
(212) 439-2345

International Health Clinic
Albert Einstein College of Medicine
1300 Morris Park Avenue
Bronx, New York 10461
(212) 430-2059

Department of Preventive Medicine &
Community Health
State University of New York Health
Science Center at Brooklyn
450 Clarkson Ave., Box #43
Brooklyn, NY 11203
(718) 270-1056

Department of Medicine
Childrens Hospital of Buffalo
219 Bryant St.
Buffalo, NY 14222
(716) 878-7751

Infectious Disease & Travel Health
One South Lawn Ave.
Elmsford, NY 10523
(914) 592-2460

Travel Health Services
50 East 69th St.
New York, NY 10021
(212) 734-3000 or 570-4000

Executive Health Examiners
Intermedic
777 Third Ave.
New York, NY 10017
(212) 486-8900

NYU Medical Center
341 E. 25th St., Room 105
New York, NY 10010
(212) 340-6764

International Travelers Health Service
New York Medical College
Valhalla, NY 10595
(914) 285-8867 or 993-4655

North Carolina
Duke Univ. Medical Center
Hospital South
1700 Woodstock Rd.
Durham, NC 27710
(919) 684-6832

Ohio
Traveler's Health Care Center
2074 Abington Rd.
Cleveland, OH 44106
(216) 844-8081

Pennsylvania
International Traveler Clinic
500 University Ave., Box 850
Hershey, PA 17033
(717) 531-8885

Travel Health Center
3300 Henry Ave.
Philadelphia, PA 19129
(215) 842-6465

Internat'l Travel & Infectious Disease
3459 Fifth Ave.
Pittsburgh, PA 15213
(412) 648-6411

Travelers' Clinic
1100 E. Orange St.
Lancaster, PA 17604
(717) 397-3711

Pittsburgh Infectious Diseases, Ltd.
1350 Locust St.
Pittsburg, PA 15219
(412) 232-7398

South Carolina
Greenville Memorial Medical Center
701 Grove Road
Greenville, South Carolina 29605
(803) 242-7889

Tennessee
Vanderbilt Univ. Medical Center
21st Ave. South
Nashville, TN 37232
(615) 322-2017

Texas
Univ. Center for Travel Medicine
6410 Fannin St., Ste. 828
Houston, TX 77030-1501
(713) 797-4317

Virginia
Traveler's Clinic
Univ. of Virginia
Charlottesville, Virginia 22908
(804) 924-9677

Washington
Travel-Tropical Medicine Clinic
Univ. of Washington Hospital
1959 NE Pacific
Seattle, Washington 98195
(206) 548-4888

Travelers Medical & Immunization
Clinic of Seattle
509 Olive St., Suite 1201
Seattle, WA 98101
(206) 624-6933

West Virginia
Marshall Univ. School of Medicine
1801 Sixth Avenue
Huntington, West Virginia 25701
(304)696-7046

Wisconsin
International Travelers Clinic
St. Luke's Hospital Emergency Dept.
2900 West Oklahoma
Milwaukee, WI 53212
(414) 649-6664

Canada
Travel Clinic
Toronto General Hospital
200 Elizabeth Street
Toronto, Ontario,
Canada M5G 2C4
(416) 340-4030

Infectious Diseases & Tropical
Medicine Clinic
1200 Main St. West
Hamilton, Ontario, Canada L8N 3Z5
(416) 521-2100, ext. 5997

McGill Univ. Centre for Tropical
Medicine
1650 Cedar Ave., Room 787
Montreal, Quebec, Canada H3G 1A4
(514) 937-8049

Infectious Diseases & Tropical
Medicine
Vancouver General Hospital
2733 Heather St.
Vancouver, BC V5Z 1M9
(604) 875-4588

International Association for Medical
Assistance for Travellers (IAMAT)
1287 St. Clair Ave., W., Ste. 1
Toronto, Ontario M6E 1B8
(416) 652-0137

Conversion Charts

D

Pound/Kilogram Conversions for Dosage Calculations
1 Kg = 2.2 lbs, 1 lb = .45 Kg

lb	Kg	lb	Kg	lb	Kg
80	36.3	125	56.7	165	74.8
85	38.6	130	58.9	170	77.1
90	40.8	135	61.2	175	79.4
95	43.1	140	63.5	180	81.6
100	45.4	145	65.8	185	83.9
105	47.6	150	68.0	190	86.2
110	49.9	155	70.3	195	88.5
115	52.2	160	72.6	200	90.7
120	54.4				

Fahrenheit/Celsius Temperature Conversions
°C = (°F-32) x 5/9; °F = (°C x 9/5) + 32

°F	°C	°F	°C	°F	°C
90	32.2	96	35.6	102	38.9
91	32.8	97	36.1	103	39.4
92	33.3	98	36.7	104	40.0
93	33.9	99	37.2	105	40.6
94	34.9	100	37.8	106	41.1
95	35.0				

Index

323

About the Authors

Bradford L. Dessery is a former Peace Corp Volunteer who served in Honduras, Central America from 1966-1968. He holds a B.A. degree in English Literature from Stanford University. He received his RN at Grossmont College, El Cajon, California. He is a member of the International Society of Travel Medicine. He has lived in Guatemala and traveled extensively in Mexico, Belize, and Costa Rica. In his spare time he enjoys SCUBA diving, photography and camping.

Marc R. Robin is the coordinator of the International Traveler's Clinic in San Diego, California. He received his Registered Nurse degree at Grossmont College, El Cajon, California and his Adult Nurse Practioner license at the University of Oregon. He is a member of the American Society of Tropical Medicine and Hygiene. He is also a freelance writer and photographer, specializing in wilderness subjects. He writes for *Footprints*, the outdoor magazine of Adventure 16, on travel medicine and environmental topics. He is an avid explorer by foot, mule, and with backpack of Baja California. He has traveled extensively in Latin America. He also writes on pre-historic rock art of Baja California.

Both authors are frequent lecturers on international travel medicine. The authors first met at a vegetarian restaurant, El Sol, in Panajachel, Guatemala, in 1973.

How To Get Your Free
Nutshell™ Guide to Healthy Traveling

For one free copy of the wallet-sized Nutshell™ Guide to Healthy Traveling, send a stamped self-addressed envelope to K-W Publications, Dept. Free Nutshell, 11532 Alkaid Dr., San Diego, CA 92126.

If your organization would like to make a bulk purchase of the Nutshell™ Guide please send inquiries to the same address.

----------------- **Order Form** -----------------

For additional copies of *The Medical Guide for Third World Travelers* visit your local bookstore, or order direct from:

K-W Publications
11532 Alkaid Dr., San Diego, CA 92126
(619) 566-6489.

Name _____

Title/Institution _____

Address _____

City/State/Zip _____

Phone ( ) _____

❏ Yes, Please send ____ copy(ies) of *The Medical Guide for Third World Travelers* @ $14.95.

Ship via:
❏ Book Post $2.00 (Slow, U.S. Post Office) for first book. $1.00 each additional book.
❏ UPS $4.00 (faster) for first book. $1.50 each additional book. Outside U.S., $4.00 for the first book. $2.00 each additional book. California residents add current sales tax per book.
❏ $_____ Total ❏ Check enclosed ❏ Bill institution PO # _____
❏MasterCard/Visa # _____ Exp. _____